Advance praise for Joseph Califano's revised edition of *How to Raise a Drug-Free Kid*

"This should be required reading for every parent of a child. Addiction has claimed the children of too many. Having the information and maintaining parental vigilance are a great start. The tools are found between the covers of this well-crafted book."

—Judge Judy Sheindlin

"This wonderful book will help you answer some tough questions and give you a road map for tackling one of the hardest tasks as a parent."

—Jamie Lee Curtis, mother, actress, and author of children's books

"The revised edition of *How to Raise a Drug-Free Kid* makes an already terrific book for parents even better. The book's focus on engaged and informed parenting is a very powerful approach. The book provides many ideas and very practical tips for parents on navigating the tumultuous waters of raising a child, and raising a child drug-free."

—Joseph Woolston, MD, Albert J. Solnit Professor of Pediatrics and Child Psychiatry, Yale Child Study Center

"This revised edition of Joe Califano's book, *How to Raise a Drug-Free Kid*, adds plenty of practical advice gleaned from both scientific literature and tips from parents. I recommend it with enthusiasm to parents and teachers."

—Herb Kleber, MD, professor of psychiatry and director, Division on Substance Abuse, Columbia University and New York State Psychiatric Institute

"As a physician specializing in adolescent medicine, I am in everyday contact with parents struggling to get their kids through the teen years without getting sucked into the abyss of drug and alcohol use teens confront today. Fortunately, Joe Califano's revised edition of *How to Raise a Drug-Free Kid* is now available. In a no-nonsense way, this book shows parents ways to do just that. It should be a 'must have' in every parent's library."

—Ralph I. Lopez, MD, professor of clinical pediatrics, Weill Cornell Medical Center, author, and physician specializing in adolescent medicine

ALSO BY JOSEPH A. CALIFANO JR.

The Student Revolution: A Global Confrontation (1970)

A Presidential Nation (1975)

The Media and the Law (1976) (with Howard Simons)

The Media and Business (1979) (with Howard Simons)

Governing America: An Insider's Report from the
White House and the Cabinet (1981)

The 1982 Report on Drug Abuse and Alcoholism (1982)

America's Health Care Revolution: Who Lives?
Who Dies? Who Pays? (1986)

The Triumph and Tragedy of Lyndon Johnson:
The White House Years (1991)

Radical Surgery: What's Next for America's Health Care (1994)

Inside: A Public and Private Life (2004)

High Society: How Substance Abuse Ravages
America and What to Do About It (2007)

How to Raise a Drug-Free Kid: The Straight Dope for Parents (2009)

How to Raise a Drug-Free Kid

THE STRAIGHT DOPE FOR PARENTS

JOSEPH A. CALIFANO JR.

Founder, the National Center on Addiction
and Substance Abuse at Columbia University

A TOUCHSTONE BOOK
Published by Simon & Schuster
New York   London   Toronto   Sydney   New Delhi

Touchstone
A Division of Simon & Schuster, Inc.
1230 Avenue of the Americas
New York, NY 10020

First Touchstone trade paperback edition September 2014

TOUCHSTONE and colophon are registered trademarks of Simon & Schuster, Inc.

For information about special discounts for bulk purchases, please contact Simon & Schuster Special Sales at 1-866-506-1949 or business@simonandschuster.com.

The Simon & Schuster Speakers Bureau can bring authors to your live event. For more information or to book an event, contact the Simon & Schuster Speakers Bureau at 1-866-248-3049 or visit our website at www.simonspeakers.com.

Interior design by Elliott Beard
Cover design by David Ter-Avanesyan

Manufactured in the United States of America

10   9   8   7   6   5   4   3   2

Library of Congress Cataloging-in-Publication Data
Califano, Joseph A., Jr., 1931–
  How to raise a drug-free kid : the straight dope for parents / by Joseph A. Califano Jr., Founder, The National Center on Addiction and Substance Abuse at Columbia University.
    pages cm
  "A Touchstone Book."
  Revised edition of the author's How to raise a drug-free kid : the straight dope for parents, published in 2009.
  Includes bibliographical references and index.
  1. Substance abuse—United States—Prevention. 2. Teenagers—Drug use—United States. 3. Parenting—United States. 4. Parent and teenager—United States. I. Title.
  HV4999.C45C34 2014
  649'.48—dc23   2014007744

ISBN 978-1-4767-2843-8
ISBN 978-1-4767-2849-0 (ebook)

For the families (mothers, fathers, siblings, grandparents) that have endured the agony of a child addicted to drugs or alcohol, with the hope and prayer that this book will help other families avoid such tragedies. And for the newest Califano grandchild, Patrick Joseph Becker.

The author is donating all royalties
from sales of this book to the
National Center on Addiction and Substance
Abuse at Columbia University (CASA).

Contents

x *Contents*

PART 2
RECOGNIZE IT

18. HOW DO I HELP MY TEEN COPE WITH THE COLLEGE YEARS?   275

PART 3
CONFRONT IT

PART 1

PREVENT IT

1

PARENTING: THE WORLD'S MOST IMPORTANT JOB

Over the past five years, I've travelled across the country talking and listening to thousands of parents about how to raise healthy and drug-free kids. I have learned so much from those parents: their ideas and anxieties, their needs and the pressures they're under. Over those same years, there has been a revolution in our scientific knowledge of developing teen brains, and dramatic changes have occurred in the environment that teens experience: new drugs such as synthetic marijuana, Molly, and e-cigarettes; new ways to get high and chill out; an explosion of social media that often glorifies teen drinking and drugging.

What I've learned from and about parents, the scientific breakthroughs, and the rapidly evolving teen world has convinced me (and many parents and colleagues who have contacted me) of the need for a revised edition of my 2009 book *How to Raise a Drug-Free Kid: The Straight Dope for Parents*. I've written this new edition to address concerns that parents have expressed to me in public meetings and private conversations, to share the good ideas I've learned from parents raising children, and to pass along new knowledge that can help you as you seek to raise healthy and drug-free kids.

I have spent many years of my life—as a White House aide; secretary of health, education, and welfare; and founder, chair, and president of the National Center on Addiction and Substance Abuse at Columbia University (CASA)—wrestling with the threat that drugs and alcohol present to you, your family, your community, and our nation. For a quarter century at CASA, we've been surveying teens and parents, talking with families; interviewing the best researchers, pediatricians, adolescent and child psychiatrists and psychologists, scientific experts, clergy of every faith, school nurses, teachers, and principals; and studying the successes and failures of schools, parents, and teens, with one objective: to find the most effective ways to raise drug-free children.

I'm often asked, "What's the most important thing you've learned about raising drug-free kids?" The most important thing I've learned is this: you, as a parent, are on the front lines every day. Whether your child smokes, drinks, or uses drugs is more likely to be determined in your living room or dining room, or over your kitchen table, than in any classroom, courtroom, or legislative hearing room. And your job gets more challenging each year. That's why I've spent the last couple of years revising *How to Raise a Drug-Free Kid*: to help you do the most important job in the world.

Whatever you achieve in life—running a Fortune 500 company, discovering a cure for some cancer, being the greatest NFL quarterback or female tennis player, becoming a university president or federal judge, serving as a US senator or four-star general—will pale against your responsibilities as a parent.

Parents are entrusted with the world's most precious gifts—their children—gifts far more valuable than the world's purest gold and largest diamonds. How you nurture, develop, guide, instill values, and inspire personal standards and character in your children is the most important task of your life. Succeeding in that task will be your greatest accomplishment and provide your greatest satisfaction.

I've added this chapter to the new edition of this book because of my experiences with parents across the nation since the first edition was published. Too many parents want to be pals with their kids. Too many think that keeping their child from smoking, drinking, and using drugs is somehow isolated from overall parenting. Too few understand the importance of setting limits and establishing consequences for teens who violate those limits.

In Miami and Minnetonka, Hartford and Houston, San Francisco and Chicago, New York and Baltimore, I was struck by how many parents want to be friends with their kids, don't want their kids ever to be angry with them, and see giving their kids pretty much whatever they want as an expression of their love. Meeting with parents in schools, public and private, religious and secular, rich, middle-class, and poor, I was struck by how many parents took it at face value that when their kids said, "Everyone does it, Mom and Dad," that indeed everyone *was* doing "it"—whether it was staying out with no curfew, not telling parents where they go, smoking pot, drinking beer, or having sex.

And I was amazed at how many parents said they felt that "my sixteen- [seventeen- or fifteen-, even fourteen]-year-old gets angry with me *if* [not *when*] I try to find out where he's going on Saturday night." After hearing this same concern again and again, I realized that far too many moms and dads put popularity above parenting. And I came to understand that somewhere along the way, for the children of such moms and dads, the line in the sand that once distinguished their folks from their friends had been washed away.

If this sounds familiar to you, my hope is that this new and revised edition of my book will help you draw that line deeply between you and your teen.

Your job is not to be your child's friend but to be your child's teacher; it is to be not only the source of parental love but also the source of parental discipline; it is to establish standards of conduct and to provide your child with a moral compass. Your children will not thank you for being a pal; at some point, they may wonder whether you care enough about them to be a parent.

Suppose your kid asks you, "Why should I tell you about what I'm doing if you won't tell me?"

You can respond, "Because we're not friends. This isn't an equal relationship. I'm the parent. My job is to make sure you grow up. Your job is to grow up."

Dr. Ralph I. Lopez, pediatrician and author
of The Teen Health Book: A Parent's Guide
to Adolescent Health and Well-Being.

What's the job of parenting? It's a hundred jobs: loving, nursing, chauffeuring, talking and listening, diagnosing, praising and punishing, healing, teaching, feeding, dressing, role modeling, encouraging and discouraging, reining in and freeing, monitoring and trusting, taking to church or temple, holding your child accountable, and knowing the right time (and the wrong time) to do many of these things. During the teen years, the job of parenting may seem like simply surviving. That's why they say grandchildren are the reward for not strangling your teenager. (I know: I've raised three kids, helped raise two stepkids, and have nine grandchildren.)

The pressure to conform and be accepted will grow substantially and your children may feel compelled to make choices based on their need for acceptance. Your best defense against this social influence is instilling positive values at an early age, so your children will recognize bad influences and unhealthy values, and not feel the need to adopt values and act in certain ways just to be accepted.

Dr. Jim Taylor, author and expert in child development and parenting, "Healthy Values Protect Your Kids from the Media's Unhealthy Messages," Huffington Post, November 19, 2012.

Most of all, parenting entails instilling values, installing that most invaluable and intricate of chips—a moral compass—and building character. There's no way to outsource that responsibility. Mark Mattioli, one of the Sandy Hook Elementary School parents who lost a son in the unspeakable Newtown, Connecticut, shootings of December 2012, put it quite well in January 2013: "Cultivating character . . . We as parents, that's our primary job. We ask the schools to contribute to that, but we are the primary caregivers and educators."

He then recalled an experience with his own mother. "At age six, my mom took me to the grocery store . . . I asked for a pack of bubblegum, and my mom said no. So I stole it . . . My mother discovered this when we pulled into our driveway. She drove back to the store, made me hand the gum back to the cashier and apologize, and say I'd never do it again. This is the kind of parenting we need. Parenting is where we need to focus our attention."

In our society, teenagers need plenty of guidance and experience in order to gain the ability not only to tell right from wrong but also to do the right thing. How well your child develops that ability is first and foremost within your power and responsibility as a parent.

IT'S NONE OF YOUR BUSINESS

If your child is an older teen, he may tell you that whether he smokes, drinks, or uses drugs is none of your business, or that he has the right to decide what he does with his body. If so, you need to establish that as a parent, your child's substance use *is* your business. Your job is to teach him to make healthy, responsible decisions. You can also stress that as a parent, you need to prevent him from engaging in self-destructive behaviors such as smoking, drinking, and taking drugs.

And it's not just about drugs and alcohol. It's about the kind of crowd they're hanging with in and out of school, and on and off the sports field. You should try to know something about the kids your child hangs out with, plays with, or goes to movies, sleepovers, and parties with.

Earl Lloyd, the first black NBA basketball player, tells a wonderful story of coming home, and his mother said, "Where have you been?" . . . He said, "I was on the court." She said, "I told you not to be out there with those boys." He said, "I wasn't doing anything."

And she said, "Look, when you're not in the picture, you can't be framed."

Now, that's the kind of stuff parents need to be doing.

Bill Cosby, "A Plague Called Apathy,"
New York Post, *June 9, 2013.*

So many parents are reluctant to tell their children not to go to some party, not to stay out as late as some of their friends do, not to see R-rated films, not to send crude messages on social media, not to go with a crowd that is drinking or smoking pot, or not to go to unchaperoned sleepovers. They don't want their children to get angry with them; some don't want their children to be in a funk, or go to their room and slam the door, saying, "I'll never talk to you again!" But living with that reaction from your teen is part of parenting.

Indeed, if your teenager doesn't tell you that he hates you a few times a year, you may not be doing your job.

It's not a popular stance, believe me, to say parents should become more involved. If you ask too many questions or make too many rules, your kid won't be one of the cool kids or a member of the popular crowd. But maybe parents need to stop and consider their roles as parents.

Diana Reese, "Should Parents Be Held Liable for Rapes at Teen Parties?," Washington Post, April 16, 2013.

PARENTAL PEER PRESSURE

When you take actions like these—setting curfews and enforcing them; telling your teen that he must do his homework before watching television or going on the internet; stopping your teen from buying or playing M-rated (for mature) video games or iTunes music that glorify sex, violence, and drugs; checking up on parties or sleepovers she is going to; and insisting on knowing where your teen is out at night—you're likely to get a response such as, "But Mom, Jack's [or Olivia's] parents let their kids do these things. They're, like, so much cooler than you." Hold your position. Remember, the children of "cool" parents are likelier to get into hot water.

Beware of parental peer pressure. In my talks to parents all over the country, I was struck by the number of mothers who were succumbing to the same kind of peer pressure they wanted their kids to be strong enough to resist. So many parents made comments to me like, "But when all the other parents of my son's classmates let their kids stay out past midnight, it's hard for me to make him come home by eleven," or "Every other mother seems to let her kids go to concerts where lots of kids are smoking pot," or "If other parents let their fifteen-year-olds go to R-rated movies, how can I tell mine that he can't?" or "When all my daughter's girlfriends are wearing this very sexy clothing, how can I tell her she can't?"

You have not only the right and obligation but also the Parent Power (more on this later) to set your own family standards. Sure, your child will balk the first few times you do, but shortly your son or daughter will get the message and, perhaps grudgingly, but happily, live within the boundaries you set. If you want your child not to be influenced by the peer pressure of friends who may smoke, drink, or pop pills, then you need to set the standard with your own conduct.

THE PARENTING QUILT

You may be asking yourself, "Why are all these other things relevant? I got your book just to learn about how to raise a drug-free kid." True, but you cannot isolate preventing your child from drinking and using drugs from your involvement with other behaviors. You cannot be a "good" parent about drugs and alcohol unless you know about your child's school, activities, and interests, have family dinners and take vacations together, watch over your child's personal hygiene, set limits such as curfews, teach respect for adults and relatives, monitor your child's use of social media, and are otherwise engaged in your child's day-to-day life.

Family matters. The entire quilt of family and parenting is one piece, not an ersatz patchwork of unrelated squares. It's all part of helping your child get through the dangerous decade from ten to twenty-one without smoking, drinking, using illegal drugs, or abusing prescription medications. If you succeed in doing that, you will have virtually guaranteed that your child will never have any such problem.

So remember as you read this book or look for some section you're especially interested in: You are a parent, not a pal. You're a mother or father, not a friend.

Your kid will make plenty of friends over a lifetime, but the number of parents your son or daughter has been allotted is limited. If you fail to assume this role in your children's life, where will your children turn, and to whom, when what they really want—and need—is not another pal but a parent.

If being your kid's friend was enough to raise him or her successfully, we would all probably parent that way. But our job is way more complicated than that. Children and teens really crave boundaries, limits, and structure. Our role as parents is really to teach, coach, and give our kids consequences when they misbehave. If you slip into that friend role, however, it is virtually impossible to lay down the law and set limits on your child's inappropriate behavior. I've noticed that a lot of parents are trying to be their kids' friends these days—many give in to their kids' demands, perhaps because they want to be the "cool" parent. Sometimes it's because the parents are simply exhausted from working so hard, managing the household, and trying to raise their kids as best they can. Being a friend is much easier and more comfortable than being a parent.

Janet Lehman, MSW, "Why You Can't Be Your Child's Friend," EmpoweringParents, 2013.

During my talks with parents across this country, I was asked, "If you had a magic wand to wave so that teens would grow up drug free and healthy, what would you do?" My answer was and is, "I would wave it over parents." Why? Because you parents will have the greatest influence over the person your son or daughter grows up to be. You have more power to raise drug- and alcohol-free kids than anyone else. I wrote this book to show you how best to exercise your extraordinary influence—what I call your Parent Power—and to help you appreciate the uncommon power of common sense as you use your Parent Power.

In this book, I give you many effective, straightforward, practical techniques to prevent substance abuse. These techniques are what the experts call "evidence based"—that is, supported by scientific analysis and evaluation. I'll describe these tools and how they work to enhance your Parent Power. Read on and learn how you can guide your child—and family—to a happy, healthy tomorrow.

2

TAKE A HANDS-ON
APPROACH TO PARENTING

As a parent, you have the greatest power to influence your children—even your teenage children. You have more power than any law; any peer pressure; any teacher or coach; any priest, rabbi, or minister; any music, film, or internet site; any rock star, movie star, or famous athlete—even more than any sister, brother, aunt, or uncle.

You have the power to empower your children to make sensible, healthy choices throughout their teen years. The key to Parent Power is being engaged in your children's lives.

Parental engagement isn't rocket science. It's hands-on parenting. It's relaxing with your kids, having frequent family dinners, supervising them, setting boundaries, establishing standards of behavior (and consequences for failure to meet those standards), showing interest in their school, friends, and social activities, loving and disciplining them, and being a good role model.

Why is parental engagement so important? Because children of hands-on parents are far less likely to smoke, drink, or use drugs.

Why is it so important to keep your teenager from doing these things? Because a child who gets to age twenty-one without smoking, abusing alcohol, or using illicit drugs is virtually certain *never* to do so. And that child is much likelier to have a healthy, happy, and productive life.

At CASA, we consider hands-on parenting so important that we have created a national day of celebration: Family Day—Be Involved. Stay Involved. It is celebrated every year on the fourth Monday in September. (See www.casafamilyday.org for more information.)

During childhood and adolescence, drug use can interfere with your child's physical, emotional, and cognitive development. We know a lot more today about the dangers of nicotine, alcohol, and illegal and prescription drug use than we did in the past. The scientific evidence is now overwhelming that teen alcohol and drug abuse interferes with brain development and can inflict serious, sometimes irreversible, brain damage in the long term. Even in the short term, such abuse adversely affects the brain, reducing a teen's ability to learn and remember, processes critical to children in school.

The earlier and more often an adolescent smokes, drinks, or uses illicit drugs, the likelier he is to become addicted. Adolescents are more sensitive than adults to the addictive properties of nicotine, alcohol, and drugs such as marijuana, Xanax, OxyContin, and cocaine. Every year, every month, every day that your child goes without taking that first puff, sip, hit, or pill decreases the likelihood that she will become addicted, develop related mental or physical illnesses as a result of substance abuse, or suffer the tragic consequences of a substance-related accident.

Through your engagement, you can influence, teach, encourage, correct, and support your children so that they develop the will and the skills to choose not to use tobacco, alcohol, and other drugs. Indeed, your Parent Power is the most effective instrument in the substance-abuse-prevention toolbox.

My focus is preventing substance abuse among tweens (ages eight through twelve) and teens (ages thirteen through nineteen), but the parental engagement I encourage begins even earlier and extends through the college years.

Communication doesn't start when your child is seventeen; it should start when your child is three. So by the time that your child is seventeen, there's a pattern of communication that has, hopefully, been going on for some time.

Dr. Ross Brower, professor of public health and psychiatry at Weill Cornell Medical College; psychiatrist at New York–Presbyterian Medical Center.

Establishing a strong connection and good communication with your kids will become more difficult if you wait until the teen years, when children become more independent. The communication foundation you set early in your child's life will be invaluable during the turbulent teens.

THE TEN FACETS OF PARENTAL ENGAGEMENT

Parenting is an art, not a science. Being engaged in your children's lives doesn't require being a supermom or superdad. It simply means using your strengths and taking advantage of opportunities to be a good parent.

Like a brilliantly cut diamond, parental engagement has many facets. Think of the ten facets of parental engagement as an action guide for good parenting, a criteria for developing a strong moral framework in your son or daughter. If they seem intuitive to you, that's great! It means you're already on the right track.

1. Be there: get involved in your children's lives and activities.
2. Open the lines of communication and keep them wide open.
3. Set a good example: actions are more persuasive than words.
4. Set rules and enforce them with consequences if your children fail to follow them.
5. Monitor your children's whereabouts.
6. Maintain family rituals such as eating dinner together.
7. Incorporate religious and spiritual practices into family life.
8. Get Dad engaged—and keep him engaged.
9. Engage the larger community.
10. Get to know your kid's friends and their parents.

With these ten facets of parental engagement, you will have the tools to create a relationship that will enable you to raise your children to be healthy and substance free, poised to develop their talents to the fullest. The benefits of such a relationship reach well beyond substance abuse prevention. But without this foundation, your admonitions to say no to drugs and alcohol will be like trees falling in an empty forest: your children will not hear them, much less be influenced by them.

1. Be There: Get Involved in Your Children's Lives and Activities

Being there—being physically and emotionally available and present—is the essence of parental engagement.

There are endless casual opportunities to be there: eating dinner together as a family; celebrating birthdays and holidays; helping your sons or daughters with their homework; going to their athletic events, school plays, and debates; attending religious services together; taking walks, watching television, going to the movies, fishing, hunting, shopping, driving. These moments are all opportunities for talking and listening to your children about all kinds of things. They are situations where you can comfortably help your children learn to make healthy, sensible decisions.

I am a big advocate of playing with your kids (Monopoly, Scrabble, card games, puzzles) and sports (catch, soccer, baseball). The family that plays together stays together.

Dr. Jeanne Reid, mother of three children.

As a parent, you are likely to see your children's strengths and weaknesses before they do, and you can reinforce their strengths and help them deal with their weaknesses by praising them for their efforts and encouraging them to strive for success. Parental praise, affection, acceptance, family bonding, and discipline are all associated with reduced risk of substance abuse. Such parental support nourishes a confidence in children that their families are sufficiently strong and durable to cope with stressful life events. That confidence is tied to a reduced risk of substance abuse. It's up to you to know the strengths and weaknesses of your children and to be there for them.

Being there also means being sensitive to the complex biological, emotional, psychological, neurological, hormonal, and social transitions that your kids are experiencing. The tween and teen years involve many difficult transitions and challenges that have an impact on your child's self-esteem, confidence, values, and sense of self-worth.

Especially during these years, your children confront a confounding array of issues regarding their beliefs, values, sexual activity, entertainments, friends, and cliques, as well as tobacco, alcohol, and drug use. At these vulnerable and formative ages, they do not yet have the emotional maturity and brain development to control their impulses or to sort out their options and make sound choices on their own. They may often be reluctant to admit it, but they both need and want your help to avoid making impulsive mistakes. Although your children will try to assert their independence, they want you close enough to catch them when they fall, soothe them when they feel hurt, and hug them when they're scared or ashamed.

Being there pays off big-time: teens who say they have an excellent relationship with their parents are less likely to smoke, drink, or use drugs. So are teens who grow up in caring and supportive family environments, where parents have high expectations of their children and welcome their children's participation in family routines and rituals.

So be there—at school and family events, breakfast and dinner, times of celebration and crisis, and religious services—and see what a difference it makes for your teen.

2. Open the Lines of Communication and Keep Them Wide Open

Too many parents assume that they are the last people on earth their teens want to talk to about their problems. How many times have we heard "My fourteen-year-old daughter cringes when I come near her to talk about her life" or "My sixteen-year-old son will never open up to me about issues like drugs or parties"?

That's not necessarily true. And even if you expect such a reaction from your child, simply expressing your interest in your child's life is helpful.

Often opportunities to discuss serious topics with your teen will occur randomly. You may be washing the dishes or the car, or driving to school or a movie when your teen pops a critical question. Take advantage of the moment. It might happen when your daughter asks, "What do you think of e-cigarettes?" Or your son asks, "Do you think they'll legalize pot?" The ball's in your court. Grab the moment for a serious talk about nicotine or marijuana. Don't punt away this golden opportunity by saying, "I'm busy washing the car," or "You'll be late for school," or "Let's talk about it later."

At CASA, we survey teens from across the nation frequently.

Without exception, the lion's share constantly tell us that drugs are their top concern. Yet a third of teens have never had a serious discussion with their parents about the dangers of alcohol or drug use, and only one in seven have had an in-depth conversation with their parents about the dangers of prescription drug abuse. Many who haven't had those conversations wish they could honestly discuss substance abuse with Mom and Dad.

Children who learn about the risks of drugs from their parents are much less likely to use them. Most girls and many boys credit conversations with Mom and Dad as their reason for deciding not to do drugs.

Your children are likely to care more about what you think than anything else they see or hear. Indeed, teens consistently tell us that "disappointing their parents" is a key reason why they don't use drugs. Signaling your disapproval by sending your children a clear message not to use substances may be the difference between your teen's saying no when offered opportunities to smoke, drink, or use drugs and your teen's trying these substances.

Teens—even older teens—may not know how to ask for your help. It may be difficult for them to be forthcoming, but they look to you for advice, encouragement, and support. These conversations may be hard for you too. Talking to your child or teenager openly about issues such as substance abuse may feel uncomfortable, or you may be unsure about what to say. In the following chapters, I offer plenty of tips on how to make those conversations comfortable and productive.

3. Set a Good Example: Actions Are More Persuasive Than Words

The most important facet of parental engagement is your own conduct. Your kids will be more affected by what they see you do than by what they hear you say. Moms and Dads who smoke cigarettes, abuse alcohol, smoke marijuana, and abuse prescription drugs are likelier to have kids who smoke cigarettes, abuse alcohol, smoke marijuana, and abuse prescription drugs.

If you don't want them to drink . . . but the message is, "This is what Mommy does every single night" . . . when they go out into the world, it's not going to be so foreign for them to say, "My mom drinks every night. I can drink every night." It really has to do with practicing what you preach.

> *Jamie Lee Curtis, actress and author of a series of children's books, who lived with the alcohol and drug abuse of her movie-star parents, Janet Leigh and Tony Curtis, and later experienced her own alcohol and Vicodin addictions.*

"Can I have that with a twist?"

Parental drinking behavior can decisively shape a child's view of alcohol use, even at the earliest ages. Dr. Stanley Gitlow, one of the nation's premier alcoholism clinicians, once told me, "When Dad comes home after work and rushes to belt down a couple of martinis, by the time his baby is three years old, that tot sees drinking as a way to relax. Years later, when that child starts bingeing on the weekends in high school, he won't even know that he picked it up watching Dad hit the martinis more than a decade before."

You don't have to be a teetotaler to be a good role model. There's a difference between rushing to belt down martinis every night and having some wine with dinner.

Even if your own behavior is not perfect, setting a healthy example and changing your behavior sends an influential message to your children. For example, if you are a smoker, the younger your children are when you quit smoking, the less likely they are to smoke at all. Being honest about your struggles and inviting your children to witness and support your efforts to stop smoking will empower your children to resist smoking in the first place and to quit themselves if they start. I experienced the influence that this kind of positive role modeling can have on a child with my own son, Joe.

When I was working in the White House for President Lyndon Johnson, and when I was practicing law in Washington, DC, I was smoking two to four packs of cigarettes a day and never thought much about quitting. That changed in the summer of 1975, though, when Joe told me that all he wanted for his eleventh birthday was for me to quit smoking. I went to a smoking cessation program, and on October 27, 1975, I officially kicked the habit. Shaking my nicotine addiction was as difficult as anything I'd ever done. But I knew that the likelihood of my son picking up the same unhealthy habit was much higher if I continued to smoke, and his health and future weren't something I was willing to risk. My son never smoked.

4. Set Rules and Enforce Them with Consequences If Your Children Fail to Follow Them

Engagement in your children's lives involves establishing expectations and limits. It means setting curfews and checking ahead with hosts of parties that your teens want to attend to make sure that a chaperone is present and alcohol is not. It means monitoring your children's internet and social media activities, the movies they see, the concerts they attend, and the video games they play. It means enforcing consequences for stepping beyond the boundaries you set.

You can expect your kids to argue about almost every line you draw. They'll say the curfew is too early, that their friends can stay out a lot later. They'll argue that they are old enough to go out without telling you where they're going. They'll claim that you're embarrassing them by calling other parents to make sure those parents will be home for the teen party at their house and that alcohol won't be served or allowed. They'll tell you that every fifteen-year-old sees R-rated movies. They'll resent what they insist is an invasion of their privacy when you restrict their internet activities. They'll say that other kids can buy M-rated video games no matter how much violence, sex, or drugs are in them, and that other kids' parents let their children go to any concert. Their common chorus will be, "All my friends can do it," or "Don't worry, I can handle it," or "Don't you trust me?"

During our teen focus groups at CASA, where we typically have a wide-open, confidential discussion with twenty to twenty-five kids, I've heard all those arguments. But when I draw them out, more often than not they admit that the rules their parents establish show that "my parents really care about me." Your children need and deserve guidance, information, supervision, and discipline. Children aren't born knowing how to set their own boundaries. The rules you establish, the lines you draw, the messages you send, and the consequences you establish for violating those rules become your children's internal compass for their own behavior.

The students made a persuasive plea for parents who set clear boundaries. What really set them off was the bad behavior of mothers and fathers who drink with kids, who supply alcohol, who seem oblivious to their children's problems. "I have less respect for those parents," said one boy. "They think they're the cool parents. But they're not responsible." What some parents don't get, several kids said, is that "nobody cares if the parents are cool." What they do crave is parents who act like parents.

Marc Fisher, "Are You a Toxic Parent?,"
Washington Post Magazine, *July 30, 2006.*

Children look to you not only to set clear rules but also to enforce them fairly. Enforcing the rules through punishment or other consequences is an essential exercise of your Parent Power and a key lesson in your children's learning process.

Your children will appreciate and respect the rules you craft—not going to parties where alcohol is served, setting curfews and restrictions on movies or video games—if they understand the reasons behind those rules and if the rules are enforced consistently. Answer their inevitable "Why?" questions. Here's a sample exchange:

Teen: "Why are you spoiling my fun when everyone else is doing it?"

Parent: "It's dangerous, illegal, and unhealthy for fifteen-year-olds to be at parties where alcohol is served. The possible consequences—drunk driving, aggressive sexual advances, alcohol poisoning—are not something I want you exposed to. It's not that I don't trust you, it's that I know how easily things can get out of hand if kids are drinking."

Jane Hambleton of Fort Dodge, Iowa, bought her nineteen-year-old son an Oldsmobile Intrigue. She set two firm rules: no booze, and always keep the car locked. Three weeks later, Jane found a bottle of booze in the car. Her son said that he was the designated driver and that a friend had left the bottle in the car. Jane believed her son, but thought that her son needed to learn a lesson about rules and consequences—she took the car away and sold it. The ad she ran in the *Des Moines Register* read: "OLDS 1999 Intrigue. Totally uncool parents who obviously don't love teenage son, selling his car. Only driven for three weeks before snoopy mom who needs to get a life found booze under front seat. $3,700/offer. Call meanest mom on the planet."

Connie Schultz, Chicago Sun-Times, *January 17, 2008.*

If you explain the logic behind the rules and limits, it will help your children tap into that logic when faced with tough decisions and to exert self-control when confronted with inevitable temptations.

To the extent possible, the consequences for breaking the rules should be laid out in advance. This way, children know what to expect if they push the limits and will be more likely to accept the consequences as fair. Another advantage of advance notice is this: when your child breaks the rules, you can focus on what caused the behavior and how to make sure it won't happen again, rather than arguing about the punishment.

Do you want to know one of the things kids criticize most about parents? Inconsistency. Kids respect and need parents who set rules and stick to them. Kids are rather unimpressed with parents who bend the rules every time their kid complains. In one focus group, a teen told me about an incident in which the high school principal enforced a rule that punished kids caught smoking pot by prohibiting them from attending the senior prom. The students' parents lobbied, and the principal reversed his decision. The other kids in the school said they had no respect for the indulgent parents who pressured the school to change the rules for their kids, or for the principal who caved in to the pressure.

Keep in mind that children will often test your limits: it's a normal part of growing up. But when your children break the rules you set, be careful to judge the *act*, not the *child*. When parents criticize children as "stupid," "worthless," or "bad," it can reinforce the bad behavior because the children may learn to think of themselves that way. When parents focus on *why* the behavior was unacceptable, children learn how to make better choices in the future.

We learned a lesson in consistency from our thirteen-year-old daughter. She was invited to a summer-camp reunion in Greenwich Village, a bus ride away. We agreed on condition that she would call us to let us know she arrived safely. We assumed she'd call by 8 p.m., but she didn't until 10 p.m. We were worried sick. She wanted to know, "Am I in trouble?"

A half hour later she came home, apologized, and asked the consequences. She didn't accept her month grounding easily, "Just because I forgot to call!"

A week later she was invited to attend a high school drama-society meeting, a great honor for a middle-school student. We were caught between the grounding and the special event. I came up with the Monopoly concept of a "Get Out of Jail" card. I drew up a "Get Out of One Grounding Free" card for use at the bearer's discretion.

"You were grounded, but we know the high school drama club is important, so we give you a choice to use the card."

To our astonishment, she said, "I can't take this. I don't like being grounded and I think it's unfair, but if you go back on this, I won't ever know when you mean things. Thanks, but no thanks."

Dr. Ralph I. Lopez, pediatrician and author of The Teen Health Book: A Parent's Guide to Adolescent Health and Well-Being.

5. Monitor Your Children's Whereabouts

Supervision serves a purpose. Adolescents who are closely supervised by their parents are much less likely to smoke, drink, or use drugs. Simply realizing that they are being monitored, that their parents insist on knowing where they are and whom they are with and on being awakened each night when they get home after a night out with friends, may deter children from doing these things.

In one of our national surveys about teen attitudes, we found that about half of twelve- to seventeen-year-olds typically go out on school nights to hang out with friends, and that most of their parents seem unaware of where their children are and what they're up to. This spells trouble. The survey revealed that the later teens are out with friends on a school night, the likelier it is that those friends are drinking or doing drugs. Half of teens who come home after ten o'clock on a school night report that drug and alcohol use was going on among their friends.

Knowing your children's whereabouts after school and on weekends positions you to make sure they're occupied appropriately, to move to prevent risky situations, and, if necessary, to intervene in time to help them. There is an important corollary to Grandma's adage about idle hands being the devil's workshop: teens left alone to fend for themselves for extended periods of time are at greater risk for getting drunk and getting high.

6. Maintain Family Rituals Such as Eating Dinner Together

Dinner makes a difference.

A decade and a half of CASA research has consistently found that the more often children have dinner with their parents, the less likely they are to smoke, drink, or use drugs.

Family dinners are so important that I have devoted an entire chapter to the subject, chapter 5, "Eat Meals Together: Dinner Makes a Difference." I also discuss other family rituals—celebrating birthdays, holidays, and family events—which are excellent examples of comfortably exercising your Parent Power.

7. Incorporate Religious and Spiritual Practices into Family Life

Religion can benefit your children immeasurably. Whatever your religion—Buddhist, Catholic, Hindu, Jewish, Mormon, Muslim, Protestant, or if you simply define yourself as spiritual—sharing your faith with your children will reduce the likelihood that they will abuse harmful substances. Teens who consider religion to be an important part of their lives are far less likely to smoke, drink, or use drugs. A 2012 Gallup poll showed that individuals who attend religious services weekly are less likely to smoke than those who never attend.

Those who are involved in their church are much less likely to be involved in drugs.

Michael J. Sheehan, archbishop of Santa Fe, New Mexico.

Faith is an effective substance-abuse-prevention tool because it offers people, including children, strength in the face of adversity. People who make religious practice a part of their lives derive strength and support from the religious community that surrounds them, from the teachings of their faith, and, if they believe in a higher power such as God, from that higher power. With these resources, youngsters are far less likely to turn to alcohol and drugs for relief.

Teen Substance Use by Religious Service Attendance

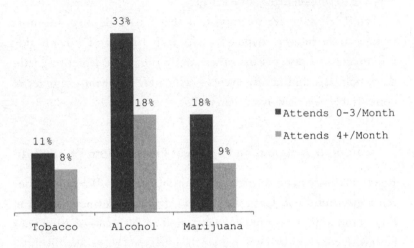

CASA. National Survey of American Attitudes on Substance Abuse XVII: Teens (2012).

For you and your children, religion can be a meaningful resource for morals and values. When you explain to your children why they shouldn't abuse substances, your religion may provide some valuable teachings. In most religions, including Judeo-Christian traditions, the body and mind are sacred. Abuse of alcohol, tobacco, and other drugs should be avoided because they harm the body and degrade the individual's dignity. The Catholic Church teaches that we are all made in God's image and with free will, characteristics incompatible with substance abuse and addiction. In Islam, alcohol and other intoxicants are forbidden because they make the body and mind impure. In the philosophy of Buddhism, alcohol and drugs are shunned because they cloud the mind, which can incite further improper behavior.

People who are actively involved in religious practices or have high levels of spirituality are less likely to use alcohol, use tobacco—if they smoke, they smoke less—and less likely to be substance users.

Margaret A. Chesney, PhD, director of Osher Center for Integrative Medicine, University of California San Francisco.

Another tangible benefit of sharing your religious practice with your children is that it strengthens the family bond and provides an opportunity to establish meaningful family rituals. Teens who attend religious services regularly—at least once a week—are at much lower risk of smoking, drinking, or using drugs than teens who never attend religious services. It is not likely that teenagers today will go to church, temple, or mosque on their own; it's usually something they do with their parents. Religious services and rituals such as first communions, confirmations, and bar and bat mitzvahs also offer excellent opportunities for parental engagement and communication, and for instilling values in teens.

If a family is positive, is healthy, if it's reinforcing, then the likelihood of its members getting into trouble with substances of abuse is diminished, and that's clearly a very strong emphasis of our [Mormon] faith.

Glen R. Hanson, DDS, PhD, professor, University of Utah Department of Pharmacology & Toxicology; former director of the National Institute on Drug Abuse (NIDA).

8. Get Dad Engaged—and Keep Him Engaged

Since parental engagement is a mom-and-pop operation, it's important that both Mom and Dad be engaged.

When Mom is engaged, children benefit. But when Mom and Dad are both engaged, their Parent Power is amplified: fathers who are involved in their children's daily lives and keep open lines of communication sharply reduce their children's risk of substance abuse.

Too often, Mom is the only engaged parent. In our surveys, teens—both boys and girls—are more likely to report having an excellent relationship with their mother than with their father.

When we ask teens who have never smoked marijuana, "Why?" they tend to credit their decision to their mothers.

When we ask teens to whom they turn to discuss something very serious, they overwhelmingly answer "Mom."

"My wife is recording everything the kids do until they leave
for college. Then I'll binge-watch them grow up."

Children need their fathers to be there day after day, talking, listening, teaching, supporting, encouraging, and loving them. Mom needs Dad to be there too. If Dad is not engaged, Mom has no support in parenting: making decisions, setting rules, enforcing consequences, setting a good example. Children in two-parent families who report only poor or fair relationships with their fathers are at higher risk for substance abuse than those in single-parent families who have an excellent relationship with their mother or father.

Parents can divide some responsibilities of parental engagement. Perhaps Dad can't make it home for dinner, but he can help them with their homework later in the evening or spend time with the kids on the weekends. What is essential is that fathers, as well as mothers, lay a foundation of frequent and open communication with their children, that they talk and listen to them, set a good example with their own behavior, and that both fathers and mothers give the same consistent messages about not smoking, drinking, or using drugs. In families where Mom and Dad start from different views, it is important for them to come to a shared position before talking to their children.

There are many activities that can help Dad engage with the kids: dinner, playing sports or games like Scrabble, taking walks, coaching a team, helping with homework, collecting things together, even just driving the kids to and from their activities. Weekend (or longer) trips are a wonderful way for Dad to get involved. The YMCA Adventure Guides program organizes camping trips for fathers and their children. Any of these activities gives Dad a chance to show his interest in his child's hobbies, friends, schoolwork, and development.

Of course, not every family has two parents. In twenty-first-century America, there are all kinds of families: those headed by Mom and Dad, Mom alone, Dad alone, Mom and Stepfather, Dad and Stepmother, grandmothers or grandfathers, aunts or uncles, two Dads or two Moms, even older siblings. Sometimes children have two families, with two sets of parents. What counts more than who heads the family, or how many heads the family has, is the engagement of those family heads—and the consistency of their messages about alcohol and drug use. An engaged single parent is more effective than disengaged fathers and mothers in two-parent families.

"Me? I thought you were raising them."

9. Engage the Larger Community

Parental engagement should extend beyond the immediate family to the larger families of a child's friends, schoolmates, teachers, neighbors, church, and community. These larger families can serve as your support groups and your child's safety nets.

You may feel as though you are the only parent struggling to enforce rules or making difficult judgment calls, but the truth is that you are not alone, and you don't need to do it alone. You are not the first parent ever to worry about how to keep your kids healthy and on the right track; I assure you that most other parents share the same concerns.

Parents need support. Just as people have exercise buddies to help motivate them to get moving and keep moving, so too parents need parenting buddies. When your children are young, you have many opportunities to get together with other parents—at school and community events, children's birthday parties, Mommy and Me class, PTA meetings—to talk about the challenges of being a parent. But as your children grow older, there may be fewer opportunities, and you may feel more isolated.

Concerned parents Thom and Deirdre Forbes created an online community chat group for local parents to share their concerns about what's going on with their kids. Parents could ask questions (even anonymously), share success stories and parenting tips (for example, appropriate curfews), and discuss incidents that happen among teens in their community (arrests, house parties).

The Forbeses have found that the ideal parenting discussion group should be:
- limited to parents of children in the same grade;
- supplemented with periodic face-to-face meetings among the parents (every three months or so); and
- completely independent from the children's school.

As a fully engaged parent, you should continue to develop meaningful relationships with the important people in your children's lives—the kinds of relationships that can make it easy to talk to parents in the community or the coach of your child's team about issues that concern you. Nurture your relationships with parents of your child's friends so that you don't have to face the challenges of raising a teenage son or daughter alone. Talk to other parents; ask what works and what doesn't work for them when they talk to their kids about risky behavior and substance use. And if your child says that you enforce the strictest curfew, check around. It's probably not true.

You can start a parent group in your own community through your church or Little League team, or on the internet by creating a Google Group or using a social networking website (Facebook, LinkedIn, Blogster) to get parents talking.

Developing close relationships with other families in your area can yield tangible benefits. Say you're concerned about what's going on at the parties your teenage son attends; you will have a much easier time calling the parents who are hosting those parties if you've met and talked with them before. Indeed, in some communities, parents have come together voluntarily and signed pacts where they all agree not to host parties with alcohol or other drugs. With other parents on your side, you're not alone in making difficult decisions about what to allow your own children to do. And your kids cannot tell you that your rules and standards are uniquely unjust; you can tell them with confidence that you happen to know their friends' parents are "just as horrible!"

Another benefit is that parents who have relationships with one another may be more inclined to step in when another's child is in trouble. Among mothers and fathers who have lost a child to a drug overdose or alcohol poisoning, there is a common, heart-wrenching refrain: "Our child's friends knew our child was using. Other parents at our child's school knew. Some of our neighbors knew. But no one said anything to us."

Engaged parents should accept responsibility to speak up when they learn that someone else's child is in trouble with drugs or alcohol, or when their own kids tell them that a classmate or friend is using. In a sense, parents need to regard themselves as uncles and aunts— members of the larger family that is the community where they and their children live.

You and your children are likely to be part of still another family:

your religious community. Religious organizations can play a significant role in preventing substance abuse and supporting substance abuse treatment in their communities. From offering substance abuse prevention programs to parents and teens, to providing substance abuse counseling, to including substance abuse as an issue in religious teachings and homilies, there are a variety of ways that religious organizations can reach out to folks in their community. If you are a member of a congregation or religious community, encourage your clergy and lay leaders to initiate programs to prevent substance abuse and learn where to refer individuals for treatment.

The Jewish community can no longer deny a problem in its midst, some rabbis and advocates say: Many Jews are addicted to drugs and alcohol. A combination of refusal to believe that addiction affects Jews and a lack of education have contributed to what some say is a dearth of services for Jewish addicts. Many of these addicts have specific religious needs related to their problems.

Lois Solomon, "A New Approach to Jews with Addictions," South Florida Sun-Sentinel, *February 3, 2013.*

Your children spend most of their time with yet another family: their school. Parental engagement in your teen's school and that school's culture, policies, and practices is so critical that I have devoted chapter 17, "How Can I Protect My Kids at School?," to this subject.

There are other larger families that can connect you to other members of your community and provide you with valuable resources.

One is the Partnership for Drug-Free Kids, which has a website with interactive tools to provide parents with help in raising drug-free children. You can volunteer online at www.drugfree.org to join your local partnership affiliate.

The PTA (Parent Teacher Association) fosters parental involvement in families, schools, and communities to help children succeed. Members are invited to come together to discuss issues, including raising drug-free kids, related to their children's growth and education. The PTA has local chapters in every state; to find yours, go to www.pta.org.

Another such family is made up of the more than five thousand community antidrug coalitions in the United States supported by the Community Anti-Drug Coalitions of America (CADCA). A community coalition is a group of parents, teachers, law enforcement, businesses, religious leaders, health care providers, and others who work locally to help make their communities drug free. At www.cadca.org, you can find an antidrug coalition in or near your community.

Another useful resource is the CASA website, where you can learn about teens and addiction, get more tips on recognizing if your child may have a problem with drugs or alcohol, and learn steps you can take to help your child stop using. Visit the site online at www.casacolumbia.org/addiction-prevention/teenage-addiction.

10. Get to Know Your Kid's Friends and Their Parents

As your child becomes a tween and then a teen, his friends, classmates, and peer groups will become increasingly important to him. As he makes his way through the often dizzying mazes of middle school and high school, the people with whom he spends his free time will help shape his identity, what activities, music, and hobbies he enjoys, and what goals he may have. For this reason, it is important that you know his friends and their parents.

Ask your daughter with whom she's going to the movies on a Friday night, who's picking her up and taking her to the party on the other side of town, at whose house she is sleeping over on a weekend night. Make sure you get to know these teens. Take the opportunity to start a conversation with your son and his buddies when they're hanging out at your home, or in your car as you're driving them to school, a soccer game, or a concert. Open your home to your son's or daughter's friends for sleepovers or supervised parties. Not only will it help you get to know and understand your son or daughter better, but it may also give you some idea about which of your child's friends may be positive influences and which may be negative. Indeed, knowing your teen's friends may give you important insights into your own teen, and even provide an early warning of a potential problem ahead.

There are no silver bullets, and there is no such thing as perfect parenting. Even the finest parents may end up suffering the anguish and pain of seeing a child become addicted to drugs or dying from alcohol poisoning in a college hazing incident. But parents have greater power than anyone else to reduce or eliminate those risks for their children.

For many parents, teen substance abuse is the boogeyman under the bed—something they fear and hope will never happen. This leads some parents to shut their eyes, pull up the covers, and hope for the best. But ignoring the threat of teen substance abuse or assuming that there's no threat to *your* child won't make it go away. Your disengagement will simply leave your child alone to navigate the treacherous rapids of tobacco, alcohol, and illicit and prescription drugs without a parental compass to guide him. That's why I've created these ten facets of parental engagement: to help give you the biggest and best boost in keeping your child substance free.

3

YOUR ADOLESCENT'S
BRAIN AND DRUGS

Why is it that your teenager at times seems to be so impulsive, so reckless? Why do teens sometimes appear to behave as if they were immortal, impervious to harm? What's going on?

Lots: puberty, hormonal changes, peer pressure, and a barrage of social media, visual and musical entertainment, and other outside forces and influences pressuring your teen to do, see, and buy things.

But most importantly, your teenager's brain hasn't matured; it's still developing.

WHY SOME TEENS USE

The process of cognitive development that started early in the womb continues into the midtwenties, when the human brain becomes fully formed. Teenagers may look like grown-ups, and sometimes some may even seem to be as smart as grown-ups, but because their brains are still maturing, they don't have the ability to control impulses or anticipate consequences the way that adults do.

Unfortunately, kids don't pull their hands away from drugs and alcohol because they don't get burned immediately. So they are left to grapple with the issue: What feels good often isn't good for you.

Priscilla Dann-Courtney, PhD, psychologist and parent.

"How am I supposed to think about consequences before they happen?"

Through adolescence and into early adulthood, the areas of the brain that regulate cognitive and emotional behavior go through a "remodeling" process. The parts of the brain responsible for self-regulation (for instance, controlling impulsive behaviors and understanding long-term consequences) are still developing at this stage and aren't complete until around age twenty-five. Because adolescents' brains are still developing, they lack some of the "wiring" that sends the count-to-ten, brake, and stop messages to the rest of the brain.

Think of the teen brain as a car with an accelerator and a brake. The accelerator works fine, while the brake is faulty. It's fun to go fast but difficult to stop. The teenage brain is in "drive" and it's hard to stop it. As a result adolescents and young adults are more prone to engage in risky behaviors such as smoking, drinking, illegal and prescription drug abuse, and reckless driving. Teenagers' brains encourage them to take dangerous risks just for fun, not perceiving those risks as dangerous in the way that adult brains do.

This kind of "just for fun" behavior may seem thoughtless or careless to you as a parent, but the science behind brain development explains it, as do teens' own responses when asked why they take such risks. In our 2012 survey, we found that the main reason teens give for why kids drink is "just to have fun."

[Studies examining image scans of teen brains] help explain why teens behave with such vexing inconsistency: beguiling at breakfast, disgusting at dinner; masterful on Monday, sleepwalking on Saturday. Along with lacking experience generally, they're still learning to use their brain's new networks. Stress, fatigue, or challenges can cause a misfire.

David Dobbs, "Beautiful Brains: Moody. Impulsive. Maddening. Why Do Teenagers Act the Way They Do?," National Geographic, October 2011.

What do you think is the main reason kids your age (12 to 17 years old) drink alcohol?

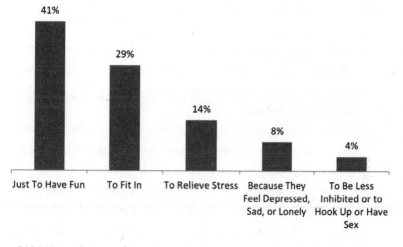

CASA. National Survey of American Attitudes on Substance Abuse XVII: Teens *(2012)*.

WHY DRUG USE LEADS TO MORE DRUG USE

You've probably heard mention of the gateway relationship among cigarettes, alcohol, marijuana, and other drugs. This refers to the fact that kids who smoke cigarettes and drink alcohol are more likely to use marijuana than those who don't, and kids who smoke marijuana are far more likely to use drugs such as cocaine, methamphetamine (meth), hallucinogens, and heroin than those who don't.

Your teen—and even some parents—will point out that not all kids who smoke cigarettes go on to drink alcohol (and vice versa), that most kids who smoke cigarettes and drink alcohol will not use marijuana, and that most kids who smoke marijuana will not move on to drugs like cocaine, meth, prescription painkillers, heroin, and hallucinogens.

That's true. But fostering good health in your children means teaching them to avoid behaviors that increase their risk of substance abuse and addiction. For some time, we at CASA have been identifying the statistical relationship among use of these substances:

- Most teens who use marijuana first smoked cigarettes or drank alcohol.
- Teens who use marijuana are much likelier than teens who don't to use cocaine.
- Teens who began smoking cigarettes by age twelve are likelier than nonsmokers to become binge drinkers and to become dependent on alcohol and marijuana.
- Teens who abuse prescription drugs are twice as likely to use alcohol, five times more likely to use marijuana, twelve times more likely to use heroin, fifteen times more likely to use Ecstasy, and twenty-one times more likely to use cocaine, compared with teens who do not abuse such drugs.

Nicotine is much more of a "gateway" drug than marijuana. More kids initiate drug use with nicotine than with marijuana. If you're a smoker, that increases the risk of marijuana use and in turn the risk of other drugs.

Nora Volkow, MD, director, National Institute on Drug Abuse.

When you tell this to your teen, he might well say, "I know lots of kids who smoke pot, and they never use any of those dangerous drugs like heroin." At that point, you have a few different resources that will be helpful in explaining to your teen how harmful drugs are. For instance, you can go to the NIDA website, search for "Drugs, Brains, and Behavior—The Science of Addiction" (www.drugabuse .gov/publications/science-addiction), and show him how each of the substances affects and disrupts the functioning of the same parts of the brain. And you can go to the National Institute on Alcohol Abuse and Alcoholism website (http://pubs.niaaa.nih.gov/publications /Hangovers/beyondHangovers.htm) and take a few minutes together to read all of the different effects that alcohol has on the brain and the rest of the body. Then ask him, "Why take an unnecessary risk, one that could mess up your brain and destroy your life?"

Parents who ignore these risky relationships among addictive substances are playing Russian roulette with their children. Virtually all cocaine users smoked cigarettes, drank alcohol, and smoked pot first. Seventeen percent of adolescents who try illicit drugs start with inhalants. If your child has started using alcohol or marijuana, he is likelier to try other drugs than a child who hasn't been drinking or smoking pot.

Cigarettes brought me to weed, weed brought me to alcohol, alcohol brought me to crank [crystal meth], crank brought me to 'shrooms, 'shrooms brought me to coke, and coke brought me to the decision to stop it all.

"Katie," thirteen years old, at High Watch Recovery Center, Kent, Connecticut, presented by Janina J. Kean at Family Awareness Program.

One reason that some teens who smoke or drink move on to other drugs is that they have a *behavioral and/or emotional problem* such as oppositional defiant disorder or conduct disorder (ODD or CD), anxiety, depression, or bipolar disorder. For these teens, drinking or drug use may be part of a larger cluster of negative, rebellious, antisocial, or destructive behaviors. The child with an emotional problem may resort to drug use as a last and easy solution to find a way to feel good; for example, a quick relief from his depression or clinical anxiety. As I point out in chapter 11, "In What Circumstances Is My Child at Increased Risk of Drug Use?," children with conduct disorders are likelier to get into substance abuse. That's why it's so important for you to seek professional help promptly if your child has such a disorder. Early intervention can prevent dangerous self-medication.

Genetic factors can sometimes explain why a teen moves from smoking and drinking to using marijuana and other drugs, as well as why one teen's response to a drug may be different from his friends' responses to the same drug. That's why it's crucial to explain to your teen any history of alcohol or other drug abuse or addiction in your family history, especially close family like aunts, uncles, and grandparents. If you're not sure when or how to talk to your child about this, discuss it with your physician or a school counselor.

Although we know what happens to the brain when someone becomes addicted, we can't predict how many times a person must use a drug before becoming addicted. A person's genetic makeup—the genes that make each of us who we are—and the environment each play a role. What we do know is that a person who uses drugs risks becoming addicted, craving the drug despite its potentially devastating consequences.

NIDA for Teens, "Drug Facts: Brain and Addiction," The Science Behind Drug Abuse, 2013.

What I call *social contagion* may also be a factor in why use of one drug can lead to use of another. Teens hanging out and using different drugs or pills often suggest that they try one another's drug or pill. For example, where a girl is drinking, one of her friends may suggest she smoke pot ("It gives a high without any calories"); another girl may say, "Try this pill!" ("It gives a high without any calories and without getting, like, a sore throat or gross taste"). The judgment of any teen is more readily clouded when in a group where most everyone is doing it.

HOW DRUGS AFFECT THE ADOLESCENT BRAIN

Another reason drug use can lead to more drug use is neurological. It has to do with how drugs affect the brain. Processed sugar, the kind you find in sweets, is in many ways just like a drug. Your body doesn't need it. It's not good for you, and the more of it you eat, the more you want it. So it is with drugs: when you put any drug in your body, your body is likely to crave more, and over time, larger doses and more intense drugs.

In recent years, scientists have identified a likely explanation for this relationship. All of the substances of abuse—nicotine, alcohol, marijuana, cocaine, heroin, methamphetamine, opioids—increase the levels of dopamine in the brain. Dopamine is the chemical messenger (neurotransmitter) that produces feelings of pleasure and excitement; it is released in the brain in response to a rewarding experience such as eating delicious food or watching your team win a big game. Dopamine is believed to be a teaching signal that helps the brain learn to repeat behaviors that are pleasurable—in the case of drugs, reinforcing drug-taking behavior.

Whatever the substance, brains of repeat drug users are "rewired," becoming predisposed to cravings. These adaptations may happen more quickly, and more profoundly, for some drugs and some teens. For example, nicotine has been shown to create especially rapid changes in the pleasure/reward pathways in the brain, and girls tend to get hooked faster than boys. The changes caused by one drug increase the brain's sensitivity to other drugs; in effect, the drug primes the brain for further and faster changes by other drugs.

Long-term abuse of alcohol and other substances can also rewire the pleasure/reward system of the brain so that normal pleasurable activities that once stimulated these pathways (enjoying a great movie or musical concert, getting straight As, and so on) are no longer sufficient. As a result, to increase dopamine levels and experience resulting pleasure, the addict needs to use drugs. And the more frequently and longer an addict uses drugs, the more drugs he or she needs to create the high.

When you talk to your child about this, use the analogy of muscles: if you lie in bed and don't use your legs for a long time, it becomes harder for you to climb steep hills or run fast; similarly, if you don't use the natural ways to increase your dopamine levels (a big personal achievement in athletics or a school play) and instead rely on drugs to increase those levels, it becomes more difficult for your body to increase dopamine levels naturally, and you become more dependent on drugs to do that.

Drugs such as heroin, OxyContin, cocaine, and Ecstasy affect the teen brain in a way more profound than (but similar to) the way alcohol and marijuana do. The chemical compounds in these drugs ape the natural compounds and neurotransmitters in the brain and flood the brain with dopamine or serotonin (a compound in the brain that also affects mood). This sudden rush causes an intense feeling of euphoria and can damage the natural neurotransmitters, thus decreasing the brain's natural production of dopamine or serotonin. Taking these drugs stimulates the brain's natural receptors, and the brain, in essence, says, "That felt good! Do it again!"

Drugs also change the teenage brain in ways that can make the brain more susceptible to addiction later. The neurological damage created by drug use during adolescence disrupts the pleasure/reward centers in such a way that the brain learns to become addicted. The result is that teenagers who abuse substances are much more susceptible to developing chronic substance abuse problems later in life. Even if a teen is able to eventually kick those habits or addictions once she becomes an adult, her brain may not reach the potential it could have if she hadn't started using in the first place.

WHAT DOES ALL THIS BRAIN SCIENCE MEAN FOR ME AS A PARENT?

Adolescent passions are normal and can be healthy, so long as they are directed in the right ways. Help to insure that your teen's natural propensity for risk taking and pleasure seeking leads him or her to get involved in healthy activities such as sports, art, music, drama, social, political, or religious causes, achieving academic success, winning a debate or chess tournament—and get her "high" from these activities.

You can help your teen understand that experimenting with drugs at an early age can change his brain permanently, even if he just "experiments once or twice" with binge drinking or drugs like Ecstasy or synthetic marijuana. To the extent that your teen grasps this, it will make it easier for you to guide him to make smart decisions and even appreciate both the immediate and the long-term risks and consequences of drug use.

BRAIN DAMAGE FROM TEEN DRINKING

Understanding what drinking means for children and teens, and the scientific rationale for delaying use until age twenty-one, will help you convey to your child a credible, meaningful argument against teen drinking in high school and the early college years. Indeed, the threat of damage to the brain from heavy drinking offers one of the best arguments you can make to your teen for saying no.

[H]eavy use of alcohol and other drugs during the teen years can result in lower scores on tests of memory and attention in one's early to mid-20s. People who begin drinking before age 15 are four times more likely to become alcohol dependent than those who wait until they are 21.

Center for Adolescent Health at the Johns Hopkins Bloomberg School of Public Health, "The Teen Years Explained: A Guide to Healthy Adolescent Development," 2009.

Research shows that, like other drugs, alcohol can negatively impact adolescent brain development. As Dr. Aaron White of Duke University Medical Center, one of the nation's experts on the effects of drug use on the adolescent brain, explains, "There are long-term cognitive consequences to excessive drinking of alcohol in adolescence." Teens who drink heavily can savage their memory, attention span, and spatial skills. Alcohol-dependent kids fare worse on language and memory tests.

Studies have shown that the hippocampus, a part of the brain that develops during adolescence and is key to memory and learning, is smaller in adults who drank heavily during their teenage years. That's because introducing lots of alcohol to the brain during those years disrupts brain development and can lead to permanently reduced brain function. In addition to damaging the hippocampus, heavy drinking has been found to permanently harm the white matter surrounding the brain. This white matter is the brain's nerve tissue and part of the body's central nervous system. When white matter is damaged, the brain cells can't communicate as efficiently or as well as a teen needs in order to learn and function at his or her best.

[U]nderage alcohol use can also cause alterations in the structure and function of the developing brain, which continues to mature into the mid- to late-20s, and may have consequences reaching far beyond adolescence.

Steven K. Galson, MD, MPH, "Preventing and Reducing Underage Drinking," Public Health Reports 124, no. 1 (January/February 2009).

SMOKING CIGARETTES OR MARIJUANA AND THE TEEN BRAIN

Like alcohol, nicotine and marijuana can harm teens' brains, sometimes causing long-term or permanent damage. Heavy cigarette smoking, for example, has been found to negatively affect the prefrontal cortex, the area that controls skills such as decision making and impulse control. The damage from nicotine use doesn't stop at decision making, though. Since the prefrontal cortex can be permanently altered from a teen's cigarette habit, other parts of the brain have to pick up the slack, causing your teen's brain to work less efficiently than it should. (More about this in chapter 6.)

Regular marijuana use can harm your teen's brain; for example, lowering IQ and sparking latent schizophrenia (a chronic, severe, and disabling brain disorder). Your teen is likely to know what such use can do, even if he doesn't want to admit it. So when you're discussing how drugs and alcohol can damage your teen's brain, ask her if she can think of anyone from school that is known as a "pothead" or a "stoner." Although she may think it's funny to see potheads and stoners acting lazy, goofy, or disinterested during class, or loopy at social events, you can point out that such conduct is also a consequence of marijuana harming their brains and altering their personalities. (More about this in chapter 7.)

ALWAYS REMEMBER

Your adolescent's developing brain is a precious, complex, sensitive device that is more vulnerable to the damaging and addictive effects of alcohol and other drugs than the brain of an adult. You have the Parent Power to protect your child's brain and help develop it in a healthy way. Use it!

PARENT TIPS

- Educate your children about how the teen brain is particularly vulnerable to the damaging and addictive effects of nicotine, alcohol, and other drugs.
- Explain to your teens that although the likelihood of someone suffering long-term brain damage from drug or alcohol use increases with the amount and frequency of drugs or alcohol he consumes, even just experimenting with drugs or alcohol can be harmful to the brain. Such experimenting can hinder his ability to make good decisions and perform at his best in school and in extracurricular activities.
- Use the National Institute on Drug Abuse (NIDA) and National Institute on Alcohol Abuse and Alcoholism (NIAAA) websites to visually show your teen how drinking and drug use can affect his or her brain.

4

TALK TO YOUR KIDS ABOUT SMOKING, DRINKING, AND DRUGS

Communication—talking, listening, guiding—is the core of parental engagement. You need to be able to talk with your children about difficult issues, including substance abuse, in order to get them to talk to you honestly about what's going on in their lives, and to guide them to make healthy, sensible decisions.

But how?

With a teenager especially, how do you connect on a level that is comfortable and natural?

How do you become engaged in your son's life without making him feel as if you are invading his space? How do you ask questions without making your daughter feel like she's being interrogated?

How do you talk about substance use or other risky behaviors without it turning into a confrontation or a fight? Without getting a "You don't trust me!" shouted back?

The first step in building good communication is to start early. Spend quality time just talking to your child—in the car, during dinner, watching TV, going to church, at ball games, walking the dog, play-

ing games, in the park, on vacation. Use those moments you have together to get to know your kids and to let your kids get to know you.
Talk about anything and everything; it doesn't matter so much what
the subject is as long as you and your children are communicating
openly. Your children won't feel comfortable talking about difficult
issues like drugs and alcohol if they don't feel that it's normal to talk
to you about what's going on in their lives.

Training for a serious teenage discussion begins in the early years.
Talking while en route to a child's sixth birthday celebration, serving imaginary tea to a seven-year-old who says it's teatime, kicking
a soccer ball with your eight-year-old—those are the kinds of talks
that lay the groundwork for a serious discussion about drugs and their
dangers when your child is ready.

With a solid foundation of open, two-way communication, ce-
mented by talking and listening to your child, you will have the
Parent Power to guide your child to make the right decisions so long
as your guidance has the ring of authenticity to both of you.

What do I mean by authenticity? Your guidance to your child on
making healthy, drug-free decisions and the discussion that accompanies it will have authenticity if based on facts and nourished by love.

[S]peaking truth in love, we may grow up in all things.

Ephesians 4:15.

KNOW THE FACTS AND
STICK TO THE FACTS

The facts I set out in this book and the "Parent Power Glossary for
Parents and Teens" at the end give you plenty of accurate information to help you make the case that your teen should stay away from

drugs. Use that information confidently. You don't need to exaggerate or embellish the dangers of tobacco, alcohol, and drug use. If you exaggerate those dangers, your kids will smell a rat.

Be realistic about why people abuse alcohol and other drugs. For example, they can make you feel good and forget about your problems—but only temporarily. Underscore that while it may seem to your child that marijuana and other drugs are everywhere, most people don't use them and haven't tried them.

When you talk to your children about alcohol, cigarettes, and other substances, it is important that you feel comfortable and know what you're talking about. Teenagers will ask tough questions; they'll challenge you. You don't have to become a psychopharmacologist or substance abuse expert, but you do need to know how to handle the difficult questions and challenges.

If you can't answer all your child's questions or you don't know all the facts about a drug your son or daughter asks about, just admit it. If you're not sure of something, tell them that and say, "Let's find out together." For instance: "I'm not sure exactly what meth does to your body, but I've seen shows on TV, and they worry me. What do you think it does? Let's learn more about this together." You and your child can start by reading the "Parent Power Glossary for Parents and Teens" in this book; you can also visit health or government websites such as the National Institute on Drug Abuse (www.drugabuse.gov), consult other resources from the library, or ask your doctor for more information.

Take advantage of opportunities in the news to talk to your teen. When there's a story on television, online, or in a magazine or newspaper about a drug overdose, celebrity antics under the influence of alcohol or drugs, a drunk-driving incident, or violent crime, use it to open up a conversation and probe your teen's reaction.

When you talk to your kids, focus on facts that are relevant to them. Let's say you're talking about why smoking is bad. Describing the long-term dangers of smoking—lung cancer, heart disease, chronic bronchitis, and emphysema—will make their eyes glaze over. Most teens have a sense of invulnerability, that they are immortal, impervious to harm; for them, those are diseases that happen to "old people."

If you see an ad for cigarettes with your child, point out that the tobacco companies are trying to manipulate kids to get them addicted to their product so that the companies can profit from their habit. Say, "Don't let the tobacco companies make a sucker out of you." If your child tells you that friends or classmates smoke, say, "The cigarettes smoke; your friends are just the suckers on the other end."

Use pithy examples. Telling your teenage children that "kissing a smoker is like licking a dirty ashtray" might make the point because they're likely to hear it from, or tell it to, their boyfriend or girlfriend.

When the time does come to talk about nicotine, alcohol, and other drugs, it's important to know the facts and stick to them. There is no need to exaggerate, lie, or try scare tactics. There is enough science, medicine, and law on your side to make a convincing case for why substance use is not worth it.

Lake Travis school district officials are using statistics to try and help students make good choices when they are confronted with pressure from their peers to drink, smoke and use drugs. "Scare tactics don't work," said Kathleen Hassenfratz, the district's health and social programs coordinator. "We do that to kids, and it lasts for about 36 hours, that effect, and then they forget."

Rachel Rice, "Lake Travis School District Using Data to Encourage Healthy Behavior in Teens," Austin American-Statesman, December 20, 2012.

COMMUNICATION STARTS WITH YOU

Let's say you want to have a conversation with your son about drugs in school. Imagine you begin by lecturing him about not using drugs. Your son listens in silence.

You say, "Are you listening to me?"

Your son says, "Yes," and then goes to his room and shuts the door. That wasn't much of a conversation, was it?

If you want to be able to talk about substance abuse (or any difficult issue) comfortably with your child, you need to establish the lines of communication well beforehand, by encouraging conversations when your child is younger. Conversations are also a give-and-take operation: make sure that you are receiving (listening) as much as you are giving (talking). Sometimes an open mind and an open ear are the best things you can bring to a conversation with your teen.

Here is an example of how a productive conversation with your child might sound:

Parent: "Why do you think someone your age would want to smoke marijuana?"

Teen: "I dunno. To be cool, probably. Maybe just to try it."

Parent: "Do you think that smoking pot is a cool idea for someone your age?"

Teen: "Well, probably you would get into trouble if you got caught, so that's dumb. But I dunno. Lots of older kids do it."

Parent: "Did you know that marijuana is addictive? It affects your ability to think and to learn. Also, smoking pot when you're young increases your risk of getting hooked on other drugs."

Teen: "Really? I didn't know all that! Well, then how come everyone does it?"

Parent: "Actually, everyone doesn't do it. Most kids don't smoke marijuana. In any case, your [father/mother] and I know that you're smart and you'll make healthy choices about what you put into your body."

When your kids say, "You don't understand what's going on," you need to say, "You're right, I don't. What I gather is that my experience was quite different from yours, that you are experiencing pressures that I never did. So what I need is for you to help me understand what you're going through by explaining it to me."

Dr. Ralph I. Lopez, pediatrician and author of The Teen Health Book: A Parent's Guide to Adolescent Health and Well-Being.

You need to get to the point where spending time alone talking to your child feels natural to both of you. The goal is to get to know your child—her hopes, fears, likes, and dislikes—and to have your child get to know you too! Your child will be comfortable discussing difficult issues with you if he knows what your views are, what your parenting style is, and that you'll react to the difficult truths your child may reveal without yelling and/or rushing to conclusions. Self-discipline on your part is important. Balancing understanding and firm guidance is no easy task, but if you master it, you will find your child more willing to talk to you about the problems he faces. Once you and your child are comfortable talking to each other, you can persuasively convey important messages about what behavior is—and is not—acceptable for your family.

Dealing with Excuses

When adolescent patients tell me that marijuana is "natural," I respond, "So is arsenic." They laugh, then they pause for a while, and then they say, "Uh."

Dr. Claudia Califano, child and adolescent psychiatrist; clinical professor, Yale Child Study Center.

Year after year in our surveys, teens name drugs as their greatest concern, with social pressures close behind. I believe that social pressures include the pressure to do drugs. These concerns are well ahead of getting good grades, getting into college, sexual pressures, crime and violence, being bullied, and getting a job. Your kids are concerned about drugs, and they want to talk to you about their concerns. But your children may hesitate, or feel uncomfortable discussing their concerns, or even refuse to talk to you if you haven't established ongoing communication with them, or if they believe you will be hostile in response to their honesty.

The better you are at listening to your child, the likelier your child is to open up and listen to you. Parents who are not good listeners should not be surprised if their children don't pay attention to them. If you want your children to listen to you and respect your opinions, give your kids lots of opportunities to talk to you about the things that matter to them.

Being a good listener takes some practice. Give your children your undivided attention. Make eye contact. Paraphrase what they've said to confirm that what you've heard is what they've been trying to tell you. Ask open-ended follow-up questions to encourage conversation. Don't interrupt or jump in too quickly; let your children fill in silences and let them express themselves fully.

WHAT IF MY CHILD TELLS ME THAT
A FRIEND IS DOING DRUGS?

It's not easy for your teens to tell you that one of their best friends (whom they know you know) or a kid at school smokes pot. Or that they are dating someone who gets drunk on the weekends. Or that a classmate sells marijuana or pills like Adderall or his father's painkillers in school. Only if you have been broadly engaged and have established a history of listening to your child is your son or daughter likely to speak to you about such things.

Teens who confide to you about a friend's drug use may plead with you not to "snitch" on their friend. Before confiding, they may ask that you promise not to tell their friend's parents. You may fear that if you talk to that friend's parents, your teen will never confide in you again. If your child is hesitant about letting you call the friend's parents, explain that a good friend would risk her friend's anger to help the friend.

If your child tells you about a friend's drug use, ask yourself why your child is telling you. Is your child looking for a reaction, curious to see if you become alarmed or think that it's "no big deal"? Is your child probing to see how you'd react if he were using drugs? Is your child signaling that he *is* using drugs? Is your child trying to figure out what she should do about her friend? Does your child genuinely want your help in getting help for her friend?

Q: If your child told you that a friend was drinking or using drugs, would you call that friend's parents and tell them?

A: That really is a tough one. As a parent, I would want someone to tell me if my child is in trouble. I would start by talking to my child and try to get details. I also know that sometimes parents say they want to know if their child drinks/smokes, but when it comes right down to it, they don't really want to hear the information. If I ever saw the child, firsthand, high, I might then go to the parent.

A: I use discretion. Once, I told a mother something I knew to be true about her daughter's use of alcohol. She told her daughter I had called, the daughter denied the accusation, and that was the end of it—for them. Unfortunately, it drove a wedge between me and my daughter that took years to heal; wasn't worth it. That said, I have also told parents who were grateful for the information and who kept the source of the information confidential. My inclination is to tell, but I am careful.

A: I would immediately notify the parents! We're also aware that our children and some parents wouldn't accept our intervention gracefully. Some families would leap into action, and some would continue in denial—to the detriment of the family.

Parent postings in CASA's "How to Raise a Drug-Free Kid" online discussion forums.

If you discover that a child in your community is drinking or using drugs, the best way to help that child is to contact the parents directly. This won't be easy, even if you caught that child drinking or smoking pot at your home. None of us wants to be the bearer of bad news, especially about someone else's child. Parents who hear that their child is drinking or using drugs may not be receptive to such news. Their denial or disbelief is part of a devastating culture of silence about teen substance abuse, fueled by stigma and parental embarrassment. So be prepared to receive an unwelcoming reaction from the parents, but rest assured that you are doing them and their child a favor. Your call may save that child.

Parents also need to instill a sense of responsibility in their own teens to watch out for one another. Explain that an essential part of friendship is getting help for friends who are using, not covering up their drug or alcohol use. Children should be encouraged to speak up when they have a friend or classmate who is dealing or using. The point is not to punish the user, but to help insure that children (and families) who need help get it—and the sooner the better, because the earlier help is provided, the greater the chance of success.

One day I was upstairs in my bedroom, and I could hear a phone conversation through the central heating duct. It was my son, Danny. Danny was organizing a marijuana buy for himself and his friends. There were about twelve kids involved, all from the "best" families in our neighborhood. I called their parents and requested that we meet to discuss the issues of drugs and alcohol. Over the phone, several parents were indignant. Of the twelve families, parents from only three showed up: my wife and I and two other parents, each without their respective spouses.

Daniel P. Reardon, DDS.

Parents should also encourage their children to seek medical help immediately when a friend is in trouble. Too often teens abandon a friend who needs medical attention because of a drug or alcohol overdose. Children who are afraid of getting "busted" or getting into trouble may be too scared to call for help. Or they may not call because they aren't aware of how serious the danger is. Teach your children that when a friend is in medical trouble, they should always call 911; the call can be made anonymously, and it can save their friend's life.

Irma was a fourteen-year-old girl from Belmont, California, who took an Ecstasy pill . . . She became sick immediately—vomiting and writhing in pain—yet her friends did not seek medical help for her. Instead, they gave her marijuana, thinking it would relax her and possibly help her because they had heard it had medicinal qualities. Irma suffered for hours, and when she was finally taken to the hospital the next morning, she was in terrible shape. Five days later she was taken off life support and died.

Drug Enforcement Administration (DEA) website, Just Think Twice.

IF YOUR CHILD ASKS, "DID YOU DO DRUGS?" IT'S TIME TO TALK

What do you do if your child asks you point-blank, "Mom [or Dad], did you ever use drugs or smoke pot when you were a kid?" Whether your answer is yes or no, the ensuing discussion shouldn't be about you but about your child and why he's asking, and how your child's choices about substance use will affect his future. Your child has just opened the window for you to start a conversation about drugs. Take advantage of the opportunity!

If your child is asking you this question, it's probably because something happened, and he is wondering what behavior is right for him. So before you disclose anything, find out *why* your child is asking the question. "What makes you ask, honey? Did you see or hear something that made you wonder if I ever smoked pot?" Maybe a friend's parents smoke pot in front of their kids, and your child wants to know if that's "normal." Or maybe a friend offered your child a joint and said, "Everyone smokes pot when they're young." Or your child may be going to a party where he knows pills and pot will be available. Or your daughter's boyfriend may have offered her a wine cooler or vodka shot. By finding out what information your child really wants to know, you can direct your response appropriately.

Q: Has your child asked whether you drank alcohol or smoked pot as a teenager? How did you respond?

A: I told my kids that I experimented with pot and used way more alcohol than I should have. I always included the bad effects it caused, whether it was bad effects with my friends, dates, driving, etcetera, to show that it was not okay. Be honest about your use, but always talk about the negative aspects of your use. Kids appreciate honesty.

A: Yes she has and I was honest. I told her I tried marijuana at the age of 28 and didn't like that it altered my perception—that I felt like I was someone else; that I wasn't in touch with reality. I told her that lots of kids in high school used it, nice kids, kids I loved, but I never felt comfortable. Not to mention my father would probably punish me severely if he ever found out. I also told her in my senior year of high school, when we went to graduation parties, I took a beer but only because of peer pressure—so I would carry one around, often taking only a sip or two.

A: As a role model, I think it is important to keep the focus on the child. Unless I was openly in recovery, I would be silent on this subject. Studies show a relationship between parents' rules and lower rates of use, so that would be what I would emphasize.

Parent postings in CASA's "How to Raise a Drug-Free Kid" online discussion forums.

Diverting the conversation back to your child—"Let's talk about you"—is a useful psychological tool, and you have every right to use it. After all, it's one of the perks of being the parent. And you don't want to miss this key opportunity to guide your child to make healthy, drug-free choices.

USE YOUR PERSONAL EXPERIENCES AS A TEACHING TOOL

There's no consensus, no hard-and-fast rule, about how you should answer your child's question about your own history of alcohol and drug use. Whether and what to tell your child will vary from family to family, depending on the situation of the child (age, risk factors, and so forth) and the experience of the parents.

If you didn't drink, smoke tobacco, or use marijuana or other drugs, the answer may seem obvious: "No." But when you tell your child that you never tried it, be prepared for the possibility that your child will say, "Then how can you say it's dangerous or bad for me?" You can point out that there are lots of things we've never tried that we know are bad for us. There are many examples you can use. Perhaps you have a story about a friend who got into trouble as a result of drinking or drug use. Or you can rely on your own good judgment. "You don't have to put your hand into a flame or jump out the window to tell your little boy or girl not to do it."

If you did use drugs when you were a teen or in college, do not lie about it. If you lie, you can lose credibility with your children, and that is a sure way of eroding your Parent Power. That doesn't mean you have to tell your kids everything about your drug use, any more than you would tell them everything about your sex life or personal or family finances. But whatever you do share, be sure to emphasize that you don't want your children to make the same mistake, and explain why. You can tell them, "We know a lot more today about the dangers of drug use than we did when I was growing up," and give examples. What we've learned about smoking over the years is a great example. So is the new knowledge about the danger that excessive drinking poses to the adolescent brain.

Remember, you are the parent; your job is to keep your kids safe and healthy. As the authority figure, you have the right to tell your child only what you think is appropriate for a parent to disclose. There's no parental obligation to disclose your childhood foibles.

Your negative experiences are important teaching points to share with your children. Say you were at a party in high school or college where everyone started smoking pot, but you didn't want to, so you went home. This story illustrates that you had the wisdom and courage to withstand peer pressure, and can inspire your children to do the same. If you or a friend or a classmate got into serious trouble because of drinking or drugs—became addicted, had a car accident, was sexually assaulted—you should use those stories to illustrate the dangers of substance abuse and to reinforce your message that your children shouldn't repeat your mistakes or those of your friends.

If you decide to tell your children about your own history of drug use or underage drinking, make it clear that in retrospect it was a big mistake. In addition, focus on the fact that we know a lot more now about how harmful smoking, drinking, and drugs can be for teens. This can ensure that your children don't take your past conduct as proof that such behavior is a normal part of growing up, or as a signal that you won't punish them for doing the same things you did. Here are some examples:

"Yes, I smoked pot, and it was a big mistake. It made me paranoid and stupid, and I got into trouble with my parents."

"Back then, we didn't know how bad marijuana can be for you.

We know a lot more about it today than we did years ago. Marijuana today is much stronger than it was when I was in college. We now know that it's addictive and can damage your developing brain and affect your memory, ability to concentrate, and learning skills."

"I had a friend who talked me into trying cocaine. I did it once and didn't really like it, but my friend got addicted to it and had to drop out of college to get treatment. It was a dumb risk to take, and I'm just plain lucky that I didn't get hooked. My parents didn't talk to me about drugs, so I didn't know better. I want you to be educated so that you can make smarter decisions than I did."

PARENT TIPS

- Early on, establish an open dialogue on a variety of topics with your children.
- Make your expectations about substance use clear to your children.
- Make talking with your children about substance use a natural part of your continuing discussion with them, rather than just a onetime event.
- When discussing alcohol and other drugs, be honest and focus on the facts appropriate to your child's developmental stage.
- Tell your child that we know a lot more today about the dangers of smoking, drinking, and drug use for teens than we did years ago.
- Use news events, TV shows, videos on the internet, or real-life occurrences as teaching opportunities.
- If your child asks about your history of substance use, don't lie, but first focus your response on your child and why he or she is asking.
- Teach your child that being a good friend means getting help for a friend who abuses substances.

5

EAT MEALS TOGETHER: DINNER MAKES A DIFFERENCE

How do you get to know your children: what makes them tick, what concerns them, what's going on in their daily lives at school and with their friends? How do you get to know when something's wrong?

By being with them daily. And there's no more comfortable or natural way to do that than having dinner together each night. That's the ideal, but if you can't have dinner together each night, I have some other suggestions for you at the end of this chapter.

FREQUENT FAMILY DINNERS PREVENT SUBSTANCE USE

In the 1996 CASA survey of teens, I noticed that kids who had dinner with their parents every night of the week were far less likely to smoke, drink, or use drugs than kids who never had dinner with their parents. In subsequent years and other surveys, we learned that kids who had frequent family dinners also tended to get As and Bs in school, were less likely to be stressed out, be perpetually bored, or have friends who smoked, drank, or used drugs.

This chart tells the story dramatically:

Teen Substance Use by Frequency of Family Dinners

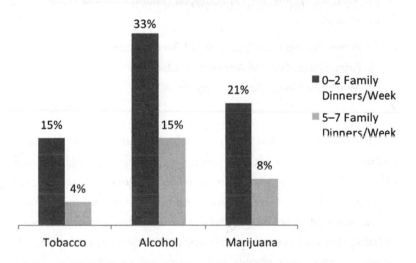

CASA. The Importance of Family Dinners VII *(2011).*

So we started calibrating our surveys and research and discovered this: as the number of days a week that parents have dinner with their children goes up, the risk that those children will get involved with tobacco, alcohol, or drugs goes down! Simply put, the more often children eat dinner with their parents, the less likely they are to smoke, drink, or use drugs. Since 1996, this finding has been confirmed year after year by our surveys and by surveys conducted by other organizations too. That's why I consider family dinner a most comfortable and powerful tool you can use to keep kids off drugs.

Families who regularly eat together know each other better. And when children—especially teens—feel that their parents understand them and know what's going on in their lives, they're less likely to smoke and abuse drugs or alcohol . . . Be sure to make family meal time relaxed and comfortable . . . make your meals electronics free. No phones, no tablets, no TV. Focus on getting to know each other well.

Armin "Mr. Dad" Brott, coauthor of The Expectant Father: Facts, Tips and Advice for Dads-to-Be, *McClatchy Newspapers, January 25, 2013.*

This phenomenon has less to do with the food that's on the plates and more to do with what's happening at the table. The nightly ritual of a family dinner gives families a relaxed, nourishing context for coming together, connecting, and communicating, talking and listening, seeing and hearing. It's where parental engagement happens. Insisting that your tweens and teens be at the family dinner table each night—without their phones and tablets—is an exercise of Parent Power at its best.

Parents who dine with their children every night know where their kids are in the evening and whether homework has been done. They get a sense of what's on their kids' minds, who their kids' friends are, what their kids are interested in, and how their moods change.

Bette Midler and her daughter, Sophie, appeared as guests on *The Oprah Winfrey Show.* Oprah asked Bette what she thought was the best thing she had done as a parent.

Midler responded, "I think the best thing that my husband and I did was we had dinner with her every single night of her life."

The nightly family dinner gives parents an opportunity to see and talk to their children on a regular basis. This helps improve communication between parents and their teens, encourages a more positive relationship, and gives parents the chance to spot any behavioral changes and mood swings in their teen that may be a sign of alcohol or drug use. And it will help keep your kids honest and accountable if they know you'll be seeing them every night.

Nightly family dinners also send your kids these important messages:

- I am here for you every night of the week.
- Need to talk about something? I'm here.
- Want to ask me something? I'm here.
- Want to boast or complain about something? I'm here.

THE DIFFERENCE FAMILY DINNER MAKES

Why is the family dinner so important in raising drug-free kids? Because it shows how much you care about your children, and this knowledge affects all aspects of their lives.

Kids appreciate it when Mom and Dad make a point of being there at dinner most every night. With both parents working, or Dad or Mom holding down two jobs to make ends meet, children realize that your being there shows a deep level of engagement. Being there for dinner creates big benefits for your children's mental, physical, and academic well-being. Here are some of them:

- You'll stay up to speed on how your children are doing in school and be able to intervene if there's a problem. If your kids are struggling with a particular subject, you'll hear about it and be able to help. A fun way to intervene may be playing a game like Monopoly if they're having trouble with math or Scrabble if it's spelling that's the struggle. If they're slacking off, skipping school, not handing in assignments, you'll be able to figure out why and try to change their behavior. If they have a learning disability, you'll pick it up faster and can deal with it in a timely manner.

- You'll be able to see how your children are doing emotionally. Are they depressed, anxious, angry, stressed out, or perpetually bored? It's important that you pick up on these things because they are all risk factors for smoking, drinking, and using drugs. You can help your children overcome these feelings if you know what's going on.

- Your children's friends can influence your child's behavior and views on substance use. Teens who have dinner with their families at least five times a week are less likely to have friends who drink, smoke pot, or go to parties where alcohol and drugs are available.

- Having dinner most every day means that it's much harder to hide smoking, drinking, or drugging from Mom and Dad. Children who think that their parents won't catch them if they smoke, drink, or get high are more likely to do so.

- Teens who have dinner with their families at least five times a week are less likely to say that they can buy marijuana within a day. The faster kids can get their hands on the drug, the greater the chances that they're using it.

Research has found that family dinners and the family engagement that occurs during them helps to enhance children's grades, discipline, and nutrition, and discourage drug and alcohol use among teenagers.

Paris Achen, *"Dinnertime Is Family Time,"*
Columbian (*Vancouver, WA*), August 22, 2011.

HOW TO GET CHILDREN TALKING AT THE DINNER TABLE

Parents of teenagers, especially older teens, often think that their kids don't want to sit around the dinner table and talk to them. But I've talked to hundreds of teens. At CASA, we've surveyed thousands. Kids do, in fact, want family dinners and the connecting that comes with them. We asked teens whether they prefer to have dinner with their families or eat alone, and more than eight out of ten of all ages preferred to have dinner with their families. And what they want at dinner is to talk to you!

Why do family dinners work? Studies suggest that frequent family dinners foster closer family ties, may be helpful in teaching children coping skills, enhance family communication, and provide good role modeling.

Debra L. Franko et al., *"What Mediates the Relationship Between Family Meals and Adolescent Health Issues?,"*
Health Psychology 27, no. 2 (March 2008).

Back in the late 1950s, there was a book about childhood and parenting titled *Where Did You Go? Out. What Did You Do? Nothing.*

That's an exchange typical in families where there is little or no communication between parents and teenagers. Parents who sit at the dinner table with their kids day in and day out can learn to turn such exchanges into more robust conversations. The key is to make talking about anything and everything part of your normal family routine, and establishing that free exchange as early in life as possible.

CONVERSATION STARTERS

One great way to get your kids talking at dinner is to use conversation starters.

For preteens, appropriate conversation starters might be questions about their world:

- What are the best and worst things that happened today?
- What's your favorite place in the house to hang out?
- If you were in charge of the music for our family vacation, which songs would you pick?
- Which TV show is the most fun to watch?
- What do you like about your friends?
- What's your favorite amusement park? What's your favorite ride?
- What's your favorite smell?
- What's your favorite toy (or game)?
- If you could have a wild animal from anywhere in the world as a pet, what animal would you choose?
- What's the greatest invention of all time?
- Using one word, how would you describe your family?
- What do you want to be when you grow up?
- What do you most like to do with the family?

When I became concerned that my teenage son might be getting involved with the wrong kids and alcohol and drugs, I wasn't sure what to do. As an immediate first step, I started requiring that he be home five nights a week for dinner. Over the next several months, I noticed a dramatic positive change in my son. I know family dinners have a positive influence on children because I watched my son change and saw improvements in his behavior, school performance, and social interaction.

Steve Burd, retired president and CEO of
US supermarket chain Safeway.

For teens, dinner conversations are the perfect opportunity to instill values in your children when they enter the teen years. Appropriate topics at this stage include current events, family matters, topics of special interest to your family (film, sports, philosophy, politics, religion), goals, difficult situations, and questions such as:

- What are the best and worst things that happened today?
- What values are most important to you?
- Who's the greatest athlete of all time?
- What can each of us do to make the world a better place? What can we do as a family?
- Did you see anything fun on YouTube today?
- Who's your favorite teacher (coach, role model) and why?
- What's your favorite subject in school?
- What's your favorite pizza topping?
- What would you do if your best friend started using marijuana (OxyContin, Xanax, cocaine)?
- What three things do you want to accomplish this year?

- What do you want to be when you grow up?
- What's your favorite movie? Band/musician? Sports team?
- What did you think of last week's sermon?

Kids know how much effort it takes to be a good parent. They know when you care enough to create a structured family life that provides a regular, ritualized forum for closeness and intimacy—the family dinner, the shared vacation, participation in their interests and activities.

Dan Kindlon, PhD, Too Much of a Good Thing: Raising Children of Character in an Indulgent Age.

You can find more great conversation starters in the CASA Family Activity Kit online at http://casafamilyday.org/familyday/tools-you -can-use/family-activity-kit. In addition, you can also find some fun activity ideas such as the Checkerboard Challenge game, family fill-in-the-blank stories, and a family recipe book. All of these conversation starters and activities can help the dialogue between you and your child grow more each day, so that when it comes time to talk about drugs and alcohol, it will feel more open, honest, and natural for everyone.

WHAT IF I CAN'T MAKE IT TO DINNER?

What if you work at night? Or can't get home in time for dinner? Or your teen has so many activities, there's no time to sit down for dinner as a family? These are all questions I've been asked by caring parents.

Family meetings counterbalance the hectic lives that today's parents and children lead; the technological distractions of the computer and video games, the extracurricular activities, school and work pressures all pull family members in different directions. Family meetings serve as a centripetal force that grounds families and encourages connections and identity. They can send a message that family time is important and is a priority in your family.

The Center for Parenting Education, "Healthy Communication Techniques: Holding Family Meetings."

Although having dinner is the easiest way to create routine opportunities for engagement and communication, you can certainly find other ways to spend time together that fit into your family's schedule. If your schedule can't be rearranged, engage in other kinds of activities with your kids, so that you are a reliable, involved, and interested presence in their lives. Remember, it's not the food that's working the magic at those dinners—it's you. Creating opportunities to connect is what's key.

A family meeting can be an opportunity to clarify expectations, celebrate accomplishments, strengthen communication, teach one another, resolve problems, and build commitment to family time. Without a regular avenue to discuss family issues, miscommunication is common, and problems are often discussed only when they have come to a boil. Such a time is hardly the best time to resolve problems in a loving and cooperative way.

Steve Dennis, dean, College of Education and Human Development, Brigham Young University– Idaho, "The Benefits of Family Meetings," 2008.

Here are some suggestions for other ways to create regular family time with your children:

- Share every available meal on the weekends.
- Have breakfast together.
- Take your child out to lunch once a week or once in a while.
- Go for walks together after work/school or on the weekends.
- Take advantage of one-on-one time in the car; offer to drive your kids to or from school, to their activities, friends' houses, movies.
- Take miniholidays together, such as afternoon trips to visit family, or go to museums, parks, or other towns.
- Have family meetings.
- Don't overschedule your child's after-school activities, and don't let those activities take away time from family dinners. You want to avoid a situation where most weekday nights your child rushes home at six o'clock, grabs a snack from the fridge, and says, "I've got to go do my homework."

Your kids need to know you are there for them. So make yourself available. Enjoy your time together.

And remember, what your kids want most, at dinner or during the time you spend together, is you.

PARENT TIPS

- Use dinnertime to ask your child about his day at school, soccer practice, or theater rehearsal; about the upcoming math test or history presentation; and about his friends.
- Use dinnertime as an opportunity to monitor your child's emotional and mental well-being. Sudden changes (beyond

typical teenage mood swings) may help you spot signs of substance use early on.

- If you can't make family dinners, seek out other times to
engage in the same conversations that you would at the dinner
table. This may be in the car on the way to school or some
activity, while watching a TV show, or playing a family board
game.

- Don't overschedule your teen with after-school activities.
Having some downtime is important and can help increase
the likelihood of everyone being able to sit down to dinner at
the same time most nights.

"I'm so overscheduled. If it weren't for timeouts, I'd have no free time at all."

PART 2

RECOGNIZE IT

6

WHAT DRUGS ARE LIKELIEST TO TEMPT MY TEEN?

The substances your teen is sure to be offered and most likely to try are cigarettes, alcohol (beer, vodka, rum, bourbon, and sweetened distilled spirits), marijuana, and prescription drugs.

Why these substances?

Because they are widely available and relatively inexpensive. Cigarettes and alcohol are heavily marketed by large corporations, like those that own Marlboro, Newport, Budweiser, and Miller beer and produce distilled spirits such as vodka. These companies make big bucks when your teen buys their products, despite the fact that it is both illegal and harmful for teens to do so.

These tempting teen drugs all share addictive characteristics. Abuse of them is associated with negative psychological, physical, neurological, and social consequences. Alcohol and prescription drugs can seriously harm your child, and can be fatal when taken in excess or mixed together. Yet many kids do just that.

There are various other drugs that your teenager might be offered or try: designer drugs such as Ecstasy (Molly) and GHB (the date-rape drug); street drugs like cocaine, heroin, and meth; drugs like salvia, an herbal hallucinogen, and Spice, a type of synthetic marijuana; and performance-enhancing drugs like anabolic steroids, especially if your child is a teen athlete. The "Parent Power Glossary for Parents and Teens" will give you a general understanding of all these drugs. But by and large, teen drug abuse involves nicotine, alcohol, marijuana, and prescription drugs. In this and the following chapters, you'll learn more about these substances so that you will be equipped to steer your children away from them.

TOBACCO: THE NUMBER ONE KILLER AND CRIPPLER

You know that tobacco use during adolescence can set kids down a path of lifelong addiction, chronic illness, and premature death. I won't repeat all those scary statistics here. What I do want to tell you is how you can keep your children from smoking burned tobacco and e-cigarettes (also called electronic cigarettes) and using other tobacco products such as dip, chew, and snuff.

Why is this so important? Because about three out of four adolescents who try tobacco products will end up addicted to nicotine as adults. Because there is now evidence that nicotine may make the young brain more susceptible to other drugs, like alcohol and marijuana. Because scientists and the US Surgeon General have recently reported that the cigarettes being sold today are actually *more addictive* than the cigarettes that were sold when you were a teen. And because if your kids stay smoke free while they're still young, the chance that they will become hooked later in life is slim to none.

The addictive power of nicotine makes tobacco use much more than a passing phase for most teens. We now know

smoking causes immediate physical damage, some of
which is permanent. Today, more than 600,000 middle
school students and 3 million high school students smoke.
We don't want our children to start something now that they
won't be able to change later in life.

Dr. Regina Benjamin, US Surgeon General,
"Surgeon General Releases New Report
on Youth Smoking," 2013.

Virtually all adult smokers got hooked on cigarettes while they
were teens or preteens. Teens are likely to experience the stress-reliev-
ing effects of nicotine more strongly than adults. Teens who smoke
develop a more deeply ingrained reward pattern than adults, which
leads to addiction. Recent scientific studies and statements made by
the National Institutes of Health indicate that nicotine can be a gateway to other drug use. Many individuals battling drug addiction at
some point in their life started out as cigarette smokers when they
were teens.

The tobacco companies have known about the addictive power
of nicotine for decades. That's why they are relentless in trying to get
your child to light up, chew tobacco, smoke flavored cigars, try snuff,
and use flavored e-cigarettes. In 2004, faced with declining sales, the
R. J. Reynolds Tobacco Company began marketing candy-flavored
cigarettes in order to disguise the harsh taste of tobacco and entice
youngsters to smoke. Public outcry forced the company to withdraw
these products from the market. But Big Tobacco has used menthol
flavoring for decades to make smoking more enticing to children.
When Congress banned flavoring of cigarettes, the big tobacco companies successfully lobbied to get menthol exempted so they could
continue to use it.

In a study of tens of thousands of US students, researchers found that kids who were dabbling with menthol cigarettes were 80 percent more likely to become regular smokers over the next few years, versus those experimenting with regular cigarettes.

Menthol is added to cigarettes to give them a minty, "refreshing" flavor. Critics have charged that menthol makes cigarettes more palatable to new smokers—many of whom are kids—and may be especially likely to encourage addiction.

Amy Norton, "Kids Who Smoke Menthol More Likely to Get Hooked," Reuters Health, October 30, 2012.

When you're talking to your child about saying no to cigarettes, be sure to discuss other tobacco-based products too. Things such as menthol cigarettes, e-cigarettes, and cigars are marketed to teens and young adults as a cooler and more fashionable alternative to traditional cigarettes. Many cigars, cigarillos, and little cigars, which are made to look like cigarettes in brown wrapping, tempt teens by coming in sweet, candy-like flavors such as chocolate, strawberry, and pineapple. Unlike the flavored traditional cigarettes created by R. J. Reynolds in 2004, these flavored cigars are still sold freely at your local store. They often contain more nicotine than a traditional cigarette. Because these flavored cigars that look like cigarettes are not taxed like regular cigarettes, they are much cheaper for children to buy. Where a pack of cigarettes may cost from $6 to $10, a pack of these flavored little cigars sells for $2 or less.

Your daughter or son might even tell you that e-cigarettes are safe because tobacco leaves aren't burned the way they are in regular cigarettes, and it's the smoke from burning that threatens to damage the throat, heart, and lungs. Tell your children that the nicotine vapor their bodies take in from e-cigarettes is just as addictive as the nicotine smoke in regular cigarettes. As this book goes to press, the jury is out on whether e-cigarettes are as dangerous to someone's health as smoked cigarettes. But the danger for your teen is that she or he will get hooked on the nicotine in e-cigarettes and then shift to regular cancer-causing ones or to other drugs. Indeed, that switch is likely one of the reasons why tobacco companies produce e-cigarettes not only with menthol but also with chocolate, strawberry, and other flavorings—something the law prohibits them from using in regular cigarettes, because such flavors entice children to smoke.

"I got an A for not smoking."

The key to preventing cigarette smoking and nicotine addiction is to understand why your child will be tempted to smoke. Advertising, movies, TV shows, and other media messages often lead children to think that smoking is cool. Many kids see smoking as a way to appear grown up or sophisticated. In chapter 15, "How Can I Mitigate the Media's Influence?," I'll give you pointers on how to teach your children to decode and resist advertising and other media messages designed to make smoking and using other tobacco products attractive.

Teens who start smoking at an early age—say, twelve to fourteen—and teens who smoke regularly are more likely than their nonsmoking peers to suffer from depression, anxiety, or low self-esteem. If your daughter voices concern or self-consciousness over her weight, make sure she knows that smoking cigarettes as a dieting technique is not healthy and not acceptable. One of the top reasons why teen girls start to smoke or continue smoking is to help them lose weight. If your teen starts smoking at a young age or is a regular smoker, try to find out if she is struggling with any of these problems. If so, seek professional advice because it may be essential to deal with the underlying problem before you can convince your child to quit smoking.

The good news is that society is on your side in this battle. There has been a seismic cultural shift away from smoking over the past thirty-five years, since as US secretary of health, education, and welfare, I mounted the nation's first antismoking campaign in 1978. Public health education campaigns, coupled with increased taxes, bans on smoking in public places, and other initiatives have reduced smoking in this country. Once marketed as the paradigm of "cool," smoking has become, in many circles—particularly among the more educated and affluent—socially unacceptable. Unfortunately, flavored smokeless tobacco use among teen boys is on the rise, as is e-cigarette use among all teens, so make sure your children know that dip, chew, and snuff are dangerous too, and e-cigarettes are just as addictive as others.

ALCOHOL: THE MOST POPULAR TEEN DRUG

It may be illegal for your teen to buy beer, wine, liquor such as vodka, and sweetened distilled spirits such as alcopops, but that hasn't stopped the alcohol industry from profiting from underage drinking. In recent years, underage drinking has accounted for almost 20 percent of alcohol industry sales. That's some $25 billion, and you can bet that the alcohol industry is doing its best to keep making those bucks, year after year, by enticing your children to drink.

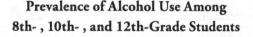

**Prevalence of Alcohol Use Among
8th-, 10th-, and 12th-Grade Students**

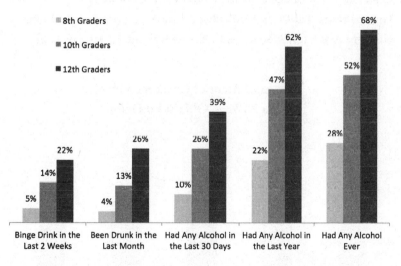

University of Michigan, Monitoring the Future survey (December 2013).

The alcoholic drinks most commonly consumed by teens are beer, distilled spirits like vodka or rum, and sweetened or flavored drinks (like Smirnoff Ice and Mike's Hard Lemonade). Your children are exposed to extensive promotion of these products, which increases their desire to drink them. For example, beer is sold and advertised heavily in sporting arenas and at concerts where teenagers congregate. In chapter 15 I'll explain these marketing strategies and how you can reduce their influence on your child.

Beer and sweetened alcohol appeal to the palates and wallets of young drinkers. These drinks are cheaper than spirits and wine. Because beer and alcopops are sold in corner stores (where drinking-age laws tend to be less diligently enforced) and supermarkets, they are often easier to purchase without a valid ID. Beer is also a large part of high school and college iconography: keg parties, beer pong, T-shirts with beer slo-gans, movies like *Animal House* and *Superbad*, and reality shows such as MTV's *The Real World*. Vodka's unique appeal is that in a bottle, from the outside, it looks like water, so it's easy to take to school. And because of its flavor, vodka can easily be mixed with or absorbed by things like gummy bears, Jell-O, and fruit slices, making it even easier for kids to consume without having to worry as much about the taste or smell.

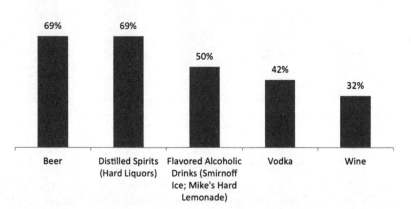

**Types of Alcohol Consumed by
13- to 20-Year-Olds Who Drink**

Michael Siegel et al., "Brand Specific Consumption of Alcohol Among Underage Youth in the United States," Alcoholism: Clinical & Experimental Research 37, no. 7 (July 2013).

One reason that underage drinking is so common is that alcohol is available in so many homes. Another reason is that teens, and many adults, tend to view drinking alcohol as a rite of passage and a normal, socially acceptable activity. Alcohol is at the heart of many cherished occasions and religious traditions. Your children are likely to see you or other family members drinking at home, at celebrations, or as part of a religious ceremony. Moderate adult drinking is widely accepted. But moderation is not a common characteristic of teen drinking.

I've seen parents who are more worried that their kid will get a disease from a mosquito bite than that their kid is out in the woods drinking beer.

Joanne Peterson, mother of a son who has been in recovery for several years and founder of Learn to Cope, a support group for parents of children addicted to opiates; Joanne's son became addicted to OxyContin after a friend's father gave it to him.

How Teens Drink

If your teen is drinking, it is likely in excess, and often with the intent to get drunk. Teens are less likely than adults to drink moderately. Adolescents drink less frequently than adults, but when they do, they drink more heavily. The US Surgeon General has reported, "When youth between the ages of twelve and twenty consume alcohol, they drink on average about five drinks per occasion about six times a month."

Beyond their penchant for taking risks and seeking thrills, scientific evidence suggests that teen drinkers are less sensitive to the sedating and discoordinating consequences of drinking alcohol: teens don't become sleepy as easily or lose their balance as quickly. Teens can physically drink more, and longer, than adults, which opens the way to dangerous binge-drinking behavior.

I don't think parents today realize that their teens are not just drinking as a social gesture, they're drinking with the intent of getting as drunk as they can. This is much different than when we were teens. This is high-risk drinking. This is drinking yourself into the emergency room.

Cheryl Sprague, prevention manager at Rushford Center, an addiction and mental health treatment program center in Connecticut for children, teens, and adults, West Hartford News, May 27, 2011.

There are immediate consequences to teen alcohol abuse: unintended, unprotected sex with several partners, poor grades, auto accidents, fighting, and rape. Alcohol is implicated in the top three causes of teen deaths: accidents (including traffic fatalities and drowning), homicide, and suicide. Mothers Against Drunk Driving (MADD), in an analysis of data from the FBI, National Highway Traffic Safety Administration (NHTSA), and Centers for Disease Control and Prevention, found that of the deaths related to underage drinking, 32 percent were traffic fatalities, 30 percent homicides, 14 percent suicides, and 9 percent alcohol poisonings. The NHTSA estimates that raising the minimum drinking age from eighteen to twenty-one has saved the lives of nine hundred teens on the road each year.

Teens who drink heavily harm their brain development and savage their memory, attention span, and spatial skills. Alcohol-dependent youth fare worse on language and memory tests.

Early alcohol initiation has been associated with greater sexual risk taking (unprotected sexual intercourse, multiple partners, being drunk or high during sexual intercourse, and pregnancy); academic problems; other substance use; and delinquent behavior in mid- to later adolescence. By young adulthood, early alcohol use is associated with employment problems, other substance abuse, and criminal and violent behavior.

American Academy of Pediatrics, Committee on Substance Abuse, "Policy Statement—Alcohol Use by Youth and Adolescents: A Pediatric Concern," April 12, 2010.

The younger a child starts to drink, the more likely he is to have serious social problems later in life: difficulty holding a job, alcohol and other drug abuse and dependency, and commission of criminal or violent acts. Children who start to drink before age fifteen are much likelier to become alcoholics than those who don't drink before they turn twenty-one.

As is the case with respect to smoking, young teens who are heavy, frequent drinkers are more likely to be experiencing emotional, social, or behavioral problems, such as anxiety, depression, conduct disorders, and antisocial behavior. If this is the case with your child, he or she will need your help addressing the underlying issue in order to stop drinking.

When it comes to reducing the likelihood of teen drinking and binge drinking, you can make a real difference. Keep track of the alcohol in your home; you may even consider locking it up, as many parents did generations ago. See and talk to your children (and, if you're suspicious, smell their breath) when they return from a night out with friends. Make it clear that drinking and driving, or being in a car with a driver who has been drinking, is absolutely prohibited; let your children know you will always provide a safe ride home if they ever need it.

Understanding what drinking means for children and teens, and the scientific rationale for delaying drinking until age twenty-one, will help you convey to your children a credible, meaningful argument against teen drinking. In addition to the immediate impact of teen drinking, in chapter 3 I set out the recently discovered threat of serious long-term damage to your teen's brain.

The Debate About Allowing Your Teen to Drink at Home

The public health message is: it is not okay for children to drink alcohol at all until they are adults, and then only in moderation. While all states prohibit selling or furnishing alcohol to anyone under twenty-one, most make an exception that allows parents to provide alcohol to their children in their homes or (in some states) in a public place.

But as a parent, you may feel conflicted about what rules to set regarding your teens drinking with the family. You may wonder if all teen drinking is bad. What about small amounts at family celebrations or at Christmas dinner? Will allowing them to drink small amounts with you teach your children to drink moderately as adults?

I will provide you with some parenting examples to consider, but how you set limits on alcohol depends very much on your knowledge of the effects of alcohol on your teen and your assessment of what will work best for your child.

Some parents believe that the best way to teach their children to use alcohol responsibly as adults is to start teaching them to drink responsibly when they are young. Parents may begin giving their children watered-down wine or small sips of beer in the tween or early teen years, and then gradually increase the portion to a half glass of wine at special dinners or family celebrations when their children are in their late teens. Parents who embrace this approach generally believe that their children will learn to drink responsibly as adults if they practice limited drinking at home as teens.

While most of us are not genetically predisposed to become addicted to alcohol, there is no way of knowing whether or not any individual teenager does have this predisposition. I was a raging alcoholic by the age of fourteen, despite my parents' European attitude toward wine with dinner and sips for children. Social drinking at a dinner table with your parents doesn't necessarily affect what you'll do as a teen at parties with your friends.

Reader's Comment, "Can Sips at Home Prevent Binges?," posted on the New York Times website.

There is no scientific research to support the idea that allowing children to drink at home will prevent them from binge drinking outside the home. In Europe, many countries have no minimum drinking age; in those that do, the minimum age ranges from sixteen to eighteen. Studies have shown that in virtually every European country except Turkey (which is Muslim), teens binge drink at higher rates than in the United States. The rate of binge drinking among teens in Ireland, Germany, the United Kingdom, and Switzerland is more than twice the rate of binge drinking among teens in the United States. The rate in Denmark is even higher.

Some parents believe that it is better to have the kids drinking under their roof than to have them drinking and driving. Other parents may be unable or unwilling to assert authority over their teens. No matter what the reason, parents who are overly permissive or who encourage teen drinking put their children at risk. Teens who believe that their parents will not care if they are caught drinking are more likely to drink, binge drink, and use other substances.

Knowledge is power, but most parents of young drinkers are unaware that their children use alcohol. On the other hand, when parents treat underage drinking as inevitable and then provide the alcohol at "supervised" parties, they are also dangerously uninformed.

As a Youth First social worker, I hear a variety of reasons why parents may provide alcohol at home. Some feel they can control the drinking and prevent driving under the influence by hosting the party and holding on to the kids' keys. However, parents who do this send the wrong message. In essence, they are saying that it's okay for teens to drink, violate the law, and harm their health.

Lauren Lesher, school social worker, "Parents Who Provide Alcohol Send the Wrong Message," Evansville (IN) Courier and Press, May 14, 2012.

Another belief that underlies permissive parenting practices is that forbidding alcohol entirely will only encourage teens to drink more and to drink clandestinely. Just as there is no evidence that letting your children drink a small amount at home on special occasions will discourage them from drinking elsewhere, there is no evidence that telling your teenager he is not allowed to drink will encourage him to do the opposite.

SOCIAL HOST LAWS

Allowing other parents' children to drink alcohol in your home is likely to violate one or more "social host" laws. These laws, which many jurisdictions have enacted, hold persons who are over twenty-one criminally responsible for underage drinking in their home. In recent years, more parents are coming face-to-face with these social host laws, and some have even been jailed.

Parents of teens: If you think a drinking disaster at your kid's party can't happen at your house, not with your kid, because he's a good kid, it's time to wake up and smell the whiskey bottle tossed on your lawn . . .

Bill Burnett, a Stanford University professor, was arrested the night after Thanksgiving over a basement party thrown by his 17-year-old son to celebrate a big high school football win.

Burnett said he and his wife had forbidden alcohol at the party and were upstairs at the time police received a call about possible drinking by minors. In fact, he said, he had twice made his way to the basement to check on the merry-making. He spent a night in jail and was booked on 44 counts of suspicion of contributing to the delinquency of a minor.

"Parents Held Responsible for Underage Drinking,"
Wall Street Journal, December 30, 2011.

As I said in chapter 2, you should encourage your kids to have their friends over or have a party at your home. But when the kids are hanging out in your living room, your backyard, or your teen's bedroom, be an attentive chaperone. And when you're talking with your child about having the party or sleepover, make sure she knows that you as the parent can be held responsible if booze or drugs show up, even if it's against your rules. If your teen knows that you could get into serious trouble for her mistake, she may be less apt to say yes when one of her friends asks about sneaking a bottle of vodka, six-pack of beer, or joint into your home. To find the most up-to-date information on social hosting laws in your state, check out the National Institute on Alcohol Abuse and Alcoholism's list on its website (http:// alcoholpolicy.niaaa.nih.gov/State_Profiles_of_Underage_Drinking _Laws.html).

IT'S UP TO YOU: YOU'RE THE PARENT

As a parent, you can learn all the facts about alcohol, but parenting is really about doing what's best for your kid. Your child is a precious individual, not a statistic. It's your job to decide what rules will work for you and your family. In making the decision regarding what message to give your children on alcohol, consider your long-term objectives. When it comes to drinking, which is more important: that your children don't damage their brains, become addicted, or accidentally kill or injure themselves or someone else by drinking too much—or that they think of you as a cool parent?

Remember this: for every year that you're able to postpone your child's first use of alcohol, his or her risk of becoming dependent on alcohol goes down.

While I can't tell you what rules will work best for your teen, I recommend that you set clear limits that teens should not use alcohol, or at least not unless they are drinking on some special occasion with you. Then stick to those limits when your teen pushes against them, and enforce them with consequences when your teen violates them.

Realistically, it may be difficult to prevent your teen from ever drinking alcohol. Your teen is prone to risk taking. This is normal teenage behavior. But even if you expect that your child may drink underage, don't make it easy for him to do so. CASA research shows that teens who are closely monitored and supervised, who believe that their parents will punish them if they are caught drinking, are less likely to drink. In fact, teens want their parents to establish and enforce limits. Despite any contrary protest, your teen really does want you to be a parent.

If you decide to allow your child to try alcohol under your supervision, a little wine at Christmas or a family wedding, you should take steps to insure that your child is not drinking outside your home without your supervision.

PERFORMANCE-ENHANCING DRUGS

In order to steer your children away from performance-enhancing drugs and other steroids, you need to appreciate what they are and why kids use them.

Is your teen an athlete?

If so, you probably appreciate the pressure that your teen is under to perform, especially if he or she is competing for a college scholarship. You may also be personally invested in your teen's athletic activities: attending practices and competitions, arranging car pools, cooking special meals. Amid all the activity, make time to talk to your teen about the dangers of performance-enhancing drugs, or PEDs.

Taken orally or injected, [steroids] are so common that they have their own slang names: D, Deca, D-Bol, Test, Roids, Juice, Slop, or Sauce . . . When taken to enhance sports performance, they are not natural and they are definitely not harmless.

Rima Himelstein, MD, "Teen Athletes and Performance-Enhancing Drugs: A Lose-Lose Situation," Healthy Kids at Philly.com, March 25, 2013.

Teens use PEDs to boost their performance, increase their strength and stamina, and enhance their physical appearance. They may feel pressure from their coach, other teammates, or even a parent to do whatever it takes to succeed. Teens can see PEDs like anabolic steroids as a quick fix to bulking up. Some teen athletes hit a plateau and think that these drugs will take them to the next level.

For teen athletes, use of PEDs is linked to their emulation of professional athletes. Some of our celebrity athletes—baseball stars like Alex "A-Rod" Rodriguez and Barry Bonds, and track and cycling stars—who have broken world records used performance-enhancing drugs such as steroids to accomplish their feats.

"Does Superman take anabolic steroids?"

Teens who witness the adulation accorded these athletes may conclude that "juicing" is an acceptable risk to gain an advantage over the competition. For high school athletes, the pressure to perform has increased, as getting into college has become much more competitive and scholarships have become so important to defray the skyrocketing cost of a college education.

Many kids see steroids as a tool to speed up the process of achieving their ideal body type and enhancing their athletic performance. And, of course, this keeps them preoccupied with an image that they feel the need to achieve at any cost. And what's even scarier is that many people who abuse anabolic steroids often use more than one kind of drug at a time—a practice that's called stacking.

The problem is that the potential effects of steroid use could be quite deadly.

Dr. Manny Alvarez, professor at New York University School of Medicine, "A Dangerous Trend: Kids and Teens Using Steroids," FoxNews.com, November 19, 2012.

Supplements

Performance-enhancing drugs other than steroids are commonly found in the form of "dietary" or "nutritional" supplements. Some performance-enhancing supplements, like creatine and dehydro-epiandrosterone, or DHEA, claim to help speed along the recovery process after a tough workout, and to increase strength and muscle mass. Similar to the hormones found in regular steroids, creatine and DHEA are both naturally produced by the body, and taking additional supplements to raise creatine and DHEA levels may give teens a boost on the wrestling mat, in the pool, or on the baseball diamond or football field. However, an excessive amount of creatine or DHEA can be harmful for your teen and produce side effects similar to those produced by steroids and described below.

Steroids

Steroids are synthetic copies of the naturally occurring male hormone testosterone. Steroids are used to treat medical conditions that result when the body's normal levels of testosterone are too low (for instance, body wasting in patients with AIDS). The doses that athletes use are ten to one hundred times stronger than the doses used to treat medical conditions.

Unfortunately, the explosion in PED use among high school and college athletes is not limited to teen athletes. Steroids are used by many teens, both girls and boys, to enhance their physical attractiveness.

Body image, especially among young women, is the leading cause of steroid use. They do it to slim down or add lean muscle, to get into "bikini shape." Guys, too, are turning to steroids to get that six-pack ab look, just to look good on the beach.

Clint Faught, educational program manager for the Taylor Hooton Foundation, created in memory of a seventeen-year-old boy, Taylor Hooton, who killed himself after taking anabolic steroids.

Girls may use steroids to improve their appearance, "get cut," lose body fat, and reduce breast size. This body sculpting may account for the increase in PED use among girls.

Serious Side Effects

Simply explaining the unattractive side effects may be enough to persuade your teen not to try PEDs.

To your son, explain that steroids can take away his masculinity: he may lose his hair, his sperm count may go down, his testicles may shrink, he might grow breasts, and he could develop severe acne.

To your daughter, explain that her voice may get deep like a man's, her breasts may shrink, she may grow dark facial hair, and she may get severe acne.

To both your son and your daughter, you can say that long-term use of performance-enhancing drugs can cause liver damage and heart disease. And you can tell them that that the National Collegiate Athletic Association (NCAA) has recognized the dangers of using PEDs. Since the 2012–13 season, the NCAA has banned the use of supplements containing DHEA and steroids by college student-athletes because of health concerns. It has also prohibited colleges and universities from giving student athletes creatine supplements.

Your teen may not realize that steroids can be addictive, and may underestimate the emotional side effects, which can be devastating. While on steroids, a teen may experience delusions or "roid rage," an increased aggression that leads to fights and hostility. Roid rage behavior can get your teen kicked off the team or thrown out of school. When a teen stops taking steroids, withdrawal can cause a depression so severe that it leads to suicide.

On December 5, 2011, we received news that no school ever wants to hear: one of our students, senior Noah Johnson, had committed suicide. The news devastated our staff and students. The grief exhibited was heart-wrenching . . .

Recently, we received a letter from Noah's mother with some disturbing news and more insight into Noah's death. While going through Noah's belongings, his family found several supplements [PEDs] that they had no idea Noah was taking. These supplements, which were all legal when

Noah purchased them, are available at several local businesses and can be purchased online. At least one of these supplements contained a synthetic anabolic steroid. The Johnson family was horrified to learn how readily available these products are to young people.

Superintendent Randy Toepke and Principal Sean O'Laughlin of Metamora Township High School, Journal Star (Peoria, IL), September 25, 2012.

Reassure your teen that your love and support are not conditioned on athletic success or an artificially shaped, good-looking body. Explain that long-term health is more important than the short-term gains of winning or appearing physically attractive—even more important than winning an athletic scholarship to college.

Discuss how an athlete's integrity is compromised by using performance-enhancing drugs. You can cite examples of athletes who have been dethroned by steroids. Marion Jones's doping forced her entire relay team to give back their Olympic gold medals. Lance Armstrong was stripped of his Tour de France victories for PED drug use, as was his team. Such incidents illustrate that using drugs to excel in sports is ultimately cheating and that it can hurt not only the athlete but also the entire team.

Talk to your child's coach about your expectations that the students not use PEDs. See that the coach is sending the same message to the kids.

Make sure your teen understands that the real recipe for success is making a long-term commitment to eating a healthy diet, getting enough sleep, and maintaining a rigorous training schedule.

PARENT TIPS

- Give your child a clear message that use of tobacco, alcohol, marijuana, and abusable prescription and over-the-counter medicines is dangerous and prohibited.
- If you smoke, quit.
- If you drink, do so in moderation.
- Don't allow anyone to smoke in your home or car.
- Educate your child about the dangers of teen drinking, binge drinking, and drinking and driving. Use news stories on TV to help point up the dangers.
- See and talk to your child upon his returning from a night out; if suspicious, when hugging your child, smell his breath.
- Alert your son and daughter to the dangers of using steroids and other performance-enhancing drugs to improve athletic achievement or sculpt attractive bodies.
- If your child is on a school team, be it football, baseball, soccer, wrestling, swimming, or another sport, let the school and coaches know that you do not want any PED use condoned.

7

HOW DO I GET MY TEEN TO UNDERSTAND THE DANGERS OF MARIJUANA?

Whats wrong with a little weed, anyway?"
Lots!

But you'd never know it after hearing about so-called medical marijuana and learning that some states are legalizing use of the drug by adults, or after seeing how movies, magazines, newspapers, and the internet have been glamorizing the drug.

When I was writing the first edition of this book back in 2007, one of the suggestions I gave parents to help convince their kids to say no to smoking pot was this: "It's illegal for anyone to smoke pot." But that suggestion may no longer carry the weight it did when *How to Raise a Drug-Free Kid: The Straight Dope for Parents* was first published. This is especially so if you're a parent who lives in a state that has legalized marijuana for all adults or "medical" marijuana for some.

Even if you don't live in such a state, these changes in laws and in attitudes over the past few years are going to make your job of raising a marijuana-free kid more difficult. Nevertheless, you can still help your teen make healthy choices. Remember, your Parent Power is greater than any outside influence.

Moreover, during these same few years, we have learned a great deal about how dangerous marijuana use can be for your teen. And what we've learned makes giving your child the skills and strength to say "No thanks" when he or she is offered a joint, pot brownie, or marijuana lollipop even more important.

If you used marijuana when you were young, you may consider smoking pot a harmless high, or you may fear appearing hypocritical if you tell your daughter or son not to do it. Perhaps you see using marijuana as a rite of passage, a phase your teen will pass through unharmed on the way to becoming an adult.

© *Steve Kelley*

Yet now is no time to be blasé about blazing blunts or bongs. Things have changed since you were a teenager. Remember how years ago, so many of us thought that smoking cigarettes was fine, and even sophisticated, macho, or sexy? Some doctors went so far as to help advertise different brands, explaining how much smoother they were on your throat when you inhaled! Well, we've since learned how wrong we—and, notably, those doctors—were about the adverse impact of cigarettes on the health of smokers and the addictive power of nicotine. Now that same kind of thing is happening with marijuana, as the medical professionals and scientists find out more about the drug. So when I tell you how much we have learned about marijuana in the past several years, you'll know how wrong it would be to write off smoking pot as a harmless or experimental teenage phase.

THE DANGERS OF USING MARIJUANA

Today's marijuana is a far more potent and dangerous drug than the pot of the 1970s or 1980s. The pot that your tween or teen would be offered today is likely to be at least ten times more powerful than the marijuana available a generation ago.

Increase in the Average Potency of Marijuana

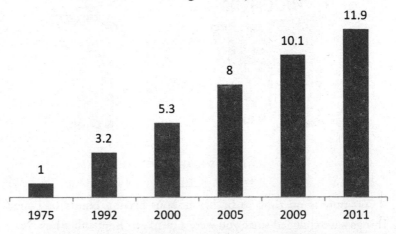

University of Mississippi, "Potency Monitoring Project"; US Department of Justice Drug Enforcement Administration, "National Drug Threat Assessment Summary" (2013).

Today's marijuana, even in small amounts, can cause a loss of physical coordination and a deterioration of motor skills. Not surprisingly, marijuana is second only to alcohol as the most frequently detected psychoactive substance among impaired drivers implicated in accidents and fatalities on the road. Not only should you make clear to your child that smoking pot is a firm no-no, but so is getting in an automobile with a driver who has been using marijuana. Just like riding with a drunk driver, getting in a car with a stoned or high driver is not worth your child's risking her safety or her life.

We know that marijuana can adversely affect your child's memory, his ability to learn and concentrate, and his neurological and emotional development. The impact of marijuana on memory and decision making is especially significant for adolescents, whose brains and bodies are still developing. For these reasons, if children smoke pot even just on the weekends, it is likely to affect their performance in school and in after-school activities. Today's pot is so strong that even small amounts smoked on a weekend can still be inside the brain during the week. Teen marijuana use can result in dropping out of school.

[R]egular marijuana use stands to jeopardize a young person's chances of success—in school and in life . . . Regular marijuana use in adolescence is known to be part of a cluster of behaviors that can produce enduring detrimental effects and alter the trajectory of a young person's life—thwarting his or her potential. Beyond potentially lowering IQ, teen marijuana use is linked to school dropout, other drug use, [and] mental health problems.

Nora Volkow, MD, director, National Institute on Drug Abuse.

If teens start using marijuana frequently, the effects on their intellectual performance, emotional development, and physical health may become even more troubling—not only now but also over the course of their lives.

Teenagers who smoke marijuana heavily show reduced brain matter and other cognitive defects later in life. We've learned that if a child continues to smoke marijuana into young adulthood, as many kids who experiment with pot at a young age do, they are at higher risk of suffering depression, clinical anxiety, panic attacks, and persistent difficulty in concentrating. Depending on the frequency and intensity of their pot-smoking behaviors, these side effects may not go away completely, even after they kick the habit. Regular marijuana use before age eighteen results in a lower IQ at age thirty-eight, even among those who stopped using at eighteen.

For kids who smoke pot often, the harmful effects of their drug use are also likely to be seen outside of the classroom. If children smoke marijuana regularly, they are at risk of suffering from many of the same respiratory problems as tobacco smokers, including chronic bronchitis, coughing, wheezing, chest sounds, and increased phlegm.

Early marijuana use is associated with the development later in life of serious mental health disorders: addiction, major depression, anxiety, and psychotic disorders such as schizophrenia . . . Daily use of cannabis in high school is associated with a sixfold increase in depression and anxiety later in life.

Elaine Gottlieb, Massachusetts Behavioral Health Partnership, "Cannabis: A Danger to the Adolescent Brain—How Pediatricians Can Address Marijuana Use," Massachusetts Child Psychiatry Access Project Newsletter, August 2012.

More frighteningly, scientific research indicates that using marijuana may cause psychotic-like episodes and increased levels of anxiety in some users. This is true for people with genetic factors predisposing them to certain mental illnesses, such as schizophrenia. For teens who are predisposed to developing schizophrenia because of a family history of the illness, smoking pot has been found to trigger schizophrenia at an earlier age and to worsen and intensify the symptoms of the disorder. If mental illness runs in your family, it's imperative to tell your children to steer clear of marijuana.

[M]arijuana use during adolescence is directly linked to the onset of major mental illness, including psychosis, schizophrenia, depression, and anxiety.

"Position Statement on Marijuana," National Association of Drug Court Professionals, December 15, 2012.

"Spice"—And We're Not Talking Cinnamon

There's a new and more destructive kid on the marijuana block: synthetic marijuana.

[U]sers [of synthetic cannabinoids] are increasingly seeking medical attention. In 2010 there were 2,906 calls to poison control centers across the United States pertaining to "synthetic marijuana"; in 2011 there were 6,959 calls.

Jason Jerry, MD, Gregory Collins, MD, and David Streem, MD, "Synthetic Legal Intoxicating Drugs: The Emerging 'Incense' and 'Bath Salt' Phenomenon," Cleveland Clinic Journal of Medicine 79, no. 4 (April 2012).

Commonly referred to as "Spice" or "K2," synthetic marijuana first began popping up in drug overdose cases several years ago, but by 2011, it had jumped to fourth place among substances abused by eighth- and tenth-grade students, falling behind only alcohol, tobacco, and real marijuana.

Synthetic marijuana is sold in colorful and eye-catching packaging, with brand names such as Scooby Snax and flavors like pineapple, blueberry, and bubblegum; there's no question that its makers are trying to tempt kids and teens to experiment with this drug. And since it's sold legally on the shelves of many local gas stations and corner convenience stores—often marketed as incense or potpourri—children can get it as easily as they can buy a bag of potato chips or a favorite candy bar, and for as little as $15 a bag.

When compared with real marijuana, synthetic marijuana is more powerful and gives a more intense high. But as too many parents and teens have learned, this high comes at an exorbitant cost.

Emily Bauer's family said that the drug that landed the Cypress, Texas, teenager, then 16, in the ICU two weeks earlier wasn't bought from a dealer or offered to her at a party. It was a form of synthetic weed packaged as "potpourri" that she and friends bought at a gas station.

"Had I thought that there was any chance that she could have been hurt by this stuff, I would have been a lot more vigilant. I had no idea it was so bad," [her stepfather] Bryant said.

"If she had bought it off the street or from a corner, that's one thing, but she bought it from a convenience store."

Emily, a straight A and B sophomore . . . complained of a migraine and took a nap at her house after allegedly smoking Spice (synthetic marijuana) with friends on December 7 . . . She woke up a different person.

Stumbling and slurring her words, she morphed into a psychotic state of hallucinations and violent outbursts, her family said.

They called 911 after they realized she had "done something," some drug.

When paramedics arrived, they . . . rushed her to a Houston-area hospital . . . She bit guardrails and attempted to bite those trying to help her. Hospital staff strapped Emily down in the bed.

"We thought once she comes down off the drug, we'd take her home and show her the dangers of this drug," said her 22-year-old sister. "We didn't think it was as big of a deal until 24 hours later she was still violent and hurting herself."

To keep Emily safe, doctors put her in an induced coma. After days in the sedated state, an MRI revealed she had suffered several severe strokes.

"In four days' time, we went from thinking everything is going to be okay and we'll put her in drug rehabilitation to now you don't know if she's going to make it," her stepfather said.

The doctors at North Cypress Medical Center told the family there was nothing more they could do.

*Christine Zdanowicz, "Teen Narrowly Escapes
Death After Smoking Synthetic Marijuana,"
CNN Health, February 5, 2013.*

[Emily survived this experience, but is legally blind, confined to a wheelchair, and unable to read or write.]

Given the newness of synthetic marijuana, doctors and other medical professionals are still discovering terrifying side effects of its use. But reports from a host of local newspapers, police departments, emergency rooms, and lawmakers across the country already tell a scary story about the dangers of synthetic marijuana. Most users are teens or under the age of twenty-five, and they have been found to suffer from a combination of overdose symptoms such as hallucinations, extreme paranoia, violence, increased heart rate, inability to feel pain, hyperthermia, and even seizures.

The synthetic drug has also been found to do serious damage to kidneys. The US Centers for Disease Control and Prevention has reported that a number of synthetic marijuana smokers, ranging in age from fifteen to thirty-three years, were found with such severe kidney damage that they had to be given emergency dialysis to avoid permanent organ failure.

MARIJUANA IS ADDICTIVE

It is estimated that 9 percent of people who use marijuana will become dependent on it. The number goes up to about 1 in 6 among those who start using young (in their teens) and to 25 percent to 50 percent among daily users . . . Marijuana addiction is also linked to a withdrawal syndrome similar to that of nicotine withdrawal, which can make it hard to quit. People trying to quit report irritability, sleeping difficulties, craving, and anxiety. They also show increased aggression on psychological tests, peaking approximately 1 week after they last used the drug.

National Institute on Drug Abuse, Research Report Series: Marijuana *(July 2012).*

We now know that marijuana is addictive, and that adolescents are more vulnerable to becoming dependent on it than adults, since their brains are still developing. In fact, the number of teens entering drug treatment for marijuana abuse or addiction has been rising sharply. Among twelve- to seventeen-year-olds, there are three times as many treatment admissions for marijuana as the primary substance of abuse than for alcohol and all other drugs combined.

Treatment Admissions by Primary Substance of Abuse, Ages 12 to 17

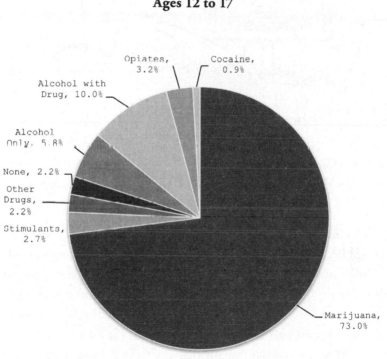

Opiates, 3.2%

Cocaine, 0.9%

Alcohol with Drug, 10.0%

Alcohol Only, 5.8%

None, 2.2%

Other Drugs, 2.2%

Stimulants, 2.7%

Marijuana, 73.0%

SAMHSA Treatment Episode Data Set (2010).

As Nora Volkow, MD, the director of the National Institute on Drug Abuse, has said, "There is no question that marijuana can be addictive; that argument is over. The most important thing right now is to understand the vulnerability of young, developing brains to these increased concentrations of cannabis."

"Wish I could!"

© *Ray Jelliffe from CartoonStock.com*

SAYING NO TO LEGALIZED MARIJUANA AND "MEDICAL" MARIJUANA

With many states saying yes to "medical" marijuana, and some legalizing the drug for adults to use, your child may ask questions like "How can smoking pot be dangerous if it's medicine and given out by a doctor?" and "If weed is such a bad drug, wouldn't it be illegal?"

So how do you go about answering these questions in an honest and thoughtful way? First, use the facts about the harmfulness of the drug. Then you should explain that the federal government's Food and Drug Administration (FDA) has a careful process in place for approving prescription drugs and medicines, and that smoked marijuana has never been through that process.

No FDA-approved medication is smoked. In addition to the concerns about potential [cancer-causing chemicals] . . . there is great difficulty in delivering the exact dose [of smoked marijuana], if a "dose" even exists . . . Medical marijuana bypasses the century-old, scientifically based drug approval procedure and the carefully regulated distribution of medications through licensed pharmacies.

> *Dr. Herbert D. Kleber, Columbia University Medical School faculty and director of Division on Substance Abuse, New York State Psychiatric Institute, and Dr. Robert L. DuPont, founding president of the Institute for Behavior and Health, and former director of the National Institute on Drug Abuse, "Commentary: Physicians and Medical Marijuana," American Journal of Psychiatry 169, no. 6 (June 2012).*

Keep in mind that the idea of marijuana now being legal or used as a medicine may be confusing for your teen. Chances are it goes against what he has learned in school health classes, and from conversations he's had with you, his pediatrician, athletic coaches, and other adults who have told him that marijuana is a dangerous and illegal drug. And seeing that marijuana doesn't necessarily have to be smoked but can easily be mixed into a brownie, chocolate bar, cookie, or piece of candy will just further blur the lines between the image your child has in his head about what drugs are and what they're supposed to look like, and what's something that he might already eat as a typical after-school snack or dessert.

Confusing messages about marijuana use that are being conveyed by proponents of "medical" marijuana perpetuate the false notion that marijuana use is harmless. These messages ignore the very real negative consequences associated with marijuana use and dependence. Given that 1 in 6 adolescents who initiate use of marijuana are at risk of developing an addiction to the drug at some time in their life, we owe it to them to make sure they understand and the people in their lives who care about them understand the real risks associated with its use.

White House Office of National Drug Control Policy, "Issues: Marijuana," 2013.

In a state that has legalized marijuana for adult use, you can point out the similarity that exists between smoking marijuana and drinking alcohol. Remind your teen that alcohol is a legal drug for adults, but illegal for those under twenty-one. Why? Because of the damage that booze can do to developing brains, just as marijuana can do.

It's important that you explain to your child that even though it may be legal for some people to use pot in some states now, everything he or she learned about marijuana before is still true. It can still make teens and adolescents more anxious, depressed, and unable to concentrate. It can still make it harder to pay attention during conversations. It can still make them less motivated and perform less well in school, sports, and other after-school activities. And just as alcohol is unsafe for kids under twenty-one years old, pot is still unsafe for them too.

Drugs as cookies mean I have to talk to my older children about drugs without the natural barriers created by the need to shoot them into veins, roll them up and smoke them, or ingest them in other complicated ways. Drugs as gummy bears mean I need to teach my younger children about eating candy found in unexpected places. Drugs as chocolate mean we're going to need to talk to our children and teenagers . . . about the dangers of treats from unexpected or unfamiliar sources.

KJ Dell'Antonia, "When Marijuana Looks Like Candy, Not Drugs," New York Times, February 11, 2014.

TEENS' PERCEPTIONS OF POT

The most important message for your children to get from conversations with you is that marijuana, even if it's legal in some states and even if it's available as "medical" marijuana, is still dangerous for kids their age. The drug's harmfulness is the key point you want to get across. To understand why that message is so important, take a look at this chart:

High School Students' Perspectives on How Dangerous Some Drug and Alcohol Behaviors Are for Teens

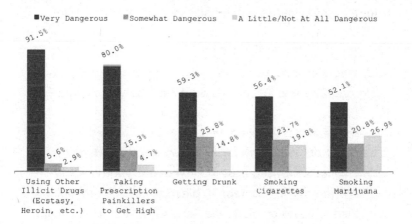

CASA. Adolescent Substance Use: America's #1 Public Health Problem *(2011)*.

As you can see, more than a quarter of high school students consider marijuana to be a harmless or only slightly dangerous drug. That's nearly twice the number of high school students who think getting drunk is harmless, and six times the number of high school students who think abusing prescription pain medications is harmless.

Why should we be concerned about teens' perceptions of how harmful pot is? Because we know from decades of research at CASA and national teen surveys that the less harmful and more socially acceptable kids think smoking pot is, the likelier they are to try it.

EVERYBODY DOESN'T DO IT

Don't fall for the age-old argument "But Mom [Dad], *everybody* does it!"

First of all, that's not true. Only about one in four teens smoke pot. That means about 75 percent don't.

If your teen tries that argument on you, take this as an opportunity to use your Parent Power and further instill the values on conduct, civility, and self-respect that you want for your child to develop. Remind your teen daughter or son of the high standards your family has set for each family member, and of the values you share as a supportive, respectful, and loving family. As the mother quoted puts it, sticking to your family's morals and expectations is important.

Q: If your child tells you that drinking or smoking pot is no big deal because lots of kids do it, how do you respond?

A: Bottom line is the expectations we have placed in our home for our family are for their own good and aren't determined or revised based on what everybody else is doing. This theme has been in place since birth and has applied to issues all along the way, so it is no new concept. Will it be tested and questioned? Of course! It already has been with smaller issues. This comes with their development of independence. We aren't surprised or angry by this process but continue to stick by our morals and beliefs and give them room to grow.

Parent posting in CASA's "How to Raise a Drug-Free Kid" online discussion forums.

IF YOU DISCOVER YOUR KID SMOKES POT

Now that you've read about legalizing marijuana and teens' perceptions on the harmlessness of this drug, it probably won't come as a surprise when I tell you that for teens, marijuana is widely used, behind alcohol and tobacco. And although high school students today are refusing that first alcoholic drink or cigarette more often than high school students did ten years ago, sadly, the same isn't true about that first joint. Today's teens are at least as likely to be getting high from pot as teens were a decade ago.

So what should you do if you catch your kid smoking pot? Don't let it slide—nip the bud in the bud. Talk to her about the risks of marijuana, and regularly check in throughout the teen years and remind your child of the drug's harmful effects.

During these talks, be clear with her about how you, as her parent, disapprove of her smoking pot just as much as you would if she drank alcohol or got high on prescription painkillers. After years of surveying teenagers, we at CASA learned how much kids are influenced by their parents' attitudes when making decisions about whether to use drugs. Teens who do not think their parents would be extremely upset to discover they had used marijuana are more than four times likelier to smoke pot than those teens who do think their parents would be extremely upset. Send a clear message about how upset you are about your child using marijuana.

This type of open communication between you and your children—letting them know clearly and consistently what your expectations are regarding marijuana and other drugs—may give your kids the final push they need to feel confident in choosing not to use the first time they're offered a joint. In chapter 19, "What Are the Signs of Use? What Should I Do If I See Them?," I provide specific suggestions for parenting steps to take if you discover that your child is smoking marijuana.

It may sometimes feel like your kids aren't listening—or, worse, like they don't care—but with your active engagement and hands-on parenting, these messages will get through to them. Don't give up or ever think you are just wasting your breath. Setting boundaries and enforcing consequences are key to raising healthy children. Holding your children accountable when they ignore those boundaries will not make them hate you, it will help teach them that smoking marijuana is not okay.

PARENT TIPS

- Dispel the myths that marijuana use is harmless and not addictive.
- Give your child a clear message that smoking marijuana goes against the values and rules developed by your family.
- Discuss how recent state actions on medical marijuana and legalization do not mean that the drug is now acceptable or safe to use, especially for kids and teens.
- Remind your child that her brain will continue to develop through her midtwenties; using marijuana now can impair that development, and cause long-term damage to her physical, mental, and emotional health.
- Alert your child to the great danger of synthetic marijuana.

8

MISCHIEF IN YOUR MEDICINE CABINET? OVER-THE-COUNTER AND PRESCRIPTION DRUGS

These days, to protect your children from the risks of substance abuse, you need to know the facts about certain over-the-counter (often called OTC) and prescription drugs: what they are, why children take them, and how children obtain them.

Why is this so important to you?

First, because among high school seniors, OTC and prescription drugs have become the fifth most commonly abused substances, right behind alcohol, tobacco, marijuana, and synthetic marijuana, and these pharmaceuticals can be addictive and do serious—even permanent—damage to your child.

Second, because potentially dangerous OTC and prescription drugs are likely to be available in your home. If there aren't any in your medicine cabinet, you can bet there are in the medicine cabinets of parents of your children's friends—and in backpacks of some of your children's classmates.

The painkiller Vicodin, cough medicines like Robitussin, the stimulant Adderall, and tranquilizers like Valium and Xanax are the top four medications abused by high school seniors. Some prescription medications have become so commonly abused that teens even have "pharming" parties, where bowls of pills in various colors and shapes are passed around like M&M's. These pills don't have the calories of beer, wine, and distilled spirits, the aftertaste of marijuana, or the stigma of street drugs such as cocaine and heroin, but their abuse can have the same grim consequences (especially if mixed with alcohol).

From 2004 to 2011, teen emergency room visits due to abuse of painkillers like Vicodin and OxyContin have more than doubled, as have such visits due to abuse of OTC cough and cold drugs and stimulants. Teen emergency room visits due to abuse of depressants such as Xanax, Valium, and Ativan are up more than 80 percent. And the incidence of teen deaths caused by prescription drug overdoses has climbed steadily since 2000.

[Austin Box, a linebacker for the University of Oklahoma Sooners football team] was upbeat, alert, and seemingly at the top of his physical game on a three-day trip to St. Louis with his father in 2011. But the day after they returned, Austin was found unconscious in a friend's home. He died after being taken to the hospital, at age 22.

The toxicology report showed five different pain medications and an antianxiety drug in Austin's system—a cocktail that ended up stopping his heart.

In the months that followed, Craig Box, Austin's father, couldn't help thinking back over their trip to St. Louis for signs of an addiction. "I saw nothing that gave me any indication that this was an issue," he said—no sign that his "all-American" son was about to become part of an increasingly American statistic.

Jason Kane, "Prescription Drug Abuse: Top 10 Things CDC Says You Should Know," PBS NewsHour, The Rundown, April 30, 2013.

Abusing prescription and over-the-counter drugs harbors the same dangers as abusing street drugs: addiction; serious emotional, social, and health problems; medical emergencies; brain damage; and overdose deaths. Teens who pop prescription pills to get high are much likelier than those who don't to use other drugs. That's why I'm going to tell you about those drugs in this chapter. I'll provide a quick summary here, but you can check out specific information on each type of drug in the "Parent Power Glossary for Parents and Teens" in the back of this book.

OVER-THE-COUNTER MEDICINES

OTC cough and cold drugs are not controlled by the federal government. They can be purchased without a physician's prescription. Although some states require an individual to be at least eighteen years old to buy certain of these medicines, it's easy for a tween or teen to buy them at most drugstores and supermarkets.

Cough and Cold Medicine

You and your child have almost certainly taken an OTC medicine to help soothe a cough or relieve the symptoms of a cold. More than a hundred typical OTC medicines, including NyQuil, Robitussin-DM, Sudafed, and Dimetapp, contain an ingredient called dextromethorphan (DXM). To get a high, teens take drugs with DXM in large doses, sometimes even twenty-five times the amount recommended on the medicines' labels. One of eighteen high school students has taken cough and cold medicines containing DXM to get high. Robitussin is the OTC drug most abused by teens.

When misused, DXM can cause slurred speech, stomach pain, hallucinations, rapid heartbeat, and vomiting, among other symptoms. If cough or cold medicines containing DXM are abused over a long period, other ingredients in them can cause liver damage.

Stuffed-up and runny noses, sore throats, and coughs happen. They're a fact of life, especially for kids. So the next time that you're at your local pharmacy to buy cold medicine, check the labels and try to pick one that doesn't list DXM as a main ingredient. If you can't find a good option without DXM, stick to the recommended dosage and keep track of how much your child takes.

PERILS OF THE PRESCRIPTION PAD

The federal government imposes special controls on three types of prescription drugs because of their high potential for abuse: painkillers, depressants, and stimulants.

Prescription Painkillers

Commonly abused prescription painkillers include Vicodin, Oxy-Contin, fentanyl, Dilaudid, codeine, Demerol, Percocet, and Percodan. The vast majority of teens who abuse prescription drugs abuse painkillers that are highly addictive, like Vicodin, OxyContin, and Percocet, and today more teens than ever use them to get high. Properly used, OxyContin, perhaps the most addictive painkiller, is time-released to provide relief over many hours. To create a "rush," teens crush OxyContin to break the time release seal and get the full dose at once. The potent prescription painkiller Zohydro ER offers teens a similar dangerous high by crushing its time release seal.

[P]rescription drug abuse . . . [is] endemic on the East Coast, [but] by the way, we're seeing it all over . . . This is not an inner-city minority problem as much as it is a suburban upper-middle-class problem.

Timothy Wilens, MD, director of the Center for Addiction Medicine and director of Substance Abuse Services in Pediatric Psychopharmacology, Massachusetts General Hospital; "Substance Use Disorders Among Youth," voted best lecture of 2013 by the American Academy of Child and Adolescent Psychiatry.

A Hallway to Heroin

Many teens who become addicted to OxyContin eventually switch to heroin, which is less expensive and can give a more intense high. As many companies have changed the formula so that crushing the painkiller no longer gives the instant and intense high that it used to, more kids have switched to heroin to achieve that same rush and numbness that they encountered on their first high with the pills.

[H]eroin isn't at all what it used to be. Not only is the drug much more powerful than before (purity can be as high as 90 percent) but it's also no longer limited to the dirty-needle, back-alley experience so many of us picture. Now it's as easy as purchasing a pill, because that's what heroin has become: a powder-filled capsule known as a button, designed to be broken open and snorted, that can be purchased for just $10. And it regularly is—on varsity sports teams, on Ivy League campuses, and in safe suburban neighborhoods.

Julia Rubin, "How Heroin Is Invading America's Schools," Teen Vogue, September 2013.

Heroin use has been rising, for example, on Long Island in New York. Heroin has become so cheap—less costly in many cities and towns than a pack of cigarettes or a six-pack of beer—that it poses a new threat to your teen.

Prescription Depressants

The most commonly abused depressants are tranquilizers, which are generally used to treat anxiety. They include medications known as benzodiazepines, such as Xanax and Valium, the two depressants likeliest to be abused by teens. Like painkillers, these can be addictive.

Another type of depressant, barbiturates such as Nembutal and Mebaral, are also sometimes used to relieve anxiety. These are more addictive than benzodiazepines and have a greater risk of overdose.

A third type is nonbenzodiazepine sleep medications like Ambien, Lunesta, and Sonata. These drugs are thought to have fewer side effects and less risk of dependence.

The effects of depressants can linger, and adversely affect cognition and memory; students who abuse them are likely to see their grades suffer.

Prescription Stimulants

Stimulants, which can also be addictive, are used to treat a variety of medical ailments, including attention deficit/hyperactivity disorder (ADHD), asthma, respiratory problems, obesity, and narcolepsy. Adderall, Ritalin, Vyvanse, Dexedrine, and Concerta are commonly prescribed to treat ADHD in children, and these are the stimulants most commonly abused, especially by early teens.

The effects of stimulants can be both short term and long term. In addition to heightened focus, a stimulant "high" for many users can mean headaches, severe mood swings, rapid heart rate, anxiety, and loss of appetite. Over time, these symptoms can lead to significant and unhealthy weight loss, high blood pressure, and depression.

Dexedrine [a stimulant] allowed me to zone out like no other drug did, not because it was better than cocaine, which I'd been addicted to at the age of 14, before being on prescription drugs, but because unlike cocaine, it was legally sanctioned and morally sanctified—my teachers, many of my peers, and society at large approved of my addiction. I'd gone through the medical establishment to get drugs, so I had a stamp of approval, a legal document that gave me permission to get high, mentally drop out of my life, and get a pat on the back in the process. That's the perversity of prescription drugs. Dexedrine was a sign of my progress, not a sign of my demise.

Peter Moskowitz, "All My Friends Are Dead," *Gawker*, May 4, 2013.

Students Using Stimulants to Get "Smarter"

It's likely that one of your kid's friends, perhaps even your own child, has been diagnosed with attention deficit/hyperactivity disorder. As ADHD becomes a common diagnosis, more children, teens, and even college-aged kids are taking prescribed stimulant drugs such as Adderall to help them improve their concentration and sit still in the classroom. Nearly twenty-one million prescriptions were handed out to adolescents in 2012.

Kids call these drugs "Good-Grade" pills or "Study Aids." Many students take them to get an extra edge in the classroom, whether or not they suffer from ADHD. The pills are easy to get, as most kids know someone at school who will sell some of their Adderall or Ritalin for as little as $5 a pill. Other teens—notably college students—have learned that they can get their own prescription from a doctor by feigning the symptoms of ADHD, and complaining about difficulty concentrating and focusing on schoolwork. Indeed, most teens know all the symptoms of ADHD.

Medications like Adderall can markedly improve the lives of children and others with [ADHD]. But the tunnel-like focus the medicines provide has led growing numbers of teenagers and young adults to fake symptoms to obtain steady prescriptions for highly addictive medications that carry serious psychological dangers. These efforts are facilitated by a segment of doctors who skip established diagnostic procedures, renew prescriptions reflexively, and spend too little time with patients to accurately monitor side effects.

Alan Schwarz, "Drowned in a Stream of Prescriptions," New York Times, *February 2, 2013.*

Whether it's because of the steady rise in the numbers of teens being diagnosed with ADHD and the large number of prescriptions being written, or the misguided thought that the drugs aren't dangerous because they're "just used to boost school performance," more kids are abusing drugs such as Adderall, and starting at younger and younger ages. Many teens don't view these drugs as risky, so they're easily induced to try them when offered by a classmate. Since 2010, the number of high school seniors who consider misusing Adderall to be harmful has dropped sharply. To keep your child from becoming one of these statistics, talk to her about the dangers of abusing prescription stimulants.

Parents, by and large, are unaware of how common use of stimulants to study has become. Although one in eight high school seniors report having used prescription stimulants as a study aid, only one in a hundred parents suspect that their child has actually used the drug. There are some parents, however, who might tell you that stimulants helped their children who did not have ADHD improve their grades and suggest you do the same to help your child. Don't listen to them. These parents are encouraging their kids to take addictive pills they don't need and on which they may become dependent in the future.

Some parents ask their doctors to prescribe stimulants to help their children with exams. After all, these parents think, what's wrong with a little extra help medication can offer? And there are some doctors who will placate the parents and prescribe the medication, thereby hurting the teenager and fostering in the child the notion of "better living through chemistry."

Dr. Ralph I. Lopez, pediatrician and author of The Teen Health Book: A Parent's Guide to Adolescent Health and Well-Being.

WHAT TO DO IF MY CHILD'S SCHOOL SUGGESTS MEDICATION FOR ADHD

Stimulant prescriptions can help children with ADHD. But whether your child has ADHD is something for you and your child's doctor to assess.

"We'll discuss your misbehavior in a moment Billy, but in the meantime, why don't you help yourself to a nice piece of candy?"

© *Loren Fishman*

Over the past decade, there has been an increase in the number of school nurses, teachers, and administrators who recommend to parents that their children take stimulant medication for emotional and behavioral issues, mainly to treat attention deficit/hyperactivity disorder. Unfortunately, some overburdened teachers and school administrators may recommend medication in cases where it is not necessary. Because stimulants like Ritalin, Adderall, and Concerta can reduce disruptive behavior, educators—and even parents—may see medication as a quick fix for rambunctious kids and may tend to use it more liberally than is medically indicated.

If a teacher, administrator, or school nurse recommends that your child should be medicated, you should get a second opinion from your child's pediatrician or a child or adolescent psychiatrist or psychologist. You can go to an education testing service that specializes in evaluating children for disorders such as ADHD. These evaluations tend to be more comprehensive than questionnaires used by many school health professionals evaluating children. If a child is having trouble focusing or is acting out in class, it does not necessarily mean that ADHD is to blame or that medication is the solution.

For children who suffer from serious ADHD, medication can be a godsend. Kids with ADHD who can't focus or sit still find that the medication makes learning possible. If your child does need medication for ADHD, keep track of your child's pills, because his or her classmates may try to get their hands on them. Make sure your child understands that prescription drugs are to be used only as directed by a doctor. Let your child's school know if he is taking a prescription stimulant. Make sure that teachers, coaches, and counselors at your child's school are vigilant about students not sharing ADHD medications and that they educate kids about why it's risky to do so. Long-acting forms of these medications may make it unnecessary for your child to take any pills to school.

© *Rob Rogers*

REDUCING THE RISK

Among teens, the abuse of OTC and prescription drugs carries much less stigma than abuse of other substances. Teens tend to think that these drugs aren't dangerous or addictive. Most believe that using prescription drugs to get high is safer than using street drugs.

With doctors prescribing these drugs to their classmates and parents, too many teens mistakenly think, "How dangerous can abusing these drugs be?" The answer is: "Very dangerous!"

Learn the truth about [prescription] pills—and don't take them lightly. In my health classes, we spent so much time talking about hallucinogens and crack and cocaine. But we barely touched on prescription drugs. I never took those other drugs seriously. I would have paid a lot more attention if they talked about the stuff in my own house [or at school].

Tim Bracaglia, nineteen years old, recovering prescription drug addict, in article by John DiConsiglio, "I Was Hooked on Prescription Drugs," Choices, 2012.

It's so important for you to let your children know that in your home, abuse of OTC and prescription drugs will be viewed the same way as other drug use, and will be subject to the same disciplinary sanctions.

If you suspect or believe that your teen may be abusing pharmaceutical drugs, check chapter 19, "What Are the Signs of Use? What Should I Do If I See Them?," where I suggest steps you should take.

Mischief Makers in the Medicine Cabinet

I call these pharmaceutical drugs the mischief makers in the medicine cabinet because most teens who abuse these drugs get them from their parents' medicine cabinet or from their friends. (And most of their friends get them from their own parents' medicine cabinets.) That's why for many teens, prescription drugs are easier to get than beer. Even if your medicine cabinet is free of dangerous prescription medications, with just the click of a mouse and a credit card, teenagers can purchase controlled prescription drugs on the internet without a prescription.

Q: If you are taking prescription painkillers such as OxyContin or Vicodin, or antianxiety drugs like Xanax, what, if anything, do you do to make sure your child doesn't have access to your pills?

A: I keep them on my person, such as in my purse, which is off-limits to my child, and she knows it.

A: I lock them up. They are a controlled substance under lock and key at the pharmacist. Home should be no different. Better safe than sorry.

Parent posting in CASA's "How to Raise a Drug-Free Kid" online discussion forums.

As a parent, you play a key role in limiting your child's access to pharmaceutical drugs. Don't leave controlled prescription pills around the house or in places where your child can find them. Your carelessness can yield inadvertent but devastating harm to your own teen. Keep track of the pills in your medicine cabinet; lock the cabinet if necessary. Carefully dispose of unused pills. For information about disposing of pharmaceuticals such as painkillers, depressants, and stimulants, check the US Food and Drug Administration (FDA) website at www.fda.gov or call toll-free at 1-888-INFO-FDA, or check with your local police department.

You have the Parent Power and responsibility to decrease your child's access to addictive pills and medicines. Indeed, since kids who experiment with pharmaceutical drugs so often get their first pills from their own home, you may have the most power to keep these drugs out of your child's hands.

PARENT TIPS

- Discuss with your child the dangers of abusing over-the-counter and prescription drugs, including overdose and addiction.

- Keep track of prescription drugs and all cough and cold medicines; don't allow them to fall into the hands of your child.
- If your child has a prescription from a doctor for a medication or is taking an OTC cough or cold medicine, make sure that he or she sticks to the recommended dose and doesn't take it too frequently.
- If your child is taking a stimulant for ADHD, let your child's school know.
- Urge your child's school to educate its students about the dangers of prescription drug abuse and of sharing prescribed pills with friends.

9

FOR YOUR TEEN, AVAILABILITY IS THE MOTHER OF USE

YOUR CHILD'S WORLD IS FULL OF DRUGS

Understanding the world your child lives in is essential. I'm going to describe that world for you. Better sit down while you read this.

Are drugs available to kids everywhere? You bet they are. Today's teens are exposed daily to a dizzying menu of addictive illegal and prescription drugs, glamorously advertised cigarettes, beer, wine coolers, fruit-flavored hard liquors, vodka, "malternatives," candy-flavored chewing tobacco, menthol-flavored cigarettes designed to make it easier for kids to inhale those first smokes, and inhalants.

Wherever you live—large city or small town, affluent suburb or rural community, the North, South, East, or West—the substances sure to be within easy reach for your kids are tobacco, alcohol, marijuana, prescription pills, and inhalants. Some other drugs are likelier to show up in specific parts of the country. Methamphetamine is more prevalent in the South, especially in Georgia, Louisiana, South Carolina, and Kentucky, and in New Mexico. Teens in some cities in Texas have gotten into "cheese"—a potent, sometimes flavored mix of heroin and an over-the-counter medicine—which has caused several deaths over the past few years. Crack cocaine is widely available in poor sections of major eastern cities. Powder cocaine is likelier to be available in affluent areas and on many college campuses. Teens are abusing painkillers more frequently in Arizona, Idaho, Indiana, Kentucky, Mississippi, Nevada, Ohio, New Mexico, Oklahoma, and Oregon. Ecstasy is more popular among teens in the Midwest and Southwest states, including New Mexico, Texas, and Colorado. And inhalants are likelier to be used by teens in Wyoming, South Carolina, Georgia, Arkansas, Arizona, and Louisiana.

There will also be times when some drugs are cheaper or more available than others. Heroin, for example, has fluctuated in price over the decades, but in recent years, it is cheaper in some communities than a movie ticket. Especially in large cities, like New York, it is cheaper than a pack of cigarettes or a beer at the neighborhood bar.

"When the teenagers can't afford the $40 price tag for OxyContin, which is getting harder to buy on the streets, or even Perc 30s, which can cost users $30 per pill, they turn to shooting heroin," [Kevin Norton, CEO of Northeast Behavioral Health,] said.

"I don't care how much disposable income you have as a teenager. When you have a choice of paying $30 to $40 for a pill, and a bag of heroin goes for as low as $6, less than a pack of cigarettes, you'll end up going for the heroin," Norton said. "I know it's a cliché, but it's almost a perfect storm."

Jeff McMenemy, "Heroin Nets Younger Users," Daily Item, April 20, 2012.

Casual and frequent exposure—especially when combined with glamorization and peer pressure—makes experimentation tempting.

Surely your teenage son or daughter has uttered these words to you at some point in his or her life: "But all my friends are doing it! Even [insert the name of straitlaced best friend who hangs out at your house after school all the time] is doing it!" Perhaps that argument was made to you in support of drinking at a party or smoking a little pot. Maybe you've even learned from other parents in your community or teachers at your child's school that yes, in fact, a lot of kids are drinking or smoking or indulging in a little drug experimentation. You may think that because you hear such behavior is relatively common in your area, it's harmless. Think again.

Teen alcohol and drug use is risky business; risky for your kid's physical and mental health and well-being in the present day, and risky for his or her future, since the younger kids are when they start to use, the likelier they are to develop addictions. My advice to you is the same that you might give to your child: just because others—your friends, your classmates—are doing it doesn't mean it's okay.

The reality is that the vast majority of teens are not using illegal drugs. National surveys suggest that about 40 percent of high schoolers have ever tried marijuana; less than 4 percent of high school students have ever tried cocaine; 1.5 percent, meth; and 1 percent, heroin. That's the good news. The bad news, however, is that teen drinking is widespread, and marijuana, prescription drugs, and alcohol are readily available to teens. Two in five high school seniors are regular drinkers, and one in four has been drunk in the last month. Resistance is an ongoing battle.

Many factors drive teen decision making about using substances, but economics and convenience are among the most important. These are factors in why government laws and policies have imposed taxes to increase the price of cigarettes, established underage purchasing bans, and prohibited indoor smoking. These steps have proven effective in driving down youth smoking rates, because the more expensive and harder it is to smoke, and the less socially acceptable, the less likely kids are to do it.

In our surveys, we ask teens to rate beer, cigarettes, marijuana, and prescription drugs by the ease with which they can get them, whether buying them at the corner store, stealing them from their parents' medicine cabinet, or taking them from a friend. In 2012 we found that cigarettes are easiest for your kids to get, but beer is a close second, followed by marijuana and prescription drugs.

Our surveys also ask twelve- to seventeen-year-olds: "If you wanted to get marijuana right now, how long would it take you?" In 2012, 43 percent could get it within a week; nearly a third, within a day, and 14 percent, within an hour. That means almost eleven million teens have ready access to the drug; nearly eight million would need no more than a day; and more than three million need only an hour to get marijuana!

If you wanted to get marijuana right now, how long would it take you to get it?

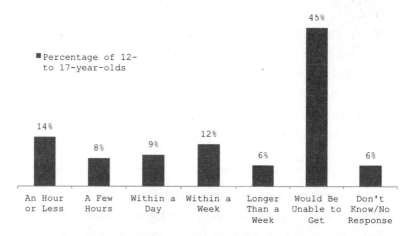

■ Percentage of 12- to 17-year-olds

An Hour or Less	A Few Hours	Within a Day	Within a Week	Longer Than a Week	Would Be Unable to Get	Don't Know/No Response
14%	8%	9%	12%	6%	45%	6%

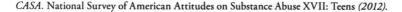

CASA. National Survey of American Attitudes on Substance Abuse XVII: Teens *(2012)*.

WHERE DO TEENS GET DRUGS?

When you think about how teens obtain drugs, you may picture a kid sneaking down a back alley to make a purchase from a street drug dealer. But in reality, kids get drugs in the most run-of-the-mill places, the places where they spend most of their time: their homes, their schools, their friends' homes, and their neighborhoods.

Teens often get two of the nation's most common legal drugs—cigarettes and alcohol—from adults or older friends. A government survey found that 40 percent of underage drinkers were given alcohol for free by an adult in the prior month. Teens can also purchase cigarettes and alcohol from careless, inattentive, or unscrupulous retailers and bartenders, on some internet websites, or by using fake IDs. These IDs can be bought on the street and are commonly passed down by siblings or other friends and classmates that are actually twenty-one years old, and have a photo of someone who looks similar enough to the teen for some overly lenient bartenders to not question.

In the Home

Parents stock a wide variety of substances in their homes: from addictive painkillers in the bathroom medicine cabinet, to inhalants in aerosol canisters under the kitchen sink, beer in the refrigerator, and liquor in the living room. Most underage drinking goes on in homes. More than half of underage drinkers had their last drink in a friend's home, and another 31 percent in their own.

When our teenagers drink, they basically are playing Russian roulette. They are toying with their lives and the lives of those around them. So, why do adults *still* turn a blind eye, say "kids will be kids"? Why do they still let kids drink in their basements? Do we let our kids party in our basements with loaded guns and say, "Sure, go ahead and fire away. We all did it. We'll be upstairs if anyone needs us." Of course not. But children who drink alcohol can get hurt or die from their actions—even under their own roofs or with people we trust.

Betsy Bethel, "Kids and Alcohol: A Dangerous Mix,"
Intelligencer *(Wheeling, WV), January 14, 2013.*

Teens and tweens sometimes inhale the fumes of common household supplies—glue, cleaning fluid, spray paint—in order to get high. These products are toxic, and their abuse can damage the heart, lungs, liver, kidneys, and brain. These substances can be psychologically addictive and, if combined with other drugs, even fatal. Be vigilant in safeguarding common household supplies and keep track of what items you have in your garage, under your sink, in your backyard shed, and anywhere else you may store them.

Special Agent Gerard P. McAleer, chief of county investigators in New Jersey and formerly in charge of the New Jersey DEA, gives talks about how teenagers often steal prescription drugs from relatives. "A woman came to me with tears in her eyes. She said that until that moment, she never realized how her daughter got hooked on prescription painkillers. She told me that she had actually been proud that her daughter had wanted to spend so much time visiting her grandmother, who was dying from cancer. The grandmother had been prescribed the painkiller fentanyl."

Ed Johnson, "Prescription for Abuse of Potent Drugs," Asbury Park Press, *June 22, 2008.*

In School

From August or September to May or June, your teen is spending a large part of his or her waking hours at school. If it's a high school, odds are that drugs are used, kept, or sold there. That sad fact is also true of up to a third of middle schools. Teens who see drugs in their schools are much likelier to be able to obtain them quickly. Compared with teens who do not know of a student drug dealer at their school, those who do are much likelier to smoke marijuana and drink alcohol. Almost half of all high school students we surveyed said they knew of at least one student who sold drugs at their school. The substance most commonly sold by students at school was marijuana, followed by prescription drugs.

Which Drugs Do Students Sell at Your High School?

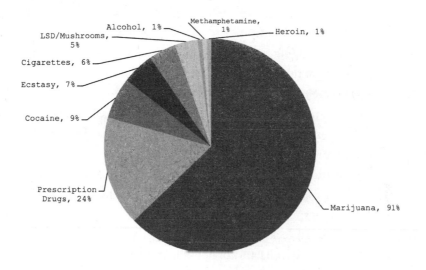

CASA. National Survey of American Attitudes on Substance Abuse XVII: Teens *(2012).*

For you, the bottom line is that each school day, your son or daughter may be in an environment where it's easy to get drugs. This means that you need to understand the school world of your teen. Understanding that environment—and your potential to change it—is so important that I have devoted chapter 17, "How Can I Protect My Kids at School?," to the subject.

A FINAL THOUGHT ON THE DANGER OF AVAILABILITY

To appreciate the danger of easy availability of substances to your teen, let me leave you with this final fact: anesthesiologists exhibit high rates of drug abuse and addiction involving painkillers, and bartenders exhibit high rates of alcohol abuse and alcoholism.

PARENT TIPS

- Learn which drugs are more prevalent in your community and discuss avoiding those drugs with your children.
- Make sure that inhalants, cigarettes, alcohol, and prescription drugs are not easily accessible in your home.
- If you are taking drugs like OxyContin, Xanax, or Percocet, please explain to your teen how dangerous these drugs can be if not prescribed by a physician for your use.
- Keep track of the number of painkillers and other addictive pills in your medicine cabinet and throw them out as soon as they are expired or no longer needed.
- If necessary, lock your medicine cabinet.
- Keep track of inhalants in household cleaners.

10

AT WHAT TIMES IS MY CHILD AT INCREASED RISK OF DRUG USE?

There is no one-size-fits-all approach to raising healthy, drug-free children. Like each mother and each father, each child is unique—in personality, strengths and weaknesses, needs and wants, emotions, and learning styles. Knowing your children, who they are, what makes them tick, and what makes them feel good (or bad) about themselves, will help you reduce their risk of substance abuse.

There are some common risk factors that you should look out for. In this chapter and the next, I will describe the times, characteristics, and situations that can increase the danger that any child will smoke, drink, or use drugs. Being able to spot these, provide appropriate support, and take timely action to modify your child's behavior can reduce the chances that your child will use tobacco, alcohol, or other drugs.

As the song and psalm say, "To everything there is a season," and there are certain times when adolescents are more likely to try drugs. During these times, you should be especially attentive and remind your children of your rules and expectations about substance abuse.

Just being a teenager in America today is a risk factor for experimenting with addictive substances. Our society showers tweens and teens with enticements to smoke, drink, and use drugs: advertising on television, radio, and websites and in magazines; stories about entertainment celebrities and sports stars; films on YouTube, television shows, video games, music, and movies glamorizing smoking, drinking, and drug use; and the conduct of other teens at their schools or in their neighborhoods.

Timing for teens can be everything: in the span of a few months, a teen's attitude toward smoking, drinking, or illegal drug use can change dramatically. Indeed, entertainment outlets aimed at teens, tweens, and even younger children repeatedly survey and conduct focus groups of teens and preteens to keep up with changing attitudes and tastes.

During any or all of the transition times described in this chapter, your child's attitudes about tobacco, alcohol, and other drugs may change. If you are on the lookout for these changes, you can provide appropriate support, encouragement, and discipline. And you can take needed actions—such as getting to know your child's new friends and the attitudes of their parents about drinking and drugs, monitoring your child's whereabouts, finding out about the parties your kid is attending—in order to help your child get through these risky times unscathed.

You may meet parents of your child's friends who drink to excess or smoke marijuana. Or you may find parents who are permissive about letting their teen drink or nonchalant about their teen smoking pot. You may learn that some parents of your teen's friends treat such substance use quite casually, as a routine rite of passage. As I've emphasized in this book, parental actions and attitudes have a profound influence on children. Discovering such conduct or views on the part of parents of your teen's friends may be a warning signal to be especially attentive to your child's relationship with those friends and even to discourage your child from getting involved with them.

*"We think it's important to meet the parents
of our daughter's bad influences."*

ENTERING MIDDLE SCHOOL

The first several months of middle school tend to be a time when a child's view of substance abuse can shift significantly. Prior to that time, while at home, in preschool, and in elementary school, children tend to develop strong antismoking, antidrinking, and antidrugging attitudes. They may see all such conduct as wrong and harmful, something that they would never do. If you smoke, drink, or use drugs, your kids are likely to urge you to stop, and their classmates will almost surely share their disdain for such activity.

As boys and girls enter middle school (fifth or sixth grade), they are exposed to the sights and sounds of substance abuse. They may see some eighth-grade school leaders who smoke, drink, and use marijuana. Your daughter may see a pretty and popular eighth grader who smokes. Your son may see a popular athlete who drinks beer. Witnessing such conduct, especially by kids they'd like to be like, or be liked by, can affect their view of substance abuse.

PUBERTY

During middle school, children start to go through puberty. Typically, girls begin puberty about one to two years earlier than boys. Physical changes that girls experience—gaining weight, developing breasts, menstruating, getting zits, perhaps becoming taller than even some boys in their class—can be especially difficult. These changes can cause girls to become insecure about their looks, their bodies, their new identities as women, and their sense of what conduct is permissible.

For both boys and girls, puberty brings emotional and behavioral changes, such as increased risk taking and pleasure seeking for boys, and anxiety and depression in girls. These emotional aspects of puberty can increase the risk that your son or daughter will start experimenting with substances. Particularly for girls, early puberty may increase the risk of substance use.

When my boys were teens and tweens, I bought a home drug test. I told them that if I ever suspected any one of them of doing drugs, that I would not hesitate to test them. I told them it was not there to intimidate them, but to assure their privacy. I would test first before I began going through their belongings.

A local drug-enforcement officer told me it was the wisest choice I could have made because it gave my sons a valid excuse to resist peer pressure. They could respond, "Hey, I can't try that because my mom tests us at home for drug use."

Many of our friends and neighbors now use the same strategy.

Parent posting in CASA's "How to Raise a Drug-Free Kid" online discussion forums.

Being engaged in your children's lives as they move through this period—by having dinner together frequently, attending religious services together, keeping communication open, involving yourself in their after-school activities, and, if at all possible, having a parent or other adult present when they get home—will help keep your children drug free.

ENTERING HIGH SCHOOL

The next transition is when your children enter high school—and it's a big one. The average risk of substance abuse *triples* when students enter high school. Students in high school are nearly twice as likely as those in middle school to say that drugs are kept, sold, or used on school grounds.

Children's attitudes about smoking, drinking, and using drugs often change during the first few months of high school because they are exposed to a new battery of influences. They may see classmates smoking, drinking, and taking drugs, not only marijuana but also pills such as OxyContin and Vicodin, hallucinogens, and perhaps even cocaine and designer drugs, like Ecstasy. In high school, your children may learn that they can purchase these substances from classmates who seem to be "nice" guys and gals. The mix of students also changes from middle school to high school; there's a vast difference between a thirteen- or fourteen-year-old and a seventeen- or eighteen-year-old.

Remember what you were like when you were just fourteen years old as compared with eighteen years old? At fourteen, a teen entering high school is more vulnerable, insecure, and dependent on friends and peers as he struggles to come into his own, and figure out who he is and what he values. As high school entrants struggle to find their place in new environments and join new social groups, they begin to shift their focus from their parents and other adults, looking instead to peer and popular culture for self-evaluation. It's easy, and tempting, to mimic eighteen-year-old seniors who appear to be cool, self-assured, and "know the ropes"—including those who smoke, drink, and use drugs.

Especially for girls, this time can be associated with less satisfaction with physical appearance, concern about weight, increased depression, and lower self-esteem—any of which can heighten the risk of substance use.

In high school, the likelihood of being offered prescription drugs, marijuana, Ecstasy, and cocaine jumps dramatically. Indeed, just about every child in America, almost certainly including yours, will be offered drugs before he or she graduates from high school, most on several occasions. That's why it's so important for you to teach your kids early on to choose not to use.

During the summer before and in the months after high school starts, find opportunities to reiterate your values and expectations. When you ask your children about their high school experiences—schoolwork, social life, sports—routinely include questions about substance use: "Are the older kids drinking or smoking pot?" "How about any kids in your class?"

MOVING TOWARD SENIOR YEAR

Getting older—moving to the later teen years—increases the chances that your son or daughter will smoke, drink, or use drugs.

Why? Because each year, these substances will become more available to them. Twenty-five percent of sixteen- and seventeen-year-olds can get marijuana within one hour; only 4 percent of twelve- and thirteen-year-olds can do so. Almost half of seventeen-year-olds have friends who abuse prescription drugs, whereas only 10 percent of twelve-year-olds do.

As [Advanced Placement] classes started adding up my junior year, I seemed to have an immense amount of work and absolutely no time to do any of it. I had always heard about people taking Adderall to focus, study longer, stay awake . . . So, as the workload piled up, my search for Adderall began. Within twenty-four hours I had five pills in my hand, costing me a mere five dollars. Five dollars for an A on an exam didn't seem as if it were any kind of price to pay at all.

Seventeen-year-old female student from Chicago,
"In Their Own Words: 'Study Drugs,'" by Alan
Schwarz, New York Times, *June 9, 2012.*

In the later teens, your children will see more of their "cool" or popular classmates, teammates, or friends experimenting with drugs, with little or no apparent harm done and oblivious to the danger to their developing brains. Your children will start dating and pushing the envelope of adulthood, increasing their independence and mobility. At seventeen, many, perhaps most, of your children's friends will drink, at least occasionally, and some classmates are likely to smoke marijuana, pop pills, and use illegal drugs such as Molly (Ecstasy).

You cannot put your teens in a risk-free cocoon. But by being aware of the shifting dangers and opportunities in their lives, you can take extra care in the later teen years to reinforce the foundation of communication and no-use messages you began to build when your children were younger.

THE HOURS AFTER SCHOOL

For children ages twelve to seventeen, the weekday is roughly divided into two equal parts: during school and after school. How and with whom your children spend those hours after the school bell rings are critical. Most smoking, drinking, and drug use that go on among high school teens occur after school while they are hanging out with one another, unsupervised by adults. Knowing where your children are and insuring that they are properly supervised after school can reduce the likelihood that they will spend that time drinking or using drugs.

The activities students typically engage in after school are also relevant to their risk of substance abuse. Those who go home to do homework are at least risk. Those who spend some afternoons participating in an extracurricular activity use drugs less often than those who are not involved in such activities. Participation in supervised sports can be beneficial both in occupying teens after school and in building self-confidence, a sense of the importance of teamwork, and physical fitness.

Not knowing where your child is and what your child is up to at ten o'clock on a school night is especially risky business. Why? Because the later teens hang out with friends on school nights, the likelier it is that drug and alcohol use will be going on among them. Half of twelve- to seventeen-year-olds who come home after ten say that's the case, as do almost a third of those who come home between eight and ten o'clock at night.

The old public service message, "It's ten o'clock. Do you know where your children are?," gets the point across, but it doesn't go far enough. Whether your children are at the mall, hanging out in the park, or at their best friend's house, if grown-ups aren't around, it's more likely that alcohol and drugs may be. The more important question for you to ask is: "Are my children being supervised by a responsible adult?"

Do not allow your children to invite friends over when you're not home. And when your child goes to a friend's house to hang out, call the friend's parents to make sure they will be present and supervising. If you decide to give your child a cell phone, do so only on the terms that your teen will use it to check in with you. Require her to call you if she decides to go somewhere different from where she was originally supposed to be, if she is going to be home later than she thought, and, of course, if she is ever in trouble or in need of a safe ride home. If your teen is of driving age, condition getting a driver's license or using your car on his being substance free and honest and clear about his whereabouts. Or if your child is younger, consider just buying her a limited-use cell phone—one that allows the user to call or send text messages to only a few predetermined phone numbers set by you or your spouse in advance. While you can't implant a GPS device in your teenager, finding ways to keep track of where they are and who they're with will greatly reduce the likelihood that your children will smoke, drink, or use drugs.

PARTIES AT FRIENDS' HOMES

Alcohol and marijuana are a big part of the high school teen party scene. One-third of teen partygoers report that parents are rarely or never present at the parties they attend.

These are unfortunate realities, but as an engaged parent, you can deal with them.

If your child is going to a party at a friend's house, investigate. Call the friend's parents to see if they'll be home during the party. Ask what they're doing to prevent drinking and other drug use during the party. If the parents are not going to be home, you should not let your child go to the party.

Why? Because at parties where parents are not present, alcohol is sixteen times likelier to be available, and marijuana is twenty-nine times likelier to be available. Moreover, teens of parents who allow their kids to go to parties where alcohol is served are much likelier to smoke, drink, and use drugs.

Percent of 12- to 17-Year-Olds Who Have Tried Substances by Whether Parents Allow Them to Attend Parties with Alcohol

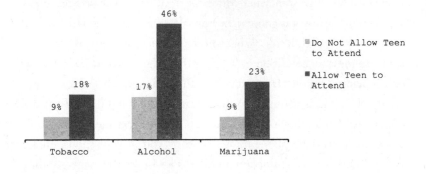

CASA. National Survey of American Attitudes on Substance Abuse XV: Teens and Parents *(2010).*

Q. Do you call the parents of your child's friends to see that alcohol will not be present and that chaperones will be there during a party or sleepover?

A. Absolutely call. I would caution that no matter how protective you are, how wonderful a child you have raised, they are human, and you just never know. It would also demonstrate to your kid that you are in touch with what they do, where they go, who they are with, what's going on, etc. They need to know you are in touch, involved.

A. Yes, my 16-year-old son knows that I'll call, usually with an offer to the parent to provide food or drinks to help share the hosting responsibility, and the parents are always grateful for my call. I'm 75 percent confident in his ability to make good choices, but this way he knows I'm involved, and so do his peers.

A. If the parent is one I do not know, I will always call. Even when I know the parent, I have at times placed a call. As my son got older, I would ask him instead, as I knew he would be leaving my house and making his own decisions on these matters very soon.

Parent postings in CASA's "How to Raise a
Drug-Free Kid" online discussion forums.

The presence of parents can reduce the likelihood that alcohol and other drugs will be available, but it does not guarantee a substance-free party. While almost all parents say that they would not serve alcohol to teen partygoers in their homes, one-third of teen partygoers say they have attended parties where teens were drinking alcohol, smoking pot, or using cocaine, Ecstasy, or prescription drugs *while a parent was present*; nearly half of seventeen-year-olds have attended such parties. Many communities have passed "social host" laws that make it a criminal offense for parents to serve alcohol to underage individuals who are not their own children or allow them to drink in their own homes. (See page 94.)

Early on, I talked to parents who assured me that they were chaperoning their children's parties. When I found out, on more than one occasion, that a parent's word could not necessarily be relied on, I put the onus on our children: no staying at homes without parental supervision.

Parent posting in CASA's "How to Raise a
Drug-Free Kid" online discussion forums.

How can you be sure your child isn't drinking or drugging while at a friend's home? As President Ronald Reagan said, "Trust, but verify." Speak with your kids about your expectations for their behavior both in your own home and in the homes of others. Call the parents of your child's friend and ask whether alcohol or other drugs will be available or allowed in their home. Ask the parents what precautions they take to insure the safety of all the kids at the party. Talk to your child when she comes home.

But the most important tool, I found, was to talk to him when he came home to assess his condition. I always told him to wake me up if I was asleep, and he did. If he hadn't, there would have been a consequence. The one time there was a problem, I was able to discover it by talking with him when he came home.

Parent posting in CASA's "How to Raise a Drug-Free Kid" online discussion forums.

If your teen has a party at your house, even a small one, *be there*, not in another part of the house, and pop in and out of the party. Take action to make sure there's no substance use: check on the kids, talk to them.

While you cannot (and should not) police your child's every action inside and outside your home, you should maintain family rules and expectations about behavior. One positive way of doing this is by having your whole family write and sign a family contract about rules and expected behaviors. I'll discuss this further and give you examples of statements to put in a family contract in chapter 12, "How Can I Make My Home a Safe Haven?"

THE INFLUENCE OF FRIENDS

Social interactions and peer influence can contribute to drug use. Having friends who smoke is one of the main reasons that teens start smoking.

Teens say that one of the pressures they feel to begin using drugs is because their friends do, with curiosity as a close runner-up. After curiosity, a commonly cited explanation for initial drug use is "to be cool." Older teens appear more susceptible to such peer influences.

Drug-using friends may encourage your teen to experiment. If your son is drinking at a party, a friend who smokes pot may suggest that he should try marijuana because "it gives you a better buzz than beer, and faster, with no hangover." Another friend may tell your teen a story about how she tried Vicodin and how "it was an amazing experience," arousing your teen's curiosity to try it too. Your daughter's friends may decide that they are all going to take Molly together at the prom, and offer your daughter a pill in the car. This kind of peer pressure is frequently associated with drug initiation among teens.

Becoming part of a social group that uses can lead your teen to drink and experiment with drugs. So get to know your children's friends. Create opportunities to spend time with them. Invite them over for dinner or offer to drive them to activities. Ask your children about their friends, what they enjoy, and whether anyone in their circle is drinking, smoking cigarettes or pot, or abusing prescription drugs. These conversations can create opportunities to help your child navigate the teen social scene and to reinforce rules and values. They can also serve as a way to dispel any curiosity your teen may have about what it feels like to be high or drunk, lowering the likelihood of her saying yes when that Ecstasy pill is offered or that bottle of vodka is passed around. If possible, make your house the "fun" place for your children and their friends to hang out. Create a recreation room or other space in your home where the kids feel comfortable. Check in on them occasionally: bring them a snack, offer to order them a pizza, or take them to the movies. You will be surprised by how much you can be there, even when your children are with their friends.

ROMANTIC RELATIONSHIPS

Teenagers fall in love. Indeed, psychiatrists say that for many people, teenage love may be the most intense love experience of their lives. These intense relationships can be magical, an important part of growing up, but they can also be times of increased substance abuse risk for your child.

If your teen is going out with a boyfriend or girlfriend, get to know this person and how much time your teen spends with him or her. Teens who spend twenty-five or more hours per week with a boyfriend or girlfriend are almost five times likelier to get drunk and smoke marijuana than teens who spend fewer than ten hours per week with their girlfriend or boyfriend. While I don't know the reason for this statistical correlation, it may be that time spent with a significant other takes away from time spent with family or otherwise engaged in productive activities. In some cases, the significant other may encourage your child to use. Or it may be that alcohol and drugs are seen as a way to relax sexual inhibitions. If your teen is spending a lot of time with a boyfriend or girlfriend, getting to know that person may help you determine whether your teen is one of those at higher risk. Try inviting your teen's boyfriend or girlfriend over for a family movie, cookout, or pizza. That way, your teen can spend more time with his crush, but you can also get to know her a bit better.

Another factor is age. Teen girls whose boyfriends are two or more years older are much likelier to drink, get drunk, and smoke marijuana, compared with girls whose boyfriends are closer to their own age or girls who don't have boyfriends. Think about how dramatically different are the worlds of fourteen- and fifteen-year-old girls compared with the worlds of sixteen- and seventeen-year-old boys.

Remember how much easier it is for older than younger teens to get drugs in a day.

Percent of Teens Who Can Get Marijuana or Prescription Drugs Within a Day by Age

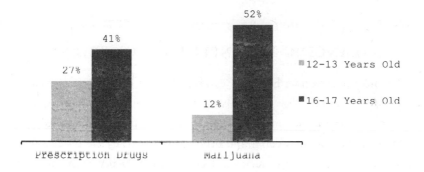

CASA. National Survey of American Attitudes on Substance Abuse XVII: Teens *(2012)*.

Alcohol and drugs are easily available in the world of the older boy; he's likely going to parties and other events, or hanging out with peers in places where such substances are common, or he may have a fake ID that he uses to buy beer or other alcoholic drinks popular with teen girls, such as wine coolers, rum, and vodka. If your daughter is dating someone who is two or three years older, spend as much time as you can getting to know that person and assess his influence on your daughter. If you're concerned, consider ways to convince your daughter to end the relationship or limit the time and activities she spends with her beau, especially time spent alone with him.

Hopefully, you will have a close enough relationship with your teen to know whether your son or daughter is sexually active, or at least you will be a savvy enough parent to suspect when this is the case. Sexually active teens are far more likely to get into alcohol and drugs. Some use such substances as sexual disinhibitors. The concern here for parents is not only drug or alcohol use. Most unplanned teen-age pregnancies occur when one or both of the participants are high at the time of conception. The combined risk of substances and sex is so important for you and your child to understand that chapter 14, "Substances and Sex: What's the Relationship Between Alcohol, Drugs, and Sexual Activity?," is dedicated to this subject.

BALANCING THE INFLUENCE OF FRIENDS

Parents often wonder how they can balance out the influence of their children's friends. The answer is by being an engaged parent. If you have a good relationship with your children, and are able to talk to them openly about alcohol and other drug use, they are much more likely to emulate your values and expectations rather than those of their friends. One of the most common reasons that kids give for abstaining from drugs is that they don't want to disappoint their parents. Your children really do care about what *you* think of them—even more than they care about what their friends think.

PARENT TIPS

- Reinforce parental messages and ask more questions about substance use during the transition times.
- Be present when children are socializing in your home.
- When your child goes to a party, ask the hosting parents what they're doing to make sure that drugs and alcohol won't be available.
- Don't let your children attend parties where adults are not present or where alcohol or drugs are.

- After school, make sure your child is supervised, especially when hanging out with friends, and engaged in extracurricular activities.
- Be awake when your teen comes home at night and talk to him.
- Know who your child's friends are and who your child is dating. Create opportunities to speak to or get acquainted with their parents as well.
- Discourage your teenage daughter from dating someone two or three years older.
- Make your home the fun place for the kids to hang out.
- Condition your teen's getting a driver's license or using your car on being alcohol free and drug free.

11

IN WHAT CIRCUMSTANCES IS MY CHILD AT INCREASED RISK OF DRUG USE?

How you deal with the characteristics and situations that increase your child's risk of substance abuse should be tailored to your family's values and your child's specific circumstances and needs. But as soon as you suspect that your child is struggling with a serious behavioral, mental, emotional, drug, or alcohol problem, seek professional help.

Why do you think some kids fall prey to substance abuse?

"Lots of reasons—to hide pain and to feel better. Students say they want an altered state instead of who they are or what they feel. In addition . . . peer influence, curiosity, availability of drugs, friends using, stress, sadness. Escape problems, family conflict, trouble in school or with a boyfriend or girlfriend."

Ginger Katz, founder of the Courage to Speak Foundation, in honor of her son who died of an accidental drug overdose at age twenty, "Giving People the Courage to Speak in Westford," by Joyce Pellino Crane, Westford (MA) Eagle, March 30, 2013.

FAMILY DISRUPTIONS AND TRAUMA: DIVORCE, FREQUENT MOVES, DEATH OF A LOVED ONE, CHILD ABUSE

Family disruptions—everything from a separation or divorce, to a death in the family, to frequent geographic moves, to traumas such as physical or sexual abuse—cause significant stress and anxiety in a teenager and can strain the relationship between you and your child. During these disruptions, your child is more susceptible to the lure of alcohol, tobacco, and drugs.

Divorce

Parental divorce can have a devastating impact on a child and sharply spike the risk for substance use. Teens with divorced parents are much likelier to drink alcohol and use drugs than those whose parents are not divorced. This increase in risk occurs, in some cases, immediately upon learning of the divorce. But for very young children, the emotional trauma of their parents' divorce may be cumulative, and the risk of substance abuse may increase over time.

Children of divorced parents confront a change in lifestyle, often including lots more—or lots less—money, a move to a new school or home, and inconsistent support and attention from Mom and Dad. These stressful circumstances can lead children to smoke, drink, and use drugs.

Sometimes divorce means that the child spends more or all of the time with one parent. The loss of a positive relationship with both Mom and Dad is disturbing, so it is important that divorced or separated spouses make arrangements that permit both parents to maintain good relationships with their children. It's critical that both parents agree to send the same messages about alcohol and drugs to their children. Teens who continue to have a good relationship with both parents and get such messages are less susceptible to engaging in risky behaviors such as substance abuse.

Moving Frequently

Moving and changing schools frequently increases teens' risk of substance abuse. Teens, especially girls, who move frequently (six or more times in a five-year period) from one neighborhood or home to another and change schools in the process are at high risk of smoking, drinking, and using marijuana. Children whose home lives are unstable due to frequent relocations are more likely to suffer from behavioral, emotional, and academic problems, all of which hike the risk for substance abuse.

Frequent moves are often associated with economic hardship (for example, when parents can't afford to stay in their home) or new family configurations (moving in with a parent's new spouse), which are stressful for children. In addition, parents who move frequently tend to have weaker ties in their community and often are able to invest less time and money in supporting and supervising their kids. Children who are uprooted frequently may resent their parents or otherwise have poorer relationships with them. Every move forces the teen to establish an identity at a new school, and most teens will prefer to be seen there as a "cool kid." Being the new kid in the class may make it likelier to be befriended by youngsters who may be more inclined to use drugs, and the new kid in the class may be tempted to do so to get accepted by that group. All of these factors can increase a child's susceptibility to peer pressure and the risk of drinking and drug use.

Death, Disability, or Illness in the Family

A death, serious illness, or disability of a family member can be profoundly stressful for children. The loss of a parent or sibling (or grandparent) is traumatic not only for the child but also for other surviving family members. Prolonged grief can negatively affect family cohesion and parental engagement. A serious illness or disability can disrupt normal family routines. The healthy family members may need to take on additional responsibilities or forgo certain activities to accommodate the sick family member. High health care–related costs can create economic instability that negatively affects the family's lifestyle.

Traumatic Incidents and Violence

God forbid, if you learn that your child is the victim of sexual or physical abuse, promptly seek professional help so that you and your child can deal with this awful situation and its dangerous consequences. Children who are subjected to incidents of such abuse are at high risk of self-medicating their pain by abusing alcohol and prescription and illegal drugs. So too are children who witness acts of domestic violence between their mother and father.

SOCIAL, DEVELOPMENTAL, BEHAVIORAL, AND MENTAL HEALTH PROBLEMS

Just about every teen will experience teenage angst; it's part of growing up. Parents need to know their kids well enough to distinguish serious emotional and behavioral issues from the normal mood swings, rebellious behavior, and boundary pushing that mark teenage development. This can sometimes be difficult; when in doubt, talk to other parents about their experiences with their seemingly moody or defiant teens or seek professional help.

Social, developmental, behavioral, and mental health problems increase the risk of substance abuse for teens—and substance abuse in turn can intensify those problems. Adolescents with social anxiety, eating disorders, learning disabilities, attention deficit/hyperactivity disorder, conduct disorders, or depression may struggle more than others to thrive, to excel, and just to fit in. These teens often use substances to help them cope and self-medicate to escape the stress of their everyday lives.

Laboring with a social, developmental, mental health, or behavioral problem does not mean that your child will drink or use drugs, only that there is a greater risk of doing so. If you see signs that your child is experiencing any of these problems, you should address them promptly by seeking professional help. But your job does not end there. Stay engaged in your child's life and monitor progress. Talk to your child honestly about the lures and dangers of smoking, drinking, and drugs. And be on guard for symptoms of substance abuse. In chapter 19, "What Are the Signs of Use? What Should I Do If I See Them?," I describe the warning signals of smoking, drinking, and illegal and prescription drug abuse that you should look out for.

Kids who use substances, especially at young ages, often have some underlying emotional or mental health problem. The research at CASA, and the work of many experts in substance abuse and mental illness, reveal that kids who smoke cigarettes at young ages may be experiencing depression or anxiety, or some other emotional or psychological problem. High school girls who smoke or drink are nearly twice as likely as those who don't to be depressed. Teens who smoke marijuana or pop pills, or who frequently abuse alcohol, are more likely than those who don't to be suffering from emotional or psychological ailments. Early and frequent use of marijuana by children who are predisposed to mental illness increases the risk of a psychotic illness. And the odds are that those who get into drugs such as methamphetamine, cocaine, and heroin may have some co-occurring mental illness such as bipolar disorder.

In these circumstances, it is not sufficient simply to say, "Stop smoking" or "Stop drinking" or "Stop using." A child who is self-medicating will need your help—and that of a pediatrician, psychologist, or psychiatrist—in order to deal with the related underlying emotional or psychological problems. You will not be able to treat the drug use, or even end the cigarette smoking, of such a tween or young teen without tackling the related problem.

She was an honors student and competitive soccer player who wrote poetry, played guitar, and often had a sketchpad under her arm.

But Caitlin Robb was also a terrified teenager. Her mind raced like a thoroughbred. Her bipolar disorder caused extreme mood swings.

Dabbling in alcohol and pot, she discovered, calmed her jangling nerves. But by the end of high school, she had spiraled into a cycle of binge drinking and getting high, trying to stop, followed by the inevitable wave of despair when she couldn't . . .

"It was all about escape . . . and just to take the edge off so I didn't have to feel," [she said].

Andrea Gordon, "Teens Facing Addiction and Mental Illness Need Services That Treat Both," Toronto Star, May 4, 2012.

Drug use has the potential to trigger certain mental illnesses in teens who have a genetic susceptibility (in other words, carry the DNA that contributes to such conditions). So if there is a history of mental illness in your family (not just you and your spouse, but grandparents and aunts and uncles), discuss it with your children when they're the appropriate age. Warn them about the added risk of substance use so that they can know how important it is for them to avoid it. (More on genetics and addiction in chapter 12.)

THE SIGNS OF DEPRESSION

Many teenagers struggle with depression, but most of them never receive treatment. This may be why so many depressed teens turn to substances to self-medicate. Drugs and alcohol may temporarily relieve your child's symptoms and make him or her feel better. But with repeated resort to those substances, the benefits will disappear, the symptoms will become worse, and addiction becomes likelier.

Signs of depression in teens are easily confused with normal teenage behavior changes and mood swings. In observing your child, if you notice a severe intensity of any of the following symptoms, or a combination of several of them, it may indicate that your child is suffering from depression.

- Sadness or hopelessness;
- Irritability, anger, or hostility;
- Tearfulness or frequent crying;
- Withdrawal from friends and family;
- Loss of interest in activities, inability to enjoy previously favored activities;
- Unexplained changes in eating and sleeping habits (too much or too little);
- Restlessness and agitation;
- Feelings of worthlessness and guilt;
- Lack of enthusiasm and motivation;
- Fatigue or lack of energy;

- Difficulty concentrating;
- Frequent complaints of physical illness, such as headaches or stomachaches;
- Talk of death or suicide.

If you observe any of these symptoms, talk to your child about what is causing them. These symptoms could be either the cause or the consequence of substance abuse or addiction. If you believe that your child is depressed, or abusing drugs or alcohol, or if the symptoms do not seem to improve, seek professional help.

For more information about the symptoms and potential treatments for the various social, developmental, behavioral, and mental health problems that are common in adolescents, visit the American Academy of Child and Adolescent Psychiatry (AACAP) website at www.aacap.org, or the National Institute of Mental Health website at www.nimh.nih.gov/health/topics/index.shtml.

EATING DISORDERS

Children and teens with eating disorders are likelier to smoke and abuse alcohol and illicit drugs. While such disorders are far more common in girls, they can sometimes be found in boys. Girls suffering from anorexia may see tobacco, cocaine, methamphetamine, and even heroin as appetite suppressants. Bulimics may abuse alcohol or self-medicate themselves with it, and then purge themselves to avoid the calories. Some teens may suffer from a new trend called "drunkorexia," which involves restricting the foods and calories they consume during the day so that they can drink more alcohol in the evenings without the added weight gain that is common among heavy drinkers. The mental distress that often accompanies eating disorders, such as anxiety and depression, increases the risk of self-medication with tobacco, alcohol, and illegal and prescription drugs.

LEARNING DISABILITIES

Learning disabilities are conditions of the brain that affect a child's ability to take in, process, or express information. They are not mental impairments, and should not be confused with genetic or developmental disorders such as Down syndrome or autism. There are four basic types of learning disabilities: reading disorders, mathematics disorders, disorders of written expression, and other learning disorders such as ADHD.

ADHD generally involves an inability to sit still, be quiet, pay attention, or focus. Symptoms of ADHD include inattention, hyperactivity, and/or impulsivity. If your child shows symptoms of ADHD, you should seek professional advice. For more information about ADHD and adolescent substance use, see the section on prescription stimulants in chapter 8, "Mischief in Your Medicine Cabinet? Over-the-Counter and Prescription Drugs."

Children with learning disabilities are susceptible to the kinds of problems that precipitate drug and alcohol abuse: low self-esteem, academic difficulty, loneliness, and depression. Their anxious search for social acceptance tends to make these children easy targets for friends and classmates offering tobacco, alcohol, pills, marijuana, and other illegal drugs to be happy, get high, and be one of the "cool kids."

The teenage years are a troubling time for many with learning disabilities (LD) and attention deficit/hyperactivity disorder (ADHD), when low self-esteem and academic failure are at their most pronounced, and the desire for social acceptance can lead to the use, abuse, and sometimes sale of drugs and alcohol.

Anne Ford with John-Richard Thompson, On Their Own: Creating an Independent Future for Your Adult Child with Learning Disabilities and ADHD.

Identifying learning disabilities early on and attending to the special needs of children with them can provide the support these children need to overcome their emotional issues and help them steer clear of alcohol and other drugs.

When she learned she had a learning disability, Carrick Forbes lost hope that she would ever be smart. Carrick numbed her pain and frustration with drugs: "I had felt stupid since I was five. Because to me, learning disabled meant nothing different than being mentally retarded . . . I think that I just sort of tried to accept the fact that I was not smart. And I would never be very smart. And so that school was not my forte. And I should go try to find other outlets."

Interview with Ann Curry on Dateline, July 31, 2005.

BEHAVIORAL DISORDERS AND CONDUCT PROBLEMS

Some children have difficulty sitting still, following rules, or behaving in a socially acceptable way. They act out, rebel, argue, talk back, resist authority, and get into trouble frequently. Such children may have a behavioral disorder.

Behavioral disorders include conduct disorder (CD) and oppositional defiant disorder (ODD). Conduct disorder involves outwardly destructive behaviors such as lying, stealing, damaging property, fighting, and aggression toward others, including parents. Children with this disorder have a hard time following rules and behaving in a socially acceptable way.

Children are naturally defiant from time to time; they may argue, talk back, and disobey their parents or teachers. But a small percentage of children are consistently defiant, to the extent that it can interfere with their social, academic, and family lives. Oppositional defiant disorder is defined as an ongoing pattern of uncooperative, defiant, and hostile behavior toward parents, teachers, and other authority figures that seriously interferes with the youngster's day-to-day functioning. Symptoms include constant temper tantrums, excessive arguing, active defiance, frequent anger and resentment, deliberate attempts to annoy, upset, or even hurt people, and seeking revenge.

If your child is exhibiting conduct problems, it signals the risk of a host of future problems, including substance abuse. For teens with conduct problems, drug use may become another way of acting out. More boys tend to exhibit conduct problems than girls, but girls who display them are even more likely than boys to abuse drugs and alcohol.

Years of research on prevention taught us that youth substance initiation and use share some common risk pathways with other problem behaviors, like aggression and other risky behaviors.

R. Gil Kerlikowske, director of the Office of National Drug Control Policy, "Remarks at Community Anti-Drug Coalitions of America National Leadership Forum," February 28, 2011.

If your teen is regularly disobeying rules, lying, stealing, fighting, being kicked out of class, sent to the principal's office, or caught breaking the rules, you should seek professional help. Your child may be struggling with some coexisting or underlying mental health problems that can be treated.

STRESS, SEXUAL ORIENTATION, BOREDOM, SPENDING MONEY

Our research has taught us that certain aspects of a teen's lifestyle may increase the chances of using drugs. For instance, high stress, frequent boredom, and too much spending money can be a dangerous combination for any American teen. Teens who share two or more of these characteristics are three times likelier to smoke, drink, and use illegal drugs.

Across the years, our focus groups with affluent teens have revealed several troubling trends regarding drinking. First, binge drinking is distressingly commonplace. Students have remarkably easy access to alcohol, with efficient systems in place to secure large amounts at a moment's notice. Second, youngsters frequently drink with the deliberate intention of getting drunk; and for every reported incident of serious intoxication, involving stomach pumping, indiscreet sexuality, and/or violence, there are many others that go undetected by adults. Third, plans to "party hard" are often made as an antidote to the unrelenting stresses of "working hard" in order to achieve excellence across multiple domains of achievement [i.e., school, sports, clubs, etc.].

Suniya Luthar and Samuel Barkin, "Are Affluent Youth Truly 'at Risk'? Vulnerability and Resilience Across Three Diverse Samples," Development and Psychopathology 24, no. 2 (May 2012).

Stress

Nearly half of teens say they feel a great deal of stress in their day-to-day lives. These high-stress teens are much likelier to smoke, drink, and use drugs. Stress in a teenager's life can be caused by a variety of factors, such as living conditions (poverty, homelessness, an abusive home environment) or typical teenage experiences (schoolwork, bullying, dating, making friends, feeling rejected by classmates). Most teens report that the main source of their stress is the pressure to do well in school. Teens who are stressed out may turn to drugs to seek relief from their anxiety or to forget their troubles.

Percent of Teens Who Have Used Substances by Stress Level

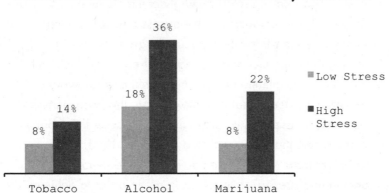

CASA. National Survey of American Attitudes on Substance Abuse XVII: Teens *(2012).*

If your child is stressed out, look for the reasons why. If it's too much schoolwork or too many extracurricular activities, talk to the school and your child about making adjustments in the schedule. If there's tension because of economic problems in the family, or the death of a close relative, spend the time with your child to explain that these are all part of the experience of life that everyone may face and let her know that you understand how she feels.

If there's a serious illness in the family, suggest things that your child can do: "Why don't you call Grandma? That'll make her feel better," or "Say a prayer for Grandpa." If the tension is from being rejected by friends, not getting invited to a party, or breaking up with a girlfriend or boyfriend, tell your child about similar situations that you went through when you were a teen and how you moved on and learned from that experience. Use your Parent Power to put things in perspective for your daughter or son.

Sexual Orientation

Some teens may experience severe stress related to their sexual orientation. For lesbian, gay, bisexual, and transgender (LGBT) adolescents, discovering and understanding their sexual identity can be a lonely journey. Such teens fear they may be rejected by you, by other family members, or by friends, and this fear can make it even more difficult for them to cope with their sexual orientation.

Resulting stress is largely why LGBT teens are up to twice as likely as straight teens to drink alcohol, use tobacco, smoke marijuana, and do other drugs like cocaine and heroin. According to the Centers for Disease Control and Prevention, being alienated by Mom or Dad even more sharply increases the chances of LGBT teens using drugs. LGBT teens that have experienced this rejection from their families are more than three times as likely to use illegal drugs as other LGBT teens.

For some parents, hearing that your child is lesbian, gay, bisexual, or transgender is not easy. It may come as a shock, and you may require some time to process the fact that your child has come out to you. At such times, it is important to show your son or daughter unconditional love. Even as difficult as it may be for you, remember that it is enormously more difficult for your teen. Your expression of unconditional love may give your child the strength he or she needs to resist any temptation that alcohol and drugs may offer.

Boredom

How often have you heard your child say, "I'm bored!" or "This is so-ooo boring!"

Boredom is a common complaint of teens when they are doing something they don't want to do: "Homework is boring." "Straightening up my room is boring." "Cleaning the dishes [or mowing the lawn] is boring." That kind of boredom is typical of teens, and every mother and father has heard their kids express it.

But nearly a fifth of teens in a CASA survey said they are bored all the time, or frequently bored by almost everything. If your teen is one of those, be careful. Such teens are likelier to drink or use drugs to relieve their boredom. Compared with teens who are not bored, teens who are often bored are more likely to use tobacco, alcohol, or marijuana.

If your child complains about constant boredom, get her involved in solving the problem. Ask her to make a list of fun things she'd like to do and then help her do those things. In addition to inspiring her to get involved in activities that interest her, this will encourage development of self-reliance and problem-solving skills. If your child is not responsive, there may be an underlying problem, such as depression, that should be professionally addressed.

Spending Money

Giving your children more money than they need, or allowing them to earn and spend significant amounts of their own money, may enable them to buy cigarettes, alcohol, and other drugs. The more money a teen has to spend in a week, the likelier that teen is to smoke, drink, and use marijuana. A CASA survey of twelve- to seventeen-year-olds indicates that teens who have too much spending money are likelier to try cigarettes, alcohol, and marijuana. Of teens with a lot of spending money, girls appear even more likely to smoke, drink, and use drugs than boys are.

You have the Parent Power to determine how much spending money your teen has each week. Use that power to place appropriate limits on your child's allowance. Since it is the amount of spending money available to your teen that is key here—not the source—it's also important for you to exercise some control over what your teen does with money made working at a part-time job. Encourage your teen to save some of it for a special occasion, like a concert or a major sports event, or for some popular clothing, electronic devices, or expensive sneakers he might want, rather than have it available as free-to-spend cash each week.

PARENT TIPS

- Seek professional advice if your child exhibits symptoms of an eating disorder, learning disability, attention deficit/hyperactivity disorder, conduct disorder, oppositional defiant disorder, or depression.
- If you're concerned about a learning disability or behavioral disorder, seek educational or professional testing for your teen so that an appropriate diagnosis can be made if needed.
- After a divorce or separation, see that you and your child's other parent remain engaged in your child's life and send consistent messages about substance use, curfews, things your child is or isn't allowed to do (such as sleepovers or time using the internet for fun on school nights), the friends you are or aren't comfortable for your child to hang out with, and so on.
- If you move frequently, find ways to create stability and to maintain relationships that are important to your child.
- Reinforce family cohesion after a death, disability, or serious illness in the family.

- Encourage your child to overcome boredom by getting involved in after-school activities, learning new skills, or finding other means of entertainment.
- Make sure your child doesn't have too much spending money.
- Get professional help if your child is the victim of physical or sexual abuse or witnesses a traumatic event such as domestic violence.
- If your child is lesbian, gay, bisexual, or transgender, be sensitive to the added feelings of alienation and stress your teen may experience.

12

HOW CAN I MAKE MY HOME A SAFE HAVEN?

Families have the greatest influence on children—for better or worse. For parents who want to raise drug-free children, looking in the mirror is critical.

You have the Parent Power to instill positive, healthy attitudes in your children, and this goes hand in hand with your responsibility to create a healthy environment for your children to grow up in. If you smoke, drink excessively, abuse prescription drugs, or use illegal drugs, it is important to stop. If you need help doing so, then get help fast: for your own sake and for the sake of your children.

Parents have profound power, but they need to engage. First and foremost, parents need to lead by example. Through your behaviors and actions, you are constantly communicating to your children. Parental actions, like their own drinking, smoking, and drug-using habits, are the main lessons parents deliver, enhanced by the occasional conversation.

Dr. Ross Brower, addiction and child psychiatry specialist, New York Presbyterian/Weill Cornell Medical College, "Good Parenting Helps Create Drug-Free Kids" by William Van Ost, NorthJersey.com News, September 16, 2010.

Parents are the number one influence, but they aren't the only ones in the family whose behavior children mimic. Other close relatives—siblings, cousins, uncles, grandparents, even close family friends—can have a significant impact on your child's propensity to use tobacco, alcohol, or illegal drugs.

Older relatives can serve as loyal protectors, their conduct can set a good example, and they can provide a support system that helps children to stay substance free.

Several of Robert and Ethel Kennedy's children developed serious substance abuse problems. One of their close family friends, Lem Billings, was reported to have been a heroin addict and facilitated the children's use. Their son David Kennedy struggled with heroin addiction and died in 1984 of a drug overdose. David's brother Robert F. Kennedy Jr. also struggled with heroin addiction but eventually overcame it.

Family members in recovery from addiction to alcohol or drugs who share their insights and struggles with your children can be a healthy and powerful positive influence. But a relative or friend of yours who uses can be a bad influence on your child. Your children may want to be cool and get high like their older cousin or big brother or aunt. Older relatives who smoke, drink, or use drugs may offer these substances to younger relatives, or otherwise encourage your children to use them.

BEWARE OF OLDER BROTHERS AND SISTERS WHO USE

When an older brother or sister smokes, uses drugs, or drinks heavily, it puts the younger siblings at high risk. These younger siblings are twice as likely to smoke, drink, or use illegal drugs as the average teen. Even if the younger sibling merely *thinks* that the older brother or sister is using—regardless of the truth—the younger sibling is still at greater risk of substance abuse than the average teen.

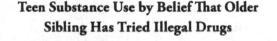

Teen Substance Use by Belief That Older Sibling Has Tried Illegal Drugs

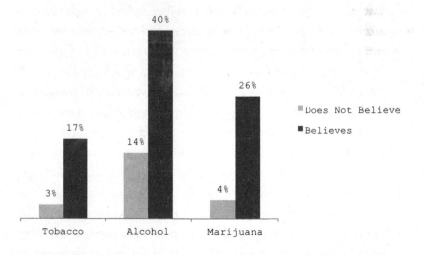

CASA. National Survey of American Attitudes on Substance Abuse, "The Importance of Family Dinners VII" *(2011)*.

In CASA surveys, more than one in ten teens said that an older brother or sister encouraged them to use illegal drugs and even offered them such drugs. Such a sibling is a "pusher" in the family, who increases the risk that your child will use.

We would have weekly sleepovers, and several of the kids I hung out with had older brothers or older sisters in high school that were experimenting with drugs. So I remember my first experience was a kid that had stolen marijuana from his brother and brought it to the house, and we all tried it.

Vincent Lobell, recovering drug user and substance abuse counselor at Outreach House in Brentwood, New York, speaking at CASA's Family Matters Conference, 2004.

When children grow up with a sibling who abuses or is addicted to alcohol or other drugs, the sober sibling suffers as well. Parents (understandably) may spend lots of energy and time to help the child with the substance abuse problem, and give less attention to their other children. Sober siblings may feel left out, angry, or ashamed that their family is different. If you are a parent in such a situation, be sensitive to what your sober child is feeling; talk openly about what is going on in the family, educate him about the other sibling's disease, and explain why you need to spend so much time working with the other sibling.

If the sober sibling is struggling to cope with his own feelings, reach out to support groups for family members of addicts, such as Al-Anon, for help. It may be natural for the sober sibling to adopt the role of the good child or the responsible child in response to the other sibling's illness. Realize that even "positive" roles such as these can be difficult to live up to and may create additional stress for the sober child. Last, your sober child will also feel pain, so make sure that child knows how much you love him, and that you would do the same for him if he got sick with a terrible disease.

Family members do not operate in a vacuum; the behavior of each family member impacts the entire unit, for good and for ill. If any of your children's relatives are smokers, use drugs, or have a drinking problem, ask them to set a good example for your child by not using around your child and by encouraging your child not to use. This may also be an opportunity to talk with your child about the relative and the consequences of the relative's use.

You don't have to have a perfect family to set a good example for your child. Let's be real: Does anyone have a perfect family? But if you strive to set a healthy example, and encourage older siblings and other relatives to do the same, your children will adopt your family's healthy attitudes about smoking, drinking, and drug use.

FAMILY CONTRACTS

Some families choose to put rules about tobacco, alcohol, and drug use in writing, in the form of a "family contract." The benefit of a family contract is that it forces everyone to discuss what parents' expectations of their children's behavior are, and insures that the rules and consequences are clear and understood by all.

It's best to concentrate on a plan for your family if your child does decide to abuse alcohol or other drugs. Lots of teens will [try] alcohol and/or other drugs before they graduate high school. Let everyone know what the plan is before it becomes an issue.

This way there are no surprises.

A written and signed contract with the consequences
spelled out will do more than anything else. Trust me, I
know!!!

Parent posting in CASA's "How to Raise a
Drug-Free Kid" online discussion forums.

Parents can also agree to certain obligations, like providing a safe
ride home, that encourage their children to uphold the commitment
to leave parties where alcohol and other drugs are available. Signing a
contract together may also increase the likelihood that children will
abide by the rules. Here's an example of what a family contract might
look like, to help you draft your own.

Sample Family Contract

Child I, (name of child), agree this is a tobacco- and
drug-free household, and that alcohol will be used only
in moderation by adults. I agree to refrain from using any
substances inside or outside our home.

Parent(s) I (we), (name of parents), agree this is a
tobacco- and drug-free household. I (we) know that smoking
and abusing alcohol or prescription drugs, or using illicit
drugs, may put my (our) child at risk and agree to set the
right example regarding substance use both inside and
outside our home.

Our family agrees on the following substance-use rules:

• Young people will not drink alcohol, or use tobacco
  products or any substances.

- Young people will not stay at parties where alcohol or other drugs are available. The consequence of doing so will be _____.
- Young people will not drive drunk or high, or accept a ride in a car with a driver who has been drinking or using marijuana or other drugs. Doing so will result in a punishment of _____.
- Parents agree to pick up kids at any time if they need a safe ride home.
- Young people will not allow their guests to bring alcohol, drugs, or cigarettes into our house.
- No one, including parents, is to make alcohol available to anyone under the age of twenty-one.
- Older brothers and sisters will encourage younger brothers and sisters not to drink, smoke, or use drugs.

We agree to abide by these rules, to treat one another with mutual respect, and to keep the channels of communication open.

_____   _____
Child   Date

_____   _____
Parent(s)   Date

You can make your own family contract easily on the Partnership for Drug-Free Kids' website at http://medicineabuseproject.org/resources/create-a-contract-with-your-teen.

DISCUSS YOUR FAMILY'S
HISTORY OF ADDICTION

Many families have at least one member who has struggled with the disease of addiction. Perhaps you have a grandfather who drank heavily every night, an uncle who never grew out of smoking pot every day, a grandmother who died of lung cancer or emphysema because she didn't quit smoking, or an elderly aunt who constantly pops tranquilizers, to the family's great amusement or alarm. If you're not sure about your own family history, ask some relatives, do a little investigating. If there is anyone in your family who has struggled with addiction, your child may be at increased risk of substance abuse and addiction.

Alcoholism devastated the Barrymore family. Patriarch John Barrymore was a great actor whose career was ruined by his drinking. His son, John Jr., followed in his father's footsteps; his acting career also collapsed due to his drug and alcohol use. John Jr.'s daughter, Drew, has been struggling to escape the same fate; she entered rehab at the age of thirteen, after drinking alcohol since the age of nine, smoking pot at the age of ten, and taking cocaine at the age of twelve.

Genetic Predisposition to Drug Use and Addiction

As I told you in chapter 3, "Your Adolescent's Brain and Drugs," we now understand that genetic as well as social and family environmental factors can play a large role in the transmission of tobacco, alcohol, and drug addiction from one generation to the next. Parents, family, friends, and the community all influence whether a child decides to experiment with substances. However, once a child has begun to smoke, drink, or use drugs, genetic factors can influence, perhaps determine, whether that child's use will descend into abuse or addiction. Similarly, the ability to tolerate a substance without becoming impaired may be strongly influenced by genetic makeup, which in turn may increase your child's tendency to abuse that substance.

Why do some people become addicted, while others do not? Studies of identical twins indicate that as much as half of an individual's risk of becoming addicted to nicotine, alcohol, or other drugs depends on his or her genes.

*National Institute on Drug Abuse, "Topics in
Brief: Genetics of Addiction," April 2008.*

Too often families overlook or conceal their own history of substance abuse and fail to warn the next generation. One big reason is shame, which stems from the stigma attached to the disease of addiction. Another reason is that addiction was not always viewed the same way in prior generations. The lecherous uncle who always got drunk and hit on the waitress at family functions may not have been labeled an alcoholic, even if that is, in fact, what he was. Another mistake that families make is thinking that addictions to various substances are not related. But the same genetic predisposition that influenced one family member to drink too much may lead another to become addicted to marijuana, cocaine, or heroin.

When you talk to your children about not smoking, drinking, or using drugs, tell them about this family risk—that addiction is a disease and that it has a genetic component. Another time you might feel comfortable discussing such a family matter is during your child's pediatric exam: "Doctor, I have something to share with you and my son about our family's medical history."

You and your children should not feel somehow doomed or marked by such a family history. As with any other disease that is linked to genetics—cancer, heart disease, diabetes—environment and lifestyle factors play a role in whether your child will develop the disease of addiction. If diabetes runs in your family, your children can learn to monitor their sugar intake and watch their weight. If certain types of cancer run in your family, your children can learn to watch their diet and get screenings at an earlier age. So it is with addiction. If this disease runs in your family, your children can choose, for example, not to drink—and you should be vigilant to watch for the signs and symptoms of substance abuse I describe in chapter 19.

It's important to understand that . . . because you are prone to addiction doesn't mean that you're going to become addicted. It just says that you've got to be careful.

Glen R. Hanson, DDS, PhD, professor, University of Utah Department of Pharmacology & Toxicology; former director of the National Institute on Drug Abuse (NIDA).

PRENATAL EXPOSURE TO TOBACCO, ALCOHOL, AND OTHER DRUGS INCREASES THE LIKELIHOOD OF FUTURE DRUG USE

Parenting Begins with Pregnancy

Children exposed to tobacco, alcohol, and other drugs in the womb are at risk for developing physical, mental, and cognitive disorders. The resulting problems that these children may face often continue into adolescence and adulthood, increasing the likelihood of alcohol and other drug abuse.

Of all the substances of abuse—including cocaine, heroin, and marijuana—studies show that alcohol causes the most damage to the brain of a developing fetus. Children with fetal alcohol syndrome (FAS) and fetal alcohol spectrum disorders (FASD)—which occur in the children of mothers who drank alcohol while pregnant—suffer behavioral problems such as hyperactivity and attention deficits, memory difficulties, poor problem-solving and arithmetic skills, lower IQ scores, and troubles with language, perception, emotion regulation, impulsivity, and motor development. These children may be impacted socially, making it more difficult for them to learn from their mistakes, grasp consequences, communicate effectively, and be cautious of untrustworthy or unsafe people. These problems in turn render the child susceptible to substance abuse.

Prenatal alcohol exposure is the leading preventable cause of birth defects in the United States. It can cause a range of developmental, cognitive, and behavioral problems, which can appear at any time during childhood and last a lifetime.

National Institute on Alcohol Abuse and Alcoholism, "Fetal Alcohol Exposure," July 2013.

Even moderate levels of prenatal exposure to alcohol can have detrimental effects on behavior and diminish a child's ability to learn. Prenatal exposure to alcohol is associated with antisocial and delinquent conduct during adolescence and young adulthood, including poor impulse control and social adaptation, aggressive sexual behavior, trouble with the law, problems holding a job, and alcohol and drug abuse and addiction.

Children exposed to tobacco in the womb may suffer a variety of long-term consequences, including lower IQ, deficiencies in verbal, reading, and math skills, and an increased risk for conduct disorders, attention deficit/hyperactivity disorder, and related alcohol and other drug dependence. In addition, pregnant women who continue smoking throughout their pregnancy typically have smaller babies with weaker lungs, which can frequently cause more respiratory issues later in life.

Marijuana exposure in the womb can slow a baby's growth and affect a child's IQ, reasoning ability, memory, and academic performance. It can also lead to mental illness, including depression, anxiety, and behavioral problems such as inattention and impulsivity. Children prenatally exposed to marijuana may be more vulnerable to the addictive power of marijuana and other drugs, including Oxy-Contin and heroin.

Cocaine exposure in the womb may similarly affect a child's attention and alertness, IQ, and motor skills. School-age children exposed to cocaine in the womb may display subtle but discernible differences in their ability to plan and problem solve. Such children may have to work harder—and need more help—to focus their attention, remain alert, and process information. Heroin and other opiate exposure in the womb may similarly affect children.

If you have a child who was exposed prenatally to nicotine, alcohol, or other drugs, be on the lookout for health and behavioral problems. Spotting these problems early and monitoring your child for the signs of substance abuse discussed in chapter 19 will help your child grow up free of drug and alcohol abuse.

PROTECT CHILDREN FROM ENVIRONMENTAL TOBACCO SMOKE

If you are a parent who is a smoker, give it up now—and not just for your own health. At the very least, make sure that you smoke outdoors, far away from your child. And never smoke in a car with your child—it's illegal in some states—although anywhere you do it, it's bad for your child's health.

The only way to fully protect nonsmokers from the dangers
of secondhand smoke is to not allow smoking indoors.
Separating smokers from nonsmokers (like "no smoking"
sections in restaurants), cleaning the air, and airing out
buildings does not completely get rid of secondhand smoke.

*SmokeFree.gov, "Secondhand Smoke," Tobacco Control
Research Branch of the National Cancer Institute.*

Exposure to secondhand tobacco smoke has both short-term and
long-term effects on children. Children who are exposed to secondhand smoke are more likely to be admitted to the hospital and to develop a range of serious infections, including meningitis. Because the
respiratory tract of a young child is not fully developed, children exposed to tobacco smoke are at greater risk for illnesses such as bronchitis, pneumonia, asthma, and sudden infant death syndrome (SIDS).
For those children who develop asthma, secondhand smoke increases
the frequency and severity of asthma attacks. Exposed children are
more likely to suffer from ear infections and to have their tonsils and
adenoids surgically removed. Exposure to secondhand smoke in the
first few months of life appears to do the most harm.

The more we learn about secondhand smoke, the more important
it is for you to keep your children out of it. Longer-term effects of
secondhand smoke include higher risks of lung cancer and other forms
of the disease, atherosclerosis (hardening of the arteries), and coronary
heart disease. There are more than 7,000 chemicals that are breathed
in as secondhand smoke. At least 250 of these chemicals may be harmful to your health, and more than 70 are known to be cancer-causing
toxins. Given the list and severity of harms caused by secondhand
smoke, it's not surprising that the late US Surgeon General C. Everett
Koop once called parents who smoke "child abusers."

If you need help to quit smoking, and many people do, there are lots of free smoking-cessation programs. Talk to your doctor or inquire whether your local health center or hospital, or your insurance plan, offers such a program. Get in touch with your state's free phone-based program, called a Quitline, by calling 1-800-QUIT-NOW. There you can speak to a Quit Coach, get a personalized plan for quitting smoking, and sign up for a free text-messaging service that gives you motivation to stay cigarette free right to your cell phone. The antismoking foundation Legacy offers a free online program, EX, at www.becomeanex.org. And another program, QuitNet, found at www.quitnet.com, has helped many people stop smoking.

PARENT TIPS

- Set a good example for your child through your own behavior.
- Encourage relatives to do the same.
- If there is a history of addiction in your family, tell your children that they may have inherited a genetic propensity for the disease.
- If one of your children has a substance abuse problem, reserve extra support and time for the sober siblings.
- Don't smoke cigarettes. If you are so hooked that you can't quit, don't smoke in front of your kids, especially in your home or car.
- Make sure to keep tabs on all the alcohol, prescription drugs, and over-the-counter medications you may have in your home. Keep them in places where your children can't easily find them, or in locked cabinets or drawers if necessary.
- If you are having trouble quitting drinking, smoking, or using drugs, get help.

13

WHAT YOU SHOULD KNOW ABOUT THE DIFFERENCES BETWEEN BOYS AND GIRLS

In America, your daughter or son can grow up to be anything: a doctor, nurse, lawyer, teacher, army general, pilot, engineer, athlete, Wall Street banker, corporate CEO, senator, or president. Daughters and sons can be at the top of their class, play the same sports with the same gusto, and socialize together on the same footing.

It should not be surprising then that where smoking, drinking, and drugging are concerned, our daughters often act like Annie Oakley, belting out with cowgirl bravado: "Anything you can do, I can do better!" On the playing field and at the after-party, girls are keeping up. The docile daughters of days past, who were left behind when the boys went drinking, are a distant memory. Young women today hang with the guys and party with the girls. Unfortunately, this means that daughters are smoking cigarettes, drinking alcohol, and using drugs just about as much as sons.

Smoking, Drinking, and Drug Use in High School (2011)

Percentage Who	High School Girls	High School Boys
Drink Alcohol	38%	40%
Binge Drink	20%	24%
Smoke Cigarettes	16%	20%
Use Marijuana	20%	26%
Try Prescription Drugs	20%	22%
Try Inhalants	12%	11%
Try Steroids	3%	4%
Try Meth	3%	5%
Try Ecstasy	7%	10%
Try Cocaine	6%	8%
Try Heroin	2%	4%

US Department of Health and Human Services, Centers for Disease Control and Prevention, Youth Risk Behavior Surveillance System (2011).

The percentages above are low because they are based on what kids say about their own behavior, and from several studies, we know that kids underreport their personal substance use. (My own sense is that teenage girls may be even likelier than teenage boys to underreport their substance use, especially if they're using drugs to hold down their weight.) *But the overarching message for parents is this: girls are smoking, drinking, popping pills, huffing, smoking pot, and experimenting with drugs like cocaine, meth, and heroin at about the same rates as boys.*

We've known for a while that binge drinking is a problem with today's youth, especially boys (who still report more

binge drinking than girls), but 20 percent of teen girls—
that's cause for alarm!

Raychelle Cassada Lohmann, MS, licensed professional counselor, "Teen Binge Drinking: All Too Common," PsychologyToday.com, January 26, 2013.

Of even greater concern for parents of daughters is that twelve-to seventeen-year-old girls are now likelier than boys to end up in the emergency room from abusing prescription and over-the-counter drugs, especially in their midteens to late teens.

Percentage of Emergency Department Visits Involving the Use of Prescription or OTC Drugs by [12- to 17-Year-Old] Teens Without a Doctor's Permission

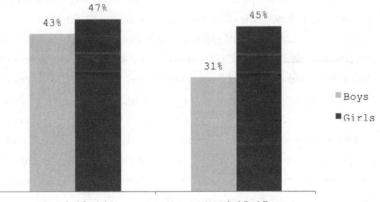

Substance Abuse and Mental Health Services Administration, Drug Misuse or Abuse-Related Emergency Department Visits Involving Nonmedical Use of Pharmaceuticals Vary by Gender Among Older Adolescents, DAWN Report (2012).

WHY TEENS USE DRUGS

By and large, teen girls and boys use drugs for many of the same reasons that adults do. Sometimes teens take drugs because they're looking for a pleasurable experience; they want to feel something new and exciting. "I smoke weed because it makes everything more fun." Other times teens turn to drugs to escape from negative feelings such as anxiety, stress, unhappiness, or boredom. "I'm getting bad grades, and I hate school. Getting high makes me feel better." Another reason teens use is social influence; teens may think it's cool, or want to fit in, or they may see people around them, even parents, doing it, and adopt their behavior. "Everyone drinks after the game; the guys would think I'm weird if I didn't."

While any teen caught drinking or using drugs may cite any of the reasons listed above, there often tend to be differences in the reasons why sons and daughters use drugs. Understanding these differences will help you identify potential risk factors in your own son or daughter and can be key to the effective use of your Parent Power.

Of course, each boy and girl is unique. But in the substance arena, you should be aware that girls share some common characteristics that differ from boys, and boys share some common characteristics that differ from girls. Boys and girls are structured and wired differently.

On the following pages, I describe these differences in stark terms, but know that some boys will try drugs for reasons likelier for girls (peer pressure, for instance) and some girls will try them for reasons likelier for boys, such as sensation seeking.

WHAT YOU NEED TO KNOW ABOUT THE DIFFERENCES BETWEEN SONS AND DAUGHTERS

1. Boys and girls often use substances for different reasons, exhibit use in different ways, respond to different risk factors, and suffer different consequences. Understanding this can help you prevent your child's drinking or drug use or intervene early to stop it.
2. The manner and situations in which boys and girls are offered substances, and the people who offer substances to them, are likely to be different. Knowing this can help you prepare your child to resist offers to try cigarettes, alcohol, and other drugs.
3. The consequences of substance use for boys and girls vary. Girls can get addicted faster and may suffer the consequences of substance abuse more rapidly and severely than boys. Boys may suffer more injuries.

Understanding these differences will give you insights regarding how you talk to your sons and daughters about the risks and attraction of substances, how you answer their questions, and how you teach them to respond to the drug offers they receive.

Overall the message is the same. However, with the girls, we've always stressed how vulnerable they become when under the influence.

For our son, we'll reinforce the bad-judgment message but also discuss the fact that violence often accompanies drugs and alcohol. We'll take him to an emergency room to hear, firsthand, from a nurse, about what she sees after midnight.

Parent posting in CASA's "How to Raise a Drug-Free Kid" online discussion forums.

BOYS WILL BE BOYS

Your son is more likely than your daughter to turn to addictive substances to satisfy his sensation-seeking impulses, show off, or be cool.

Sensation Seeking

What do I mean by sensation seeking? Scientists measure sensation seeking in terms of the extent to which someone seeks thrills and adventure, desires to have new experiences and cast off inhibitions, or can't stand boredom. Sensation seeking is a perfectly normal impulse in teenagers, especially boys, but it can lead to trouble. It may prompt teenage boys to take dangerous risks, such as drag racing, driving while drunk, or using drugs.

If your son exhibits sensation-seeking behaviors, you probably wish you could tie him to a tree until he turns twenty-one. But you don't need to lock him up, just channel his impulses! You can reduce the likelihood that he will turn to drugs or other high-risk activities by encouraging him to take equally exciting, but safer, risks.

There are many activities that can satisfy your son's need for adventure and excitement, depending on his interests. He may enjoy rock climbing, skateboarding, dirt biking, taking trips (with you), doing outdoor activities such as survival training or being a scout leader, playing in a band, getting involved with social, political, or religious causes, or learning how to DJ. Sports in particular have been shown to have a protective effect against drug abuse (but keep him away from performance-enhancing drugs such as steroids). Another benefit of channeling sensation-seeking behavior is that you can build your son's confidence by getting him engaged in activities that develop life skills.

Showing Off and Being Cool

Boys are more prone to use drugs or drink to show off or be cool. The best defense here is helping your child develop critical-thinking skills and a strong sense of self. Ask your children if they would jump off a cliff to show off or be cool like some other guys, and they'd be quick to say, "No way!" That's probably because it's obvious to them that jumping off a cliff will maim or kill you and is stupid.

Other activities, like having a few beers at a party, may not seem as obviously stupid, even to you. So how do you get your son to think twice before doing that? When it comes to steering away from trying to be cool like other guys, your son needs to think critically about the activity. Smoking or drinking a few beers may feel good, but is it healthy for athletes to pollute their bodies like that? Try to help your son understand that when making important decisions, what really matters is what's best for him. What are his expectations for himself? Will drinking help him win the track-and-field event? Will he be able to ace his math test the next day? Is it worth losing his driving privileges? Teenage boys with good self-esteem—with a strong sense of who they are and what they want for their own lives—are less likely to drink and use drugs to appear cool.

GIRLS WILL BE GIRLS

Girls tend to use alcohol or drugs to improve their mood (in other words, to self-medicate), to increase their confidence, to "fit in" better with their friends, to reduce tension, to cope with problems, to lose their sexual and social inhibitions, or to be thin.

Self-Medicating

Your daughter's low self-esteem, lack of confidence, depression, or anxiety is easily masked and easy to overlook. But there may be physical signs, and you can catch them if you're attentive. Pay attention to your daughter's sleeping habits; too much or too little sleep can be a symptom of a problem. Getting a sense of your daughter's self-confidence may require observing her interactions with others and listening to how she talks about herself. Or you can try a more direct approach and ask her questions about how she views herself or how she thinks others see her.

As a parent, you can help build your daughter's self-esteem and feelings of self-worth through encouragement and positive reinforcement. Good old-fashioned love does wonders for children's self-esteem. Praise her, hug her, kiss her, and tell her she's great. Make sure she knows that you love her no matter what, even if she gets a bad grade, or talks back to you, or confesses that she got drunk. You can also help your daughter build her confidence and self-worth by getting her involved in activities such as sports, public speaking (for instance student government or teaching), community-service activities, an exciting job or internship, arts, music, and taking care of others.

If your daughter is disappointed about a bad grade or not making a team or breaking up with a boyfriend, let her know that feeling disappointed is normal, and help her put the situation in perspective and refocus her energy in productive ways. (All this can work for your son too.)

Finding constructive ways to work through and release negative feelings is a challenge that everyone faces at some point in their lives, but not one that everyone masters. Simply talking to your daughter or son about her or his feelings and acknowledging that it's normal to have those feelings can be helpful. Teaching your child healthy ways to cope with negative feelings will prepare him or her to deal with the emotional crises that are sure to arise in life.

If you're worried that your daughter may suffer from depression or severe anxiety, you should seek professional help.

I'm no different [from] anyone else and those same doors
were opened to me and they were very easy to walk
through—drugs, alcohol, being in inappropriate places where

you shouldn't be at a certain age—it's a very tough position to be in, but I had great people to pull me back from it.

Hayden Panettiere, television and movie actress who began her career at eleven months old, in an interview with BBC Breakfast, *June 6, 2013.*

Dieting Dangers

Some girls today are literally killing themselves to be thin and achieve that rail-like figure they see in beautiful models on magazine covers and in movies and television. Whether your daughter is simply dieting or engaging in more extreme measures of weight control, she is at greater risk for smoking, drinking, and using drugs.

Girls who are dieting may smoke and use drugs to suppress their appetites. Those who engage in extreme dieting behaviors, such as not eating for twenty-four hours or more, taking diet pills, and bingeing and purging, drink more alcohol than those who don't engage in such behaviors. All girls who diet, even if they don't otherwise engage in unhealthy dieting behaviors, are likelier to smoke, and to smoke more cigarettes, than those who don't diet. In extreme situations, girls may use methamphetamine or cocaine as appetitive suppressants.

Drunkorexia, as scientists have called it, is the habit of saving calories on food to save them up for drinking. The idea? To prevent weight gain, to save money, and to get drunk faster—ignoring, of course, the potential for alcohol poisoning and long-term liver damage—and adopted, in the main, by female students.

Jasmine Gardner, "My Life as a Drunkorexic," London Evening Standard, *December 14, 2011.*

If your daughter is taking extreme weight control measures or is obsessed with being thin, she is likely being influenced by fashion magazines and pictures of ultrathin models. You can help her put the advertisements in *Vogue* and the pictures in *People* or *Us Weekly* in perspective. Talk to her about how unrealistic those figures and lifestyles are. Tell her about the history of "heroin chic" in the 1990s, when models took heroin or made themselves up to help project a toothpick-thin, washed-out image in fashion magazines.

Susan transferred to a new school in January. She was the new kid and had to make friends quickly and fit into the scene. Unfortunately, two things were very important in her new peer group. One was being thin and the other was doing everything possible to stay that way. So she became bulimic. Other than losing a little weight and feeling terrible, the experiment failed. In desperation, she resorted to cocaine. It took away her appetite, and the pounds began shedding. However, her grades slipped, and she became irritable. She lost the very friends she was trying to win over.

If your daughter is overweight, underweight, or overly concerned about her weight, be on the lookout for signs of substance use. Monitor her behavior for signs of bingeing or starvation, which can signal an eating disorder. You may need to make adjustments in your own behavior. For example, be careful about the comments you make. Here again, what you do will be far more persuasive than what you say. Modeling positive eating behavior can be more effective in changing your daughter's eating habits than verbal pressure for her to shed pounds.

If your daughter is at an unhealthy weight (too much or too little), consider seeking the advice of a doctor or a nutritionist, or someone who specializes in eating disorders. Eating disorders require professional treatment.

Peer Influence

Though both guys and girls are subject to peer pressure, your daughter is more likely than your son to go with the flow of the crowd. Your daughter's peer group is one of the most important influences on whether she will smoke, drink, or use drugs. Indeed, recent studies have shown that teen girls are much more susceptible than boys to peer influence about cigarette smoking and marijuana use. If she has friends who smoke, drink, or use drugs, your daughter is more likely to do so herself, and the more friends she has who do these things, the more likely she is to do them too.

Understanding why your daughter may be influenced by her friends' behavior will enable you to use your Parent Power to help her make her own decisions and stand by them, including a decision not to use substances.

Peer influence can work in many ways. Your daughter may respond to her peers' overt or perceived approval of smoking, drinking, or drug use. She may try to copy the substance using behavior of her new role models: the popular girls at school. Sometimes friends or classmates may pressure your daughter to try a cigarette, have a beer, pop a pill, or take a hit of marijuana.

When your daughter goes through puberty, she may start to compare herself physically, socially, and academically to her new peers. She may have doubts or insecurities about how she measures up. As a means of coping with these insecurities and fitting in, your daughter may begin to model her own behavior after that of her peers. She may suppress her own thoughts, beliefs, and desires in favor of those of her peers, which leaves her vulnerable to peer influence to smoke, drink, or use drugs.

Your daughter is likely to spend a lot of time with her friends and to be involved in their lives. Her relationships with her friends are also likely to be intimate and somewhat exclusive. She may look to friends, rather than family, for support when she is stressed out or in need of comfort. This dependence on her friends and her fear of rejection may cause your daughter to copy her friends' behaviors in order to cement the bond between them.

Even if your daughter is one of the popular girls, she is not immune to peer influence. Many popular girls feel that they are under more pressure to smoke and drink than other girls in order to maintain their sophisticated, independent image.

You—Mom and Dad—can balance the influence of your child's peers by being engaged parents. Having a strong, positive relationship with your child will bolster her against peer pressure and reduce her risk of substance use. Having a strong bond with your daughter or son may also reduce the likelihood that she or he will maintain friendships with peers who smoke, drink, or use other drugs.

SEXUAL AND PHYSICAL ABUSE

As I said in chapter 11, boys and girls who are the victims of physical or sexual abuse—date rape, or an abusive relationship with a friend or family member—or who witness such abuse in their families are at high risk of resorting to alcohol and other drug use to self-medicate.

SAYING NO VERSUS SAYING YES

By this point, you are well aware that your child will be offered illegal drugs, alcohol, and tobacco before graduating from high school. Several factors distinguish the children who say yes from the children who say no. Although some of those factors may be out of your hands, the biggest factor is you!

Your children need to be prepared for that moment when the offer comes. Tweens and teens need to develop the will and the skills to decline when they are offered cigarettes, alcohol, marijuana, or illegal or prescription drugs. They want your help to do that. You can do role-playing exercises together, so that your children can practice turning down an offer to drink, smoke, or take drugs. Role playing is a good way for your children to explore responding to different kinds of pressure; for example, "C'mon, all the cool kids are doing it," or "It will make you feel good." Also, you should take turns with your children and have them try to pressure you into doing something dangerous too. This is a nice way for you to throw out some examples of responses that your children can use in real life, without sounding too preachy.

You may prefer to simply discuss the situations your children are likely to face. However you approach the subject, you will be most effective if you know the different circumstances under which boys and girls are commonly offered substances.

Coaching Boys to Turn Down Drug Offers

Your son is likelier to be offered drugs at an earlier age than your daughter.

The offer is likely to occur in a public place where boys hang out, such as a park or playground, or on the street, often by a male stranger. This means that it may be easier for your son to walk away from the situation when it happens—but it may be harder for your son to avoid places where drug offers occur.

Boys are more likely to be offered alcohol, marijuana, and other drugs by a male relative (an uncle, a cousin, or an older sibling), or a male friend. These men may be role models, or they may be intimidating to your son, depending on his relationship with them. The person offering is more likely to emphasize the "benefits" of doing the drug, like the fact that it will improve your son's macho social standing or self-image, or make him feel great. Such an explanation may be convincing to your son, or it may appeal to your son's ego, making it harder for him to refuse.

When you talk to your son about refusing drug offers, you can help him imagine the scene realistically by incorporating these facts into the scenario. Rather than picturing a drug dealer in an alley, ask your son to imagine that it's a good friend who is offering the joint, and the friend says, "C'mon, everyone'll think we're cool." Coach your son to explain why doing drugs isn't cool: "It's addictive; it messes with your memory and intelligence; it can do serious damage to your brain; most kids aren't doing it." Another response that might feel comfortable to your son is suggesting an alternative cool activity: "No, thanks, I'm really into staying healthy and looking good, and pot makes you dumb and lazy. Hey, let's go shoot some hoops instead!"

Coaching Girls to Turn Down Drug Offers

When your daughter is offered cigarettes, alcohol, or drugs, it's more likely to be in a private setting; say, at a friend's house, or when alone with a boyfriend, especially an older one.

Because it happens in an enclosed and intimate setting, it may be harder for your daughter to simply walk away or get out of the situation. When girls are offered substances, the person offering is less likely to give an explanation. For example, they may simply say, "You want some?" If there is an explanation, it's usually that the substance isn't that bad for her. ("Don't worry, it isn't going to hurt you.") Unlike your son, when your daughter says no to a drug offer, she may feel more comfortable just saying no. But she should anticipate that saying no may not be enough to get the person offering to leave her alone.

Your daughter is more likely to get drug offers from girls her own age, like a female friend or a young female relative—a sister or a cousin—or from an older boyfriend. These are people that your daughter probably trusts and with whom she feels comfortable and wants to maintain a good relationship.

When you talk to your daughter about how to refuse a drug offer, remind her that she can control her situation. Help her imagine what responses would make her feel confident and comfortable. Use the facts above to paint a few realistic scenarios for her to think about. For example, ask her to pretend that her boyfriend offers her a joint and says, "Would you like to try it? All the girls your age smoke marijuana; it's no big deal." You should acknowledge that saying no may be hard for your daughter because she wants her boyfriend to like her, but you should also warn her that drinking or smoking pot, for example, will make her more vulnerable to sexual advances, and is bad for her brain and body.

Ask your daughter to pretend that she is a girlfriend and that you are the daughter, and have her practice offering you drugs. You may learn something about what your daughter's world is really like. She may say, "Hey, my mom has Vicodin in her bathroom drawer, wanna go take some?" or "Want one of my brother's Adderall? It will help you lose weight." You can answer, "No way, that stuff is addictive."

I knew that my daughter would most likely be riding with a boy to some place where there might be partying/drug use, so I gave her options for how to get out of that situation and get to a safe place. And I talked to my daughter more about the skills she might need to get out of a situation where she was feeling sexually pressured by a boy who had been using something that would affect his inhibition.

With my son, I addressed more the importance of not driving with substances in the car if he gave someone that had any a ride, and not riding with someone under the influence.

Because my son is older and my children are very close

to each other, I had them talk to each other when they had made mistakes and also to "call each other out" if they were sensing that one was doing something I would not approve of. The support system I taught them when they were younger carried over into their high school and college years.

Parent posting in CASA's "How to Raise a Drug-Free Kid" online discussion forums.

Your daughter may feel more comfortable simply saying no than debating whether drugs are a big deal. For example, she could practice saying, "No, thanks" or "I can't do that; my parents would kill me." Yes, it's okay to encourage your child to use you as an excuse! Sometimes, when your child is uncomfortable with a situation, blaming Mom and Dad is the easiest way out for both your son and your daughter.

You, as Mom or Dad, can also agree on a code word with your kids so that they can text you to let you know that they want you to get them out of an uncomfortable situation, with the understanding that they can tell their friends that they're annoyed or furious with you for taking them home.

Dr. Jeanne Reid, mother of three children.

THE CONSEQUENCES OF SUBSTANCE USE DIFFER FOR BOYS AND GIRLS

As I noted in chapter 2, teens are more likely to follow your rules and to develop their own responsible decision-making skills if you involve them in discussions about why you set the rules you do. When it comes to substance abuse, one reason you set clear limits is because you are concerned about your child's health and safety.

You should encourage your daughter to believe that she can keep up with the boys—but not when it comes to smoking, drinking, and using drugs. Both boys and girls will suffer common consequences of drug use: ill health, addiction, and crippling or even fatal disease or accident. But if your daughter goes for a drink with the boys, she will do more harm to herself than she realizes. Even when using the same amount or less of a particular substance, girls get hooked faster and suffer harsher consequences sooner than boys.

Between 1959 and 2010, lung cancer risks for smokers rose dramatically. Among female smokers, risk increased 10-fold. Among male smokers, risk doubled.

US Department of Health and Human Services, The Health Consequences of Smoking—50 Years of Progress: A Report of the Surgeon General, *2014.*

Alcohol is the substance that teens are most likely to use, and it is perhaps the best example to cite when explaining to your daughter that she is more vulnerable to the effects of substances than her male peers. You and your daughter can discuss the US government dietary guidelines for alcohol, which underscore the physical differences between the genders: for a woman, nonexcessive drinking is defined as no more than one drink per day; for a man, it is no more than two drinks per day. The impact that one drink has on a woman is equivalent to two drinks for a man. Men's bodies contain more water, which dilutes the alcohol; women's have more body fat, which retains the alcohol.

Substance-Use-Related Risks
That Are Greater for Girls

Smoking
- Becoming addicted to nicotine faster and at lower levels of use. In one study, girls became nicotine dependent after three weeks; boys, after twenty-three weeks.
- Increased risk of stroke in young women.

Alcohol Use
- Faster progression from regular alcohol use to alcohol abuse.
- Greater susceptibility to the development of alcohol-related medical disorders such as liver disease, cardiac problems, and brain impairment.
- Increased likelihood of engaging in risky sexual behaviors, of becoming a target of unwanted sexual advances or sexual assaults, and of the unique consequence of becoming pregnant.

Drug Use
- Increased likelihood of becoming addicted to cocaine.
- Increased likelihood of ending up in an emergency room and of hospitalization from the nonmedical use of pain medications.

Unique Substance-Use-Related Risks for Females
- Risk of coronary heart disease and stroke for women who smoke and use oral contraceptives.
- Risk of breast cancer for women who drink excessively or begin smoking in early adolescence.

When boys drink alcohol and use other drugs, the consequences tend to be exhibited in more outwardly directed ways. Typical drunken behavior for boys can lead to serious injury and trouble with the law. Sons are more likely to drink and drive, and to engage in other physically dangerous conduct, such as climbing things, diving off things, or joyriding on moving vehicles. Sons are also more likely to get into verbal and physical fights with other people while under the influence.

For either gender, drinking more than the limits established by health authorities can damage the brain and increases the risk for high blood pressure, stroke, and some types of cancer.

PARENT TIPS

- Get your son and daughter involved in healthy activities that will satisfy their sensation-seeking impulses.
- Teach your son and daughter to think critically about whether using drugs to appear cool is in their best interest.
- Monitor your daughter for signs of an eating disorder, anxiety, depression, or poor self-esteem; early intervention is the best prevention.
- Balance peer influence by being fully engaged in your son's and daughter's lives, and by encouraging them to talk to you and to think critically about their friends' smoking, drinking, or drug-taking behavior.
- Prepare your son and daughter to turn down drug offers by helping them anticipate such offers and practice responding to them. Role-play to help them.
- Teach your daughter about her higher risk for addiction and substance-use-related illnesses and sexual assaults.
- Warn your son about the increased risk of accidents and violence while under the influence of mind-altering drugs.

14

SUBSTANCES AND SEX: WHAT'S THE RELATIONSHIP BETWEEN ALCOHOL, DRUGS, AND SEXUAL ACTIVITY?

Whatever your moral values or religious convictions, it is important that your children understand how drugs and alcohol are implicated in teen sexual activity.

Whether you set firm rules about abstinence or let your child determine what's best, you should exercise your Parent Power to discuss the relationship between substance use and sex. Substance abuse can stoke impulsivity, which in turn can trigger risky sexual behavior—the results of which, including pregnancy or contracting a sexually transmitted disease (STD) such as HIV/AIDS, could change your teen's life.

Parents hold a range of beliefs when it comes to their teens' sexual conduct. Some think that teen sex is morally wrong: for example, according to the teachings of the Roman Catholic Church and evangelical Christians, sex outside of marriage is a sin. Other parents believe that their children should not have sex until they are married, or until they are in love or engaged, or until they are adults. Some parents may believe that teen sex is simply a health issue, not a moral one. Some parents preach abstinence, while others are resigned to their teenagers having intercourse so long as they practice safe sex to protect themselves against pregnancy and disease.

Whatever your personal views, you and your teen need to know that teen drinking and drug use increase the likelihood of risky sexual activity: having intercourse, having unsafe sex, having an unintended pregnancy, becoming the perpetrator or victim of sexual assault. The relationship between teen sex and substance abuse is so extensive that I believe parents cannot protect their children against the risks of either one without discussing the relationship between the two.

Whether you feel strongly that sex before marriage is wrong or you simply want your teen to postpone sex until he or she is more mature, explain your feelings to your teen. If you share the reasons behind your beliefs, your teen may be more likely to understand and adopt your values.

Mayo Clinic, "Teens and Sex: Protecting Your Teen's Sexual Health," August 8, 2013.

THE COMBUSTIBLE COMBINATION OF SEX AND DRUGS

Because of their inexperience with both sex and substances and their still-developing ability to control impulses and appreciate consequences, teens are less able than adults to manage the combustible combination of sex and substances. The Kaiser Family Foundation reports that a quarter of sexually active high school students admitted to drinking alcohol or using drugs during their most recent sexual experience. The number of such drinkers and drug users is almost certainly larger, since teens are likely not to admit such use.

Often teens use drugs or alcohol as a crutch to overcome anxiety, loosen up, make dating more comfortable, or reduce inhibitions. Some teens drink or use drugs to get high deliberately; some (particularly boys) encourage their dates to drink in order to increase the likelihood that they will have sex.

Alcohol use encourages risky sexual behavior. Youth who drink may be more likely to have sex, become pregnant, or contract sexually transmitted diseases.

Office of Juvenile Justice and Delinquency Prevention, US Department of Justice, "Effects and Consequences of Underage Drinking," September 2012.

The media shares some responsibility here. Movies and television shows often portray people, including teenagers, having instant sex in an emotional vacuum, which makes it hard for children to learn how healthy relationships are developed or what the consequences of having sex will be. Many kids mimic the scenes they see of instant sexual gratification.

Girls today . . . are coming of age in a more dangerous, sexualized, and media-saturated culture. They face incredible pressure to be beautiful and sophisticated, which in junior high means using chemicals and being sexual.

Mary Pipher, PhD, Reviving Ophelia: Saving the Selves of Adolescent Girls.

Self-esteem is another factor. Having low self-esteem puts young people at risk both for experimenting with alcohol and other drugs and for experimenting with sex at an early age. It may lead teens to take drugs or drink alcohol in order to give them the social confidence that they lack and have sex to gain acceptance, simulate intimacy, or feel desired or loved.

Bolster your children's self-esteem by reinforcing their strengths and providing unconditional love. Teach your child about romantic relationships, about developing trust and emotional intimacy. This will help your child build healthier relationships. Children who feel valuable and worthy of love are less likely to turn to drugs or sex to seek acceptance.

- High school students who drink are more than twice as likely to be sexually active as those who do not.
- High school students who have ever used marijuana are four times likelier to have had sex before the age of thirteen, and seven times likelier to have been pregnant or gotten someone pregnant than those who are nonusers.

CASA, Adolescent Substance Use: America's #1 Public Health Problem, *June 2011.*

DRUGS, ALCOHOL, AND TWEEN OR EARLY TEEN SEXUAL ACTIVITY

The younger your teen starts to drink or use drugs, the younger your teen is likely to become sexually active. And vice versa: the younger your teen initiates sex, the younger he or she is likely to use alcohol or marijuana.

If you discover that your child is having sex and using substances at an early age, it may signal mental health problems such as depression. Find a professional that you and your child (or your child alone) can talk to confidentially; for example a doctor, social worker, counselor, or clergy member. This trusted confidant may be in a better position than you to unearth the other problems and to know how to address them.

DRUGS, ALCOHOL, AND DOING MORE THAN PLANNED

Some teens turn to alcohol and drugs to reduce their sexual inhibitions. And it works. But being uninhibited may lead your teen to engage in unintended sexual behaviors that he or she will later regret. Lots of teenagers admit "doing more than they planned" sexually because they were under the influence of alcohol or other drugs at the time.

Teens often report that their first sexual experience was one they didn't plan or foresee, but, rather, that it "just happened." Alcohol and drugs increase the chance of sex just happening. Having an open dialogue about sex and substances may help your child resist their alluring combination. Use your Parent Power to instill your child with confidence, self-esteem, and the skills needed to avoid occasions and situations that increase the dangers of unintended sexual behavior.

DRUGS, ALCOHOL, AND UNSAFE SEX, PREGNANCY, AND STDS

Teens who use alcohol or other drugs and engage in sexual activity have increased chances of unintended pregnancy and infection with STDs, because teens under the influence are more likely to have sex and have unsafe sex.

According to the Kaiser Family Foundation, one in five teens report having unprotected sex after drinking or taking drugs. Teenage girls who smoke pot three or more times a month are less likely to use condoms than those who have never used marijuana.

Most unintended teen pregnancies occur when one or both of the partners are high on drugs or alcohol. Teen pregnancies are an all-too-common occurrence. For fifteen- to nineteen-year-old girls, the birth rate of 29.4 per 1,000 girls means that in a typical high school of two thousand students, like many of the schools found in big cities, on average some 30 girls get pregnant every year.

© *The New Yorker Collection 2005 Drew Dernavich from cartoonbank.com. All Rights Reserved.*

There is a relationship between drinking and using drugs and the number of sexual partners a teen has. Teens who drink or use drugs are likelier to have sex with four or more different partners during their teen years than teens who don't drink or use drugs. Having several sexual partners can double a teen's risk of getting an STD.

There is a rise in sexually transmitted diseases among teenagers. One in four teenage girls has an STD. The most common STDs among teenagers are human papillomavirus (HPV), chlamydia, herpes, and trichomoniasis. HPV, by far the most common STD (one in five teenagers has it), causes genital warts in some cases and can increase a woman's risk of developing cervical cancer.

When talking to your teen about sex, substance use, and STDs, make sure to explain that intercourse is not the only sexual activity that might be affected by substance use, nor is it the only one carrying risk. Teens can contract STDs from other forms of sexual contact, such as oral sex and anal intercourse.

Most teens learn about STDs in school—how to get them and how to avoid them. But when drunk on alcohol or high on marijuana, they not only lose their inhibitions, they forget what they learned about STDs. High school nurses and counselors well know the Monday morning moments when a student says, "I've got to see you right away," and tells them about a weekend sexual encounter and the student's fear that he or she has contracted an STD.

DRUGS, ALCOHOL, AND SEXUAL ASSAULT

Substance abuse is a common culprit in sexual assault and rape. Alcohol is found more frequently than any other drug in the systems of those who commit acts of sexual violence: rape, date rape (rape committed by an acquaintance during a voluntary social engagement), and child molestation. Some perpetrators ply their victims with alcohol and other sedatives in attempts to obtain sex. Perpetrators—including teens—are more likely to succumb to their impulses to commit sexual assaults when under the influence.

You don't have a lot of strength [when drunk] . . . If I hadn't been drunk, it probably wouldn't have happened because I could have gotten up and run out.

Female college student who experienced
alcohol-related sexual assault.

One of the key safety precautions that people can take to reduce the likelihood of becoming a victim of sexual assault is staying sober. Alcohol and other drugs make it harder for potential victims to recognize and escape from dangerous situations, or to resist force. Intoxicated victims are physically vulnerable; sexual assaults are more likely to be attempted and executed when the potential victim is intoxicated, because she is less likely or able to fight back, scream for help, or run away from her assailant.

[A seventeen-year-old high school girl in New York City] told me about parties where girls "literally wear nothing" and kids take Molly, MDMA. "The 'in' thing for girls to do is to really just go nuts at parties, just go insane. They feel like the more they drink and the crazier they act, the more guys will come to them." Crazy how? "Dancing around, flashing their boobs."

At these parties, she said, which take place "at people's houses or a space somebody rents out to make money . . . people hook up with more than one person. It's dark and, like, 100 kids are there. It's not considered a big deal. Guys try and hook up with as many girls as possible."

"At one party?" I asked.

"Yeah," she said. "They have lists and stuff. This kid in my grade has this list of 92 girls he's hooked up with."

Nancy Jo Sales, *"Friends Without Benefits,"*
Vanity Fair, September 26, 2013.

Alcohol is the most common drug used, but your daughter should be warned about other date-rape drugs such as GHB, ketamine, and Rohypnol (sometimes called a "roofie"). These drugs can be slipped into the victim's drink, causing dizziness, mental fuzziness, inebriation, and loss of muscle control, which can occur within fifteen minutes and can last several hours. They can erase the victim's short-term memory, making it less likely that the crime will be reported.

Teach your teenage daughter to protect herself from date-rape drugs by taking the following precautions:

- Don't drink alcohol.
- Drink soft drinks only from bottles and cans that she has opened herself.
- Pour her own drinks or watch them be poured.
- Set up a "buddy system" with a good and trusted friend so they can act as an additional set of eyes and ears for each other, keeping close watch on each other and each other's drinks, and calling for help if necessary.
- Never drink from a communal container (such as a punch bowl).
- Always keep an eye on her drink, and get a new drink if she loses sight of the old one.
- Call home if the party's getting out of hand.
- Immediately ask (or shout) for help if she thinks she has been drugged.

When you talk to your teens about substance abuse and sex, emphasize that one bad choice to drink or get high may lead to sexual activity they will later regret. Practicing abstinence or safe sex is much less likely when their mind is clouded with drugs or alcohol. For daughters, the dangers of unintended pregnancy and of sexual assault can be life changing. For both sons and daughters, the consequences of STDs are persistent, and in the case of HIV/AIDS, life threatening.

PARENT TIPS

- Discuss the risky connection between sex and drugs with your children.
- If your teen is sexually active and using substances at a young age (say, thirteen or fourteen), seek professional help to identify any underlying problems.
- Tell your teenage son that when under the influence, he might take sexual actions that could result in his being accused of sexual assault.
- Teach your teenage daughter to protect herself from sexual assault, including rape and date rape, by not drinking alcohol and by taking precautions against date-rape drugs.
- Take the time to read more about date-rape drugs with your daughter to help her learn the signs and symptoms on the government's office on Women's Health website at www .womenshealth.gov/publications/our-publications/fact-sheet /date-rape-drugs.cfm.

15

HOW CAN I MITIGATE THE MEDIA'S INFLUENCE?

TRUMP MEDIA MESSAGES WITH PARENT MESSAGES

Your child's brain is filling up with ideas. That is, in fact, its job.

Every day, like a sponge, your child absorbs new information and forms new ideas about the world and how things work. Much of this information comes from the media messages your child is exposed to: internet sites, billboards, TV shows, text messages, movies, music, magazines, video games, pictures on social media. Unfortunately, as I'll explain, not all this information is accurate, and some is intended to mislead your child.

In 1964 Marshall McLuhan coined the phrase "the medium is the message" in his book *Understanding Media: The Extensions of Man*, to alert the world to the power of the electronic image to affect our consciousness. Nowhere is that warning more warranted than with respect to the seduction of the innocent by the barrage of messages glorifying drinking, smoking, and drug use.

I'm going to show you how to use your Parent Power to protect your teens from the excesses of the worlds of advertising, television, music, the internet, and entertainment that might otherwise lead them to experiment with various substances.

Starting at a very young age, children are exposed to messages that make smoking, alcohol, and drugs look attractive. They see cartoon characters drinking and smoking, and TV stars popping pills. They listen to songs about smoking pot and using Molly. They see alcohol and tobacco ads that make people who use these products seem chic and sexy. These messages are so cleverly done, and so common, that your child, and even you, may not notice how persistent they are. But these messages are crafted by sophisticated professionals who know how to reach your kids. The messages can lead your child to think that smoking cigarettes and drinking alcohol are cool.

Unfortunately, children are not always able to sort through the messages they hear, separate the wheat from the chaff, and determine which ones are misleading. As a parent, you can teach your child how to distinguish facts from fictions, the truth from the hype, and how not to be manipulated by tobacco and alcohol merchants and entertainment that glorifies drugs such as marijuana and cocaine.

WHY TEENS ARE IMPRESSIONABLE

Media messages may exert more powerful influences upon adolescents, whose brains are still developing and who are struggling to define who they are and who they hope to become. Adolescents want to be independent, but they also want to fit in with their peers (who in turn are influenced by media messages); they form their own ideas about what it takes to be cool and sexy.

Unfortunately, your children are going to think that their ideas about being cool and sexy are totally original. They probably won't realize just how much advertising and the entertainment media influence what they think about themselves.

We began at an early age to always bring up substance abuse whenever our kids see it in the media. We are careful what we allow them to watch, but we also do not prevent them from seeing the reality of life. We want them to know what is going on in the world around them without glorifying what they see. We want them to understand there are choices they will make and there are consequences to those choices.

Parent posting in CASA's "How to Raise a Drug-Free Kid" online discussion forums.

BALANCING MEDIA INFLUENCES

What can you do to limit the influence of these messages?

- Monitor and limit your child's exposure to the media.
- Look at movie ratings and make sure that your children are watching age-appropriate movies (but don't just rely on the rating system).
- Watch the TV shows that your kids watch. Even shows geared toward young children may contain misleading messages about smoking, drinking, and drug use.

Children whose parents monitor their media exposure are at lower risk of substance use.

You can control the amount and types of TV and other media that your children are exposed to by setting limits. On average, children and teenagers are exposed to nearly eight hours of media (watching

TV, movies, and videos, listening to music, using a computer and social media websites, playing video games) each day. That's almost as much time spent plugged in to electronic media as most people spend working!

You can provide your children with the right messages to replace the wrong ones. As susceptible as your children's brains are to ideas from the world at large, you are still their most trusted source of information. Consistent messages from you can counteract all of the junk they may hear and see in the media, read in magazines, and watch on popular television shows.

Talk to your child about media messages. Explain where particular messages come from, who is paying for the commercials on TV, and what they're after. Teach your child that not everything she sees on TV or reads in popular magazines such as *People* and *Cosmopolitan* is sensible, or true, and explain why. You can help your young adolescent make healthy choices by teaching him to think critically about advertising and the media.

Start having these conversations before your children reach the teen years. Children are targeted by the media at a young age, and their heads are filling up with ideas right from the cradle. As soon as they are allowed to turn on a TV and watch it by themselves, be alert to opportunities to inform them about the dangers of drugs and alcohol.

Having discussions about what is being portrayed in the media is key. Our hope is to raise kids that are critical thinkers about these issues. Is it really cool to smoke cigarettes or pot? Is it really sexy to drink/get drunk? Being able to assess a situation or media portrayal accurately within one's own circumstances and drawing one's own conclusions is imperative to being a resourceful and resilient person.

Parent posting in CASA's "How to Raise a Drug-Free Kid" online discussion forums.

THE ADVERTISING ASSAULT
ON CHILDREN

Children are bombarded with glamorous or macho images of substance use. Advertising campaigns from tobacco and alcohol merchants can be extremely effective: at the height of R. J. Reynolds Tobacco Company's Joe Camel campaign in the 1990s, more children recognized the Joe Camel cartoon character than Walt Disney's Mickey Mouse; most kids knew the Budweiser frogs.

Don't be fooled. These companies are spending billions of dollars to get your child to start drinking and smoking at an early age. Why do they target your kids? Because all pushers of addictive or mood-altering products have long known what the public health community and scientific research have now confirmed: that unless they get kids to start drinking and smoking when they are young, those kids may never start. Getting kids to experiment—take their first puff, have their first beer (smoke their first joint, pop their first pill, snort their first line)—is key to developing long-term customers and adult addicts.

It's a money-winning formula: get 'em hooked young, and they'll be hooked for life. But wait until they're twenty-one, and you've got one less loyal customer. With almost 450,000 smoking-related deaths a year, the tobacco industry merchants need to get at least 5,000 kids a day to try cigarettes just so they can maintain their markets. For the alcohol industry, there's an even more immediate reason: almost 20 percent of its sales are for underage drinkers.

Remember, just as parent knowledge is Parent Power, so your child's knowledge can be his power to resist manipulation by tobacco and alcohol ads. Use advertising examples as teaching moments to help your children resist media messages. Talk to your children openly and honestly about how to decode tobacco and alcohol media messages. Teach your children that advertising is meant to change the way they think—and teach them how to unscramble these messages and think for themselves.

I taught my son from the earliest age that *advertising lies*. All advertising is designed to sell something, and most of it is something no one *needs*. Its goal is to make you think you need it and to increase your desire for it.

Parent posting in CASA's "How to Raise a Drug-Free Kid" online discussion forums.

Let your children know that there are a lot of shrewd salesmen out there who care more about selling their cigarettes, beer, vodka, and sweet alcoholic drinks than about protecting your child's health. Your adolescents will understand and appreciate that advertising is manipulative, and that with your help, they can resist. The truth® antismoking campaign of the Legacy foundation has been successful for this reason. This campaign educates teens about tobacco advertising. It recognizes that teens are rebellious and want to view themselves as independent; accordingly, it says to kids, "Don't let these guys manipulate you." Like Legacy, you too can use your teens' rebellious nature to keep them smoke and drink free! Use the Legacy website, www.legacyforhealth.org, and the truth® ads on it to start a conversation about the media with your kids.

ALCOHOL MARKETING TO TEENS

Alcohol manufacturers spend billions of dollars on television, radio, print, and outdoor advertising, much of it capturing the attention of kids. As the beer, wine, and liquor marketers have long known, exposing children and teens to alcohol advertising influences not only how they perceive drinking but also whether and how much they intend to drink.

Independent researchers have found that the more children know of beer brands and slogans, the more positively they view drinking—

and the more frequently they express a desire to drink beer. In other words, the cumulative impact of advertising is potent: the more ads children see, the more they want to drink. When you watch sports on TV or attend games with your children, notice how many beer ads there are on the air and in the stadium. More than one in five TV alcohol (mostly beer) commercials are placed on programming that is geared to twelve- to twenty-year-olds, and the likelihood of your child seeing an alcohol ad while watching television has been increasing since 2001.

Getting your children to drink is so important to the alcohol industry that it devises special products to make alcohol more appetizing. These kid-friendly products include sweet-tasting and colorfully packaged malt or other alcohol-based beverages known as malternatives or alcopops, such as Smirnoff Ice, Mike's Hard Lemonade, and Bacardi Ready to Serve Cocktails, available in flavors such as peach, pineapple, coconut, and watermelon. Designed to look like soft drinks, these sweet, fruity, alcohol-spiked drinks have become a favorite among teens, especially girls. Smirnoff has even introduced low-calorie vodkas in sorbet-inspired flavors such as raspberry pomegranate and mango passion fruit, a play to the female teen obsession to be thin. Girls aged twelve to twenty-one are exposed to twice as many alcopops ads as women over twenty-one. In addition, dessert-like liquors are becoming more and more popular for teens who want to try the new marshmallow-flavored vodka or red velvet cake–flavored malt drinks. And the alcohol merchants know what they are doing: hard liquor is now tied with beer as the favored drink of thirteen- to twenty-year-olds, with sweetened drinks like alcopops close behind.

Products like alcopops are designed not only to be more palatable but also to make drinking easier for your child. They come in bottles with twist-off tops, which are simple to open outside the home, where children are often drinking. They have a higher percentage of alcohol than beer, because companies know that many young drinkers drink to get drunk. And they are often sold in small grocery stores and corner markets, places where drinking-age laws tend to be less strictly enforced.

If you suspect that your child has been drinking, smell her breath for alcohol. But don't limit your investigation to the smell; mints and chewing gum can disguise the odor of alcohol. Talk to her and look into her eyes when she comes home at night after a date or party.

MONITOR MOVIES

You may be surprised to learn that movies contain advertising and other messages that influence children and teenagers to smoke, drink, and use drugs. Movies sell images and ideas about lifestyles and personalities; they set the standard for what's cool. Companies know that if their product appears in the right movie scene, sales increase. That's why so many companies, including alcohol and tobacco companies, like to place their products in movies.

American Horror Show

- 425,000 young people start smoking every year.
- 187,000 start because of smoking in the movies.
- 60,000 of those eventually die from it.

Legacy foundation, "Smoking in Movies," 2014.

Beyond advertising specific products, movies often glamorize smoking, drinking, and using drugs. Teens' smoking behavior is affected by what they see in films: the more movie characters your child sees smoking cigarettes, the more likely he is to start smoking. Close to half of all movies depict a lead character smoking in a way that associates smoking with physical attractiveness and social status. Most

R-rated movies show attractive characters smoking. Many of the millions of teens under fifteen who have tried smoking say that they did it because they saw it in a movie.

The movie industry has reps that do nothing but sell product placement, from shoes, to computers, to cars, to phones in the movies! We point out the "commercials" for drugs and soda and booze in the movies! "Look at that advertisement!" They now say, "Look at that product placement, Mom!" The kids hate to see how they are duped into liking something because it was in a movie. When they can spot it, they see what the advertisers are doing.

Parent posting in CASA's "How to Raise a Drug-Free Kid" online discussion forums.

Chances are your teen is watching more R-rated movies than you think, either in theaters or in your or someone else's home on DVD or cable. R-rated movies contain graphic and mature images of substance use, and studies reveal the relationship between exposure to these images and teen smoking, drinking, and other drug use. Teens who see three or more R-rated movies in a typical month are much likelier to smoke cigarettes, drink alcohol, and try marijuana than teens who do not typically watch any R-rated movies.

Altogether, the 134-top grossing films of 2011 depicted nearly 1,900 tobacco "incidents."

Elizabeth Fernandez, "Smoking in Movies Increases in 2011, Reverses Five Years of Progress," University of California San Francisco, September 27, 2012.

Even movies geared toward young audiences may contain favorable depictions of smoking and drinking. Although the number of smoking incidents in youth-rated movies (those with a rating of G, PG, or PG-13) steadily dropped from 2005 through 2010, it has been on the rise again, and movies have been consistently showing more scenes involving tobacco and smoking since 2010. Here are some scary facts about G, PG, and PG-13 movies taken from several studies in 2012:

- Most films rated PG or PG-13 feature someone smoking.
- Smoking incidents in top-grossing G, PG, or PG-13 movies rose 54 percent from 2011 to 2012.
- Nearly half of movies with a G or PG rating, and two-thirds of movies with a PG-13 rating, depict both alcohol use and violence by a character.

Youth who are exposed to images of smoking in movies are more likely to smoke; those who experience the most exposure to on-screen smoking are approximately twice as likely to begin smoking as those who receive the least exposure.

US Department of Health and Human Services,
The Health Consequences of Smoking—50 Years of Progress: A Report of the Surgeon General, *2014.*

With DVDs, TV clips on cell phones, YouTube, iTunes, video on demand at the click of a remote or a mouse, and multiscreen theaters in virtually every neighborhood, it's difficult to monitor your children's viewing habits, but it's worth the effort. Movies that glorify smoking, drinking, and drug use influence impressionable teens and make it more difficult to raise a child who has the will and the skills to say no.

MESSAGES IN MUSIC

One in three popular songs are anthems to the joys of getting drunk or stoned. Rap music is by far the worst. Nearly 80 percent of rap songs mention alcohol or marijuana. That's why ministers such as Rev. Calvin O. Butts III have criticized rappers and the music industry that records them. But rap isn't the only genre to blame when it comes to *Billboard* magazine's top hits: nearly 22 percent of country music and almost 15 percent of pop music sing about alcohol.

The 2009 hit track "Shots," by electronic dance group LMFAO, could be considered the perfect storm, referencing alcohol (by brand or otherwise) 89 times in 4 minutes, 14 seconds—that's one reference for every 2.85 seconds of music.

Vaughn Wallace, "The Alcohol Brands That Get the Most Play in Hip-Hop, Pop and Country Music," Time, August 28, 2013.

Here are some examples of lyrics of Top 40 songs that children sing along to:

- Miley Cyrus, the former Disney television star, made national headlines for the racy and drug-promoting lyrics she recorded in her hit song "We Can't Stop," in which she sings, "Red cups and sweaty bodies everywhere / Hands in the air like we don't care . . . We like to party, dancing with Molly, doing whatever we want."
- Amy Winehouse (who died of a drug overdose) sings in "Back to Black," "I love you much / It's not enough / You love blow and I love puff and life is like a pipe."

- Blake Shelton, in his country hit "Boys 'Round Here," sings, "With the boys 'round here / drinking that ice cold beer . . . chew tobacco, chew tobacco, chew tobacco, spit."
- Music mogul and rapper Jay-Z raps about Ecstasy and sleeping pills as part of the New York City party scene in "Empire State of Mind": "MDMA got you feelin' like a champion / the city never sleeps but it'll slip you an Ambien."
- The song "Blah Blah Blah" by Ke$ha talks about sex and alcohol when she sings, "Meet me in the back with the Jack . . . just cut to the chase, kid, . . . I wanna be naked, and you're wasted."

All the iTunes bills come to my email. I check lyrics of songs our son has bought and discuss them with him. He has to pay me back for those that end up being deleted from the hard drive. There's discussion more than mandate.

Parent posting in CASA's "How to Raise a Drug-Free Kid" online discussion forums.

Why do I point out these lyrics repeatedly?

Because:

There is a correlation between the amount of time teens spend listening to popular music and their substance abuse risk.

Teens who spend the most time listening to music report repeatedly getting drunk and are at higher risk of using illegal drugs.

Learn what music your son or daughter likes and talk to your child about it. Don't let your child spend your money (or any he might have earned) to download or purchase songs that glorify drugs and drinking. Talking to your children about the messages they hear in music can make a difference; so will making sure that their time is spent engaged in productive activities under adult supervision.

TRIM TELEVISION TIME

Did you know that American children and teens see more ads on television for beer than for fruit juice, gum, skin care products, cookies, sneakers, or jeans? About one-quarter of ads for Miller Lite, Coors Light, and Samuel Adams Boston Lager beers are shown on television stations with high rates of preteen and teenage viewers.

Not only do we monitor what our children watch on TV and listen to, we also monitor what other families' kids watch and listen to when they're in our presence. We have satellite TV and have blocked and restricted much of what is available and preview almost everything. We also restrict quantity of viewing time.

Parent posting in CASA's "How to Raise a Drug-Free Kid" online discussion forums.

Television abounds with favorable and funny depictions of smoking, drinking, and using drugs. TV characters misbehave all the time without having to face any real-world consequences for their actions. Seeing someone smoking on TV looks cool only because you don't see that person suffering from lung cancer or emphysema later. In the hit comedy *Cougar Town*, almost all of the characters drink wine and get drunk together regularly, and none of the negative side effects and health risks that go along with risky drinking or alcoholism are depicted.

This very funny series . . . is more pro-wine than the Pinot Grigio lobby. Jules . . . and her gang of friends consume wine all of the time, often in the morning, with great joy, little embarrassment, and many uproarious drinking games. Just about every episode contains an extended bit about the group's drinking habits, delivered with zero judgment— no one's peeing themselves or losing their jobs here, just having a gay ol' time.

Willa Paskin, "Cougar Town: The Most Pro-Alcohol Show on TV," New York magazine's Vulture, September 30, 2010.

It's not just adult characters in adult shows; teenagers are drugging it up on shows that are aimed at teenagers. *Gossip Girl*, the TV show most watched by twelve- to seventeen-year-old girls in recent years and whose reruns are still a hit among tweens and teens, chronicles the lives of affluent New York prep school students. The teenage characters routinely smoke, hang out in bars, drink martinis and champagne; they also smoke pot and even snort cocaine. In one episode, two girls abandon a boy who is dying from a cocaine overdose in a hotel room; the deceased boy's parents say the girls weren't to blame because the boy had been using heavily and could have died at any point. The main characters in *Gossip Girl* aren't depicted as kids with drinking or drug problems; their antics are portrayed as normal fun for teenagers.

We also talked about movies and TV shows from the beginning of his viewing. We always talked about the difference between reality and fantasy. I kept the true picture of alcohol and other drug use constantly before him so that he could see for himself that this subject is one that nearly all movies and TV lie about.

Parent posting in CASA's "How to Raise a Drug-Free Kid" online discussion forums.

Parents, hear this: every additional hour your teenager spends in front of the TV makes it more likely that he will start drinking, simply because he is exposed to more messages that make drinking look attractive. Research has demonstrated a relationship between the number of hours spent watching TV and music videos (both of which contain more references to drinking than video games do) and the likelihood that a teenager will start drinking.

MOVIE STARS, ROCK STARS, AND ROLE MODELS

Celebrity gossip infatuates America. We are inundated with details about how celebrities eat, dress, date, drink, smoke pot, get high. Look at any magazine rack, and you're sure to see headlines about the latest teenage idols and their partying antics.

Lindsay Lohan became more famous as a teenager for partying than for acting. Photos posted online, sometimes even by the celebrities themselves, show teen idols like singers Rihanna, Miley Cyrus, and Justin Bieber, actresses like Amanda Bynes, and athletes like Michael Phelps smoking marijuana or acting high on drugs or drunk. These photos are then seen everywhere, from the internet to popular teen magazines, and across entertainment news shows on television. Every week, another celebrity checks into or out of rehab. Some magazines suggest that rehab is the new in thing for celebrities to do. Far from ruining their careers or reputations, these celebrities become even more notorious as we watch them drink, get high, go to rehab, come out, and go back to their hopped-up lives.

I think weed is the best drug on earth. One time I smoked
a joint with peyote in it, and I saw a wolf howling at the

moon. Hollywood is a coke town, but weed is so much better. And Molly [Ecstasy], too. Those are happy drugs— social drugs. They make you want to be with friends.

Pop singer–actress Miley Cyrus, interviewed by Josh Eells, "Miley Cyrus on Why She Loves Weed, Went Wild at the VMAs and Much More," Rolling Stone, September 27, 2013.

The media stories about celebrity drug abuse offer perfect teaching moments to talk to your children about drugs and drinking. Tell them: this is not the real world. In the real world, people's lives are ruined when they get addicted to drugs. In the real world, people who drink and drive may wind up dead or in jail for killing someone else in an automobile accident. Use celebrities, whose serious problems illustrate how no one—not even the young, rich, and famous—is immune to the dangers of substance abuse. You can also point to the stories of the many celebrities who have died of an accidental overdose—actors Heath Ledger, Cory Monteith, Brittany Murphy, Philip Seymour Hoffman, and Marilyn Monroe, singers Elvis Presley, Whitney Houston, Amy Winehouse, and Michael Jackson, and rapper ODB (Russell Jones)—as examples of how dangerous drugs can be.

Some of the recent headlines involving stars who were once in wholesome family entertainment and have now spiraled out of control have offered the perfect chance to illustrate what can happen when you abuse substances.

Parent posting in CASA's "How to Raise a Drug-Free Kid" online discussion forums.

PARENT TIPS

- Listen to your children's music, watch their TV shows, read the ratings before they see a movie in order to limit your child's exposure to entertainment that has adult content or positive messages about smoking, drinking, or drug use.
- Point out media messages that encourage substance use when you see them. Explain who pays for these messages and what they're trying to make your children believe.
- Use celebrity drug and alcohol antics and tragedies as an opportunity to teach your child about the dangers of alcohol and other drug use.

16

FACEBOOK FEARS AND TEXTING TROUBLES: HOW DO I PARENT MY TECH-SAVVY TEEN?

With doing homework assignments and school research projects on laptops, text messaging friends, downloading music, watching videos online, and talking on cell phones, today's teens grow up in a world of technology that their parents never experienced. Virtually every twelve- to seventeen-year-old uses the internet, and more than a third have smartphones that provide instant, on-the-go access to the internet.

Such technology tools can provide teens with information you could only have dreamt of having at their age. But just as positive, appropriate, and healthy information is available online to your child, so too is negative, inappropriate, and unhealthy information about drugs and alcohol.

This world of technology can be intimidating for parents. From your years as a teenager, I'm sure you can remember some things that you saw or knew that your parents did not realize you saw or knew: a sexy magazine, where to buy cigarettes or beer, which theaters would let you in to watch an R-rated movie, which girls were considered promiscuous, which boys bullied. Nevertheless, your parents likely were confident that they had a pretty good sense of your teenage world. Today, because of all the opportunities for mischief available to tech-savvy teens with cell phones and iPads and laptops, few parents are likely to have that same confidence.

In a typical family system, there should be a hierarchy of knowledge and power with the parents at the top and the children at the bottom. When it comes to technology, however, often that hierarchy gets turned upside down. When children know more about technology than their parents, parents can feel intimidated by how facile their children are with new media, often even before the parents know that something new exists.

Larry Rosen, PhD, expert on the psychology of technology, "The TALK Model of Parenting High-Tech Children, Teens and Young Adults," Huffington Post, *November 19, 2012.*

As you read this chapter about the challenges that technology can pose to raising a drug-free kid, keep this in mind: you still have more sway than anyone else as to how your child uses the internet and social media. When teens are asked who has the biggest influence on what they consider appropriate or inappropriate behavior when going online or using a cell phone, 58 percent say their parents, 18 percent say friends, and 11 percent say siblings.

So what you may lack in tech savviness you can more than make up for in Parent Power. Nevertheless, if you have a good sense of what's available to him or her at the touch of a computer key, mouse, or cell phone button, you will enhance your Parent Power. That's what I want to give you in this chapter. And remember, you can use tech-nology to show your child the danger of using drugs.

We are often absent, distracted, or unaware when our children take missteps online; we miss the teachable moments, and they miss the needed guidance . . . [I]t is amazing how little all of us, as parents, know about our children's lives online and the identities they are creating for themselves there. It is where they regularly hang out and socialize, and they are wildly unsupervised. Kids want to—and need to—own their identity in a way that's not accessible to parents, and the online world has given them a place for that. But the sad truth is that it is not as protected a place as they need.

Catherine Steiner-Adair, EdD, with Teresa H. Barker, The Big Disconnect: Protecting Childhood and Family Relationships in the Digital Age.

SURFING THE INTERNET

The internet offers all sorts of information about smoking, drinking, and drugs. Anyone can find out how to buy and make drugs, how to grow marijuana, where to get seeds and starter pot plants— even how to make meth. Websites provide detailed descriptions of mind-altering pills, chemicals, herbs, and plants. Chat rooms, notoriously on Bluelight and Erowid, host discussions among drug users about their experiences getting high, and how to mix and prepare alcohol and other drugs to get high rapidly or slowly, how to come down from a high, how to shoot up, how to snort cocaine, what pills to mix with alcohol to control the intensity of a high, and more.

We had four computers in the house, and I had a personal laptop. Because of my drug habit, I also had messed-up sleep patterns, so I'd log on when everyone else was asleep. During the day hours, anytime my mom walked by me, I'd close out all my screens or have a new game of solitaire up. While I was buying drugs online, my mom was on the internet looking up ways to help me with my suspected addiction. But she hadn't learned how to monitor where I was going online.

"Sean," as told to TheAntiDrug.com's Real Teen Stories.

Through the internet, your teen can get cigarettes just by clicking a box saying she's eighteen years old. And as I said in chapter 8, the internet is full of offers to sell controlled prescription drugs—OxyContin and Vicodin, Valium and Xanax, Adderall and Ritalin—without a prescription, just with the click of a mouse and a credit card or bank account information.

As a parent, you can take some steps to make sure your children are not using the internet to learn about using drugs, making drug paraphernalia, or acquiring prescription painkillers. In your home, you can restrict computer use to public rooms, such as the living room and the kitchen table, rather than in the privacy of your child's bedroom.

Limit the time your teen spends online, [and] put computers in a common area of the house to more easily monitor their use. Set limits on which websites, chat rooms, games, or blogs they can and cannot visit, and discuss consequences for breaking these rules.

White House Office of National Drug Control Policy.

If you have any concerns about your child, you can periodically review internet websites that your child has viewed by clicking "History" on your internet browser's toolbar. If you suspect that your child may be deleting his browser history, depending on the computer operating system, you can block use of the "Delete History" function. You can also be on the lookout for charges on your credit card or deliveries from international companies and online pharmacies. They may not be obvious; look for unfamiliar but generic corporate names on your credit card bills, and screen your mail for unexpected packages.

SOCIAL NETWORKING SITES

Eighty percent of twelve- to seventeen-year-olds have personal profiles on at least one of the various social networking sites, so it's important for you to know something about how and why teens use them.

Social networking sites can be a helpful tool for your child. Online communities and groups easily accessible on these sites focus on a wide variety of topics, shared hobbies, common interests, sports, games, and religion. Your teen can pursue different interests through these online groups. However, social networking sites are double-edged swords that can make drug and alcohol use seem appealing and fun. That's why I offer this primer on the four social networking sites most widely used by teens.

You have to learn which aspects of technology have nutritional value and which are the equivalent of candy, snacks, and soda. You must educate yourself about how technology influences your children's physical and mental health, both positively and negatively. Given the ready access of information through the internet, there are no excuses for being ill informed.

Dr. Jim Taylor, author and expert in child development and parenting, "Feed Your Children a Balanced 'Diet' of Technology," Huffington Post, June 3, 2013.

Facebook

Facebook (www.facebook.com) is an online social media site that lets users connect to other users as near as next door and as far away as the other side of the world. Facebook users can create personal profiles that display information like their birthday, phone number, address, photos of themselves and friends, favorite books, movies, musicians, and any kind of personal comments. Users can make their profile "public" (visible to all other Facebook users), or "private" (visible only to users they approve as "Facebook friends").

Facebook users can share events in their day-to-day lives by public messages they write, photos, and videos. Some kids post pictures of themselves and others drinking and drugging and write comments about "what a blast the party was last night, plenty of booze, pot, and pills."

To sign up for a Facebook account, all that's needed is an active email address. Facebook states that all users must be at least thirteen years old, but it doesn't require any proof of age.

YouTube

YouTube (www.youtube.com) is an online social media site where users post videos they've made and watch videos of others. YouTube users can easily find a variety of videos, from lessons in baking chocolate cakes to lessons in rolling marijuana joints; from episodes of a television show to home videos of teens drinking and popping pills. Anyone with a video camera, including those on most cell phones, can show videos he or she has recorded, including some that glamorize alcohol and drug use. Individuals can post videos of how to grow potent marijuana in your closet, feign symptoms for getting stimulants from a physician, sell drugs, and make crystal meth in your kitchen.

Some videos are spoofs, but they're not so labeled. Spoofs or not, children watching them can get the idea that drugs are fun and everyone is doing them. No personal account or profile is needed to use YouTube, but users may create one if they wish.

In CASA's 2012 teen survey, we found that three in four teens thought that seeing pictures posted on Facebook and YouTube of kids partying with alcohol and marijuana encourages other teens to want to party like that.

Q: Should parents talk to their kids about how social media and websites, like Facebook and YouTube, may make drinking and drug use look glamorous or cool?

A: I talk to my kids about social media. I want them to understand how dangerous it can be if Facebook is used inappropriately. We talk about the dangers of Facebook and how people make it dangerous. I have my kids explain why they have to get on the computer in front of me or their dad.

A: Absolutely YES! When . . . my daughter "became of age"—middle school!—she was allowed to be on the computer one hour a day and no more. Also, she had to give us her passwords to everything so we could check in regularly, or we wouldn't pay for it.

A: Lessons on the risks and realities associated with social media are one component of a larger media awareness education we should be providing our children.

Parent postings on CASA's "How to Raise a Drug-Free Kid" online discussion forums.

YouTube states that all users must be at least thirteen years old, and some videos require viewers to be eighteen before the videos will play, but in neither case is any proof of age required.

Twitter

Twitter (www.twitter.com) is an online social media site that offers users an abbreviated way to stay in touch with others. Twitter users can write comments limited to 140 characters known as "tweets." Tweets are published in a user's brief identifying profile and visible to other users. Twitter features tweets by actors, rock stars, politicians, and other celebrities about their day-to-day lives. Often some write how high they got on drugs or alcohol and what fun it was. Anyone can register with Twitter to post his or her own comments and see those of others.

Instagram

Instagram (www.instagram.com) is an online social media site concentrating on photos. Users can take pictures with their cell phones and post them for others to see and comment on. Instagram is commonly used to view pictures that celebrities post to keep attention on their activities and antics. Anyone can get an Instagram account, and many teens do so to follow celebrities, display their own pictures, and see those of their friends. Pictures of teens and celebrities often glamorize illegal drug use, popping pills, and excessive drinking.

Though Instagram says users must be at least thirteen, no proof of age is necessary.

If you allow your child to join a social networking site such as Facebook, YouTube, Twitter, or Instagram, you might do so on the condition that you can monitor your child's activities. Many parents do this by joining the site themselves, creating their own profile, and adding their child as a friend. This enables a parent to view the content on their child's profile: comments, pictures, conversations, relationship updates, and party invitations. My son Joe and I have been Facebook friends of my teenage grandson Joe IV (nicknamed Jack) since he was a young teen.

CYBER BULLYING

Some teens use social networking sites to tease nastily or to cyber bully a child they don't like. The anonymity some kids feel when sitting behind a computer screen can lead to anything from isolated incidents of name-calling to repeatedly tormenting another teen. Fake Facebook profiles can be created (even though it breaks the site's policies and guidelines) and used to anonymously disparage a teen or start false rumors about one. Talk to your child about cyber bullying and encourage her to come to you if she or someone she knows is bullied online. In CASA's 2011 teen survey, we learned that kids who are cyber bullied are twice as likely as those who are not to smoke, drink, and use marijuana.

CELL PHONES AND TEXT MESSAGES

By the time your child is twelve, the odds are that he or she has a cell phone. And, if your son or daughter doesn't, then I bet you have heard many pleas for one, like "All my friends have one." "It's not fair for me not to have one." "I'll be safer; I can call you, and you can get in touch with me any time."

Some 80 percent of teens have a cell phone, often a smartphone with instant access to the internet and the capacity to send text messages, and take and email photographs. That's more than double the percentage of teens with such phones when the first edition of this book was written. With these phones, teens can talk to one another from any place and send text messages instantly. Cell phones provide a sense of privacy in talking, messaging, and sending photos. No wonder that cell phones have become the most popular way teens communicate. This makes it important for you to establish standards you expect your teen to observe in cell phoning and text messaging.

How Teens Communicate/Socialize on a Daily Basis with Friends

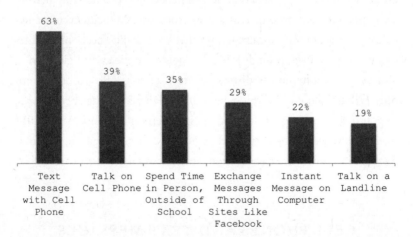

Pew Research Center Project, Teens, Smartphones, and Texting *(2012).*

With the prevalence of smartphones, the world rests in the palm of your children's hands. But think of it as a trip to a major city. There are places where we can walk safely among its crowds and wonders, and yet it can be all too easy to quickly and unexpectedly run into danger by taking the wrong turn.

Risa Ferman, district attorney and expert in internet safety for children, "What Are Your Kids Really Doing on Their Cell Phones and How Can You Keep Them Safe?," Huffington Post, *April 3, 2013.*

There's no uniform or best time for a child to have a first cell phone. Some parents give their son or daughter a cell phone in middle school, others in high school, and still others when their child gets a driver's license. Your timing depends largely on your assessment of your child's maturity and responsibility and your confidence that your child will abide by the standards you set, because a cell phone opens up a vast new world for your child. For example, some teens use cell phones for sexting: sending sexually provocative messages and pictures (often of themselves) to other teens. Your child could be the recipient of such messages, which frequently also glamorize the use of drugs and alcohol.

[T]een girls who engaged in sexting behaviors also had a higher prevalence of risky sex behaviors, including multiple partners and using drugs or alcohol before sex.

Jeff Temple, PhD, et al., "Teen Sexting and Its Association with Sexual Behaviors," Archives of Pediatrics and Adolescent Medicine *166, no. 9 (September 2012).*

On a cell phone, there's even a way for a teen to hide photos he knows his parents wouldn't approve of, like one showing a friend smoking pot or drinking beer. Photo apps, such as Snapchat, allow users with camera phones to take and send a picture to another user who can look at it for a few seconds before the photo is automatically deleted and erased. Of course, cell phone apps like these aren't used only in teens' efforts to deceive their parents or hide inappropriate behaviors; they can be used in fun and harmless activities too. But if you're concerned that your teen may be drinking or using drugs, or closely associating with classmates who do so, then it's important for you to be aware of his ability to disguise his use of his cell phone.

"I want to make my mark on the world—and have it disappear in ten seconds."

So how did I become so addicted? It was actually very easy, thanks to my cell phone . . . I kept all my drug dealers close by. In fact, I could press a couple of buttons on my cell phone, and there they were—in my address book. Whether I was at school or on vacation with my family, I always had a dealer within ten minutes from me. With a press of a "detail" button for each contact, I had all the information I needed: what types of drugs they sold, where they lived, and how to get a hold of them. Normally, I'd call or text message a dealer around two during the school day, and by the end of classes, I was hooked up.

"Amy," as told to TheAntiDrug.com's Real Teen Stories.

If you have concerns that your teen may be using drugs, it may be advisable to check what he is doing on his cell phone. You can skim through his text messages and the list of phone numbers called recently. But an errant teen is likely to know ways to hide calls and messages that would reveal such conduct.

It's heartbreaking as a parent to feel that your teen may be deceiving you. But if you suspect he may be abusing substances or spending time with others who are, his cell phone activity may help allay or confirm your suspicions. Talk to your teen about your concerns, and if he has a personal cell phone, consider monitoring its use. Depending on the seriousness of the situation, you can restrict your teen to using the cell phone only during specific hours, or change the settings so that only you can enter a password to download a new app or program. Small changes like these can make a big difference in helping your teen grow up healthy and safe.

If enforcing stricter rules about when and where your teen can use the computer isn't enough, and you think that your child may be experimenting with alcohol or drugs, it may be desirable (and necessary) to increase supervision on his use of technology. You can download computer programs called spyware so you can learn what websites your teen frequently visits, videos he watches on YouTube, and words or phrases he searches for on Google. You can install passwords to prevent your child from accessing, online or on a cell phone, inappropriate content relating to using drugs. But keep in mind that with every new program of protection developed for parents to use, another may be developed to help kids circumvent the security you put in place.

"The sandbox is safe, and it's even safer without the sand."

YOUR PARENT POWER: COMMUNICATION AND POSITIVE VALUES

With so much technology at your teen's fingertips, it's impossible to monitor all of your son's or daughter's social media activity. Indeed, by middle school, your child may become even more adept than you at using communications technology.

What can you do? At an early age, be the one who shows your child how to search for something on Google, talk to him about Facebook, and watch his first video on YouTube with him. Have conversations about social media, just as you'd talk about other things that are part of your child's growing up: respect for herself and her friends, staying away from dangerous neighborhoods, not listening to music or watching movies and TV shows that glorify sex and drugs. Become familiar enough with the internet and social media sites to use them together. That can be a comfortable way to explain what is safe and appropriate and what is in-line with your family's values and rules.

Just as we teach our children how to ride a bike, we need to teach them how to navigate social media and make the right moves that will help them. The physical world is similar to the virtual world in many cases. It's about being aware. We can prevent many debacles if we're educated.

Amy Jo Martin, author and expert in social media, "The Truth About Kids and Social Media," Fast Company, May 24, 2013.

Teaching your child what's good and bad about the internet and cell phones should be no different than instilling other values at a young age, like telling the truth and not lying, or being fair and honest, and not cheating on tests or in games. That's the best way to insure that your child will use technology responsibly—even as she becomes more proficient on a cell phone or iPad.

If you do decide to use protective strategies such as those mentioned above, make sure that is not the only action you take. Technology is no substitute for parental engagement or for getting your child the help he may need in order to stop drinking, smoking pot, or abusing prescription drugs.

"My parents are so busy checking the computer that they never think of this."

It is critical that you openly, honestly, and frequently communicate with your child early on about use of the internet, social networking, and cell phones. Be sure to talk not only about the dangers but also about the benefits—like using the internet to help with a research project, a cell phone to call you in case of an emergency, and social networking websites to keep in touch with friends and family members.

While some people choose to monitor their kids' [cell] phone use, or withhold passwords, this is a very personal choice, whereas the need for open communication between parent and child is universal.

Holly Seddon, editor in chief of Quib.ly, an online community about parenting and technology, interviewed in "Teenagers, Nudity, Cell Phones and Social Media: The Parenting Nightmare of 2013," Huffington Post, March 19, 2013.

Indeed, the values and standards you establish for your family are the best protection against your child's inappropriate use of modern technology. How your child reacts to videos of other teens drinking and drugging, partying with pills, or smoking pot is going to be influenced most powerfully by values you have instilled and standards of conduct you have made clear you expect of your child. To paraphrase the famous football coach Vince Lombardi, if you want to protect your child from being enticed by modern technology that glamorizes smoking, drinking, and drug use, family values aren't everything— they're the *only thing* likely to work.

PARENT TIPS

- Just as you teach your children to say "Please" and "Thank you" when they're still young, start talking to your child about the safe and healthy use of technology and social media *early on*. If you wait until she's in middle school or high school, you'll find that she's explored these things with friends and may have picked up unsafe online habits already.

- Find opportunities to surf the internet together, and explain how dangerous or inappropriate some websites can be for kids and teens.
- Keep track of which social media sites—Facebook, Instagram, Twitter, or YouTube—your child may have profiles on, and gain access to your child's personal pages.
- "Friend" or "follow" your child on social media sites so that you can regularly monitor his online activity.
- Ask your child for his or her passwords to everything, including his cell phone, so that you can check up on what he's doing and whom he's speaking to or texting with regularly if you become concerned.
- Restrict computer use, for nonschool purposes, to a limited number of hours or specific time slots each day.
- Warn your child about cyber bullying and let her know that if she or one of her friends is ever being harassed online, she should tell you.
- If you are concerned about what your child is doing online or on his cell phone, or if you feel that he may be deleting his internet history or text message activity, install spyware programs so that you can see this information when you need to.

17

HOW CAN I PROTECT
MY KIDS AT SCHOOL?

Walk around the outside of your child's school. Do you see a sign that announces it is a Drug-Free School Zone?

Maybe you and your children pass that sign every day, during school drop-off and pickup. Have you thought about whether the sign is true or false? Does it give you a sense of comfort? Do you think it's baloney?

Have you asked your kids what they think about that sign?

At my organization, CASA, we have.

No, we may not have spoken directly to *your* child, but we have talked to thousands of middle and high schoolers in small towns, medium-size cities, and major urban centers all over the country. And most of them tell us that the words on that sign aren't worth the paint they're printed with.

For more than two decades, we have been asking American teens about the presence of drugs within the corridors, classrooms, and grounds of their schools. We have surveyed kids in public and private schools and secular and religious schools. What we've learned is shocking: Most high school students we spoke to told us that there is a place on or nearby school grounds where students go to drink alcohol, smoke, or use drugs in the middle of the school day. And more than eight out of ten high school students say that they've seen schoolmates possessing, using, or dealing drugs, or high or drunk, at school.

Even more disturbing, when we have discussion groups of high school juniors and seniors and tell them that 80 percent of high school students say there are drugs in their schools, several of them laugh and say: "The other twenty percent must be lying."

For too many American teens, the concept of a drug-free school, that highly touted, comforting catchphrase among parents and educators, has become an oxymoron.

WHY SHOULD I BE CONCERNED ABOUT DRUGS IN SCHOOL?

Witnessing Drug Use, Possession, or Dealing Puts Kids at Risk

During the school year, teens spend about half (or more) of their waking hours at school. Whether they spend that time in a drug-free environment or in a drug-infected school—one where drugs are used, kept, or sold—has a big impact on their substance abuse risk. When CASA surveyed twelve- to seventeen-year-old students across the country, we learned that almost one in three knew of someone at their school who sold marijuana or other drugs during the school day. The chart below illustrates drugs that students sell at school.

Of the 12- to 17-Year-Olds Reporting That Students Sell Drugs on School Grounds, the Types of Drugs Most Commonly Seen for Sale

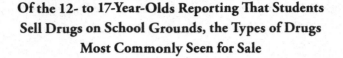

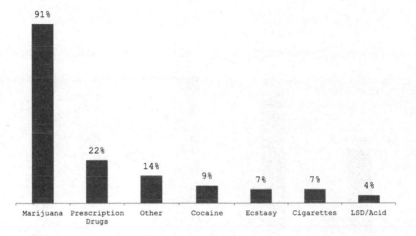

CASA. National Survey of American Attitudes on Substance Abuse XVII: Teens *(2012)*.

Sending your child to a drug-infected school dumps him into a culture where smoking cigarettes, popping pills, drinking alcohol, and using marijuana, hallucinogens, or other illegal drugs to get high is often accepted as a teen rite of passage. It forces your child to adapt to a climate where peers and older teens make it cool to smoke, drink, get drunk, and use drugs. Kids in schools like these are at much higher risk of falling prey to drug use themselves.

Compared with teens who say there are no drugs at school, those who see drugs at school are:

- two and a half times likelier to use alcohol;
- three times likelier to use marijuana; and
- nearly three times likelier to use tobacco.

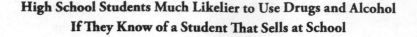

High School Students Much Likelier to Use Drugs and Alcohol If They Know of a Student That Sells at School

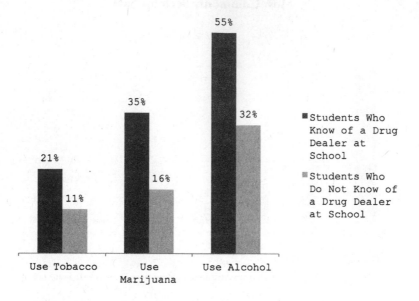

CASA. National Survey of American Attitudes on Substance Abuse XVII: Teens *(2012).*

Remember, availability is the mother of use. This is especially true at drug-infected middle schools and high schools. Teens at such schools say they can quickly obtain drugs. Compared with twelve- to seventeen-year-olds who say their schools are drug-free schools, those at drug-infected schools are two and half times likelier to be able to get marijuana, and one and half times likelier to be able to get prescription drugs, *in one hour or less!* That's about as quickly as they can buy candy.

Drugs Infect the Entire Student Body

Next to parents, schools—everything about them, including class-mates—exert the most influence on teen behavior, and that's bad news for most high school students and lots of middle school students.

When schools are infected with drugs, there is a contagion consequence that can strike any student, even student leaders. Substance abuse at schools is not limited to "difficult kids" who exhibit discipline problems or fail or cut classes.

Our research indicates that all too often, popularity and drug use go hand in hand. The school environment can foster a culture in which drug use is seen as cool. The chance of becoming "one of the popular kids" can be an enticing carrot to dangle in front of a teen. Kids who say they are among the most popular at their school are twice as likely to say that most of their friends drink, smoke, and use pot. Nearly one-third of teens say that the main reason kids their age drink alcohol is just to "fit in" with the other kids. Among teens at drug-infected schools, popular kids have a reputation for drinking a lot and using illegal drugs.

The scariest thing I ever hear a parent say is "not my kid—he's a good kid—he would never abuse a prescription drug." The reality is that *every teen* is at risk.

Addiction expert Dr. Drew Pinsky, October 19, 2011.

Drugs Threaten Academic Performance

Substance use can adversely affect student performance. Alcohol and drug abuse can change the brain and body in ways that can interfere with thinking and make learning and concentration more difficult. The more a student uses substances such as alcohol, marijuana, cocaine, Vicodin, or other drugs, the lower his grade point average is likely to be, and the more likely he is to drop out of school. On the flip side, poor academic performance can propel students toward substance use. If your child is struggling in school, there is a risk that he may abuse substances to alleviate the pain or shame of his troubles there.

It's a lot of good kids from good families who are making poor choices. In my experience, I've found kids can hide their drug use from parents for about two years [before related issues such as academic and social problems begin to arise].

Detective Tony Marcocci, quoted by Paul Peirce,
"Western Pa. Drug Overdoses Reach 'Epidemic Levels,'"
Pittsburgh Tribune-Review, *October 3, 2012.*

Alcohol at School

Make sure that your child's school is attentive to drinking as well as drug use, because the biggest drug problem among teenage students is alcohol, particularly beer and hard liquor like vodka, and sweetened alcoholic beverages.

Students who abuse alcohol are less likely to do well in school or to be committed to doing well in school. Heavy and binge drinkers between the ages of twelve and seventeen are four to five times more likely to cut classes or skip school. Students at high risk for alcohol abuse are at high risk of being left back, getting suspended from school, and performing poorly in reading and math.

Marijuana at School

As you know from reading chapter 7, the use of marijuana, one of the top drugs of choice among teens, is related to lower grade point averages, less satisfaction with school, negative attitudes toward school, school absences, and poor academic performance. Long-term regular marijuana use can impair memory, attention span, and the ability to comprehend information.

Before the mid-1970s, most people first tried marijuana during college. Today many first-time users are in middle school.

A disturbing discovery has police investigating on the Clovis North High School Campus.

Clovis police are actually looking into students selling marijuana lollipops at the school in Northeast Fresno.

They look innocent enough, but these lollipops are infused with THC, the active ingredient in marijuana. The candied drug was popular at medical marijuana dispensaries, favored by users who'd rather not smoke to get the benefits. Now students at Clovis North say it's a favorite for high schoolers trying to use drugs undetected.

"It looked like one of those caramel pops with the green on top and stuff, and I just thought, you know, it's just a lollipop, until I started hearing people talk about it," said [a] Clovis North senior.

Corin Hoggard, "Pot Lollipops Caught on Clovis North High School Campus," KFSN-TV, March 7, 2013.

Most teachers and school administrators attempt to do all they can to keep drugs out of schools, but beware those teachers and administrators who believe that student drug use is no big deal. They are wrong.

CASA's surveys have shown that some middle school teachers think marijuana users can still be good students, and some high school teachers believe that a student who uses marijuana every weekend can still do well in school. But the effects of marijuana on attention, memory, and learning last up to a day or more, so kids who smoke pot on the weekends can experience poor concentration and memory on Mondays and Tuesdays as a result.

"I have noticed that Nic is being pulled by the students who the others see as cool," [the teacher] says. "They're the ones who sneak cigarettes and—I'm only guessing—probably smoke pot. They may. But I don't think you have to be overly concerned. It's normal. Most kids try it."

"But," I say, "Nic is only twelve."

"Yes." The teacher sighs. "That's when they try it. There's only so much we can do. It's a force out there. The children have to figure it out sooner or later. Often sooner."

David Sheff, whose son later got into other drugs and almost died of a meth addiction, Beautiful Boy: A Father's Journey Through His Son's Addiction.

ZERO-TOLERANCE POLICIES

Many schools enforce a zero-tolerance policy regarding alcohol and other drug use. Zero-tolerance policies vary. Some require students who are caught using to be severely punished—suspended or expelled—no matter how minor the infraction. Other policies distinguish between use and sale; still others provide treatment and counseling and a second (or third) chance to help the student remain substance free. Zero-tolerance policies are meant to reduce drugs in the school and to make students feel safer on school grounds. They place pressure on parents to keep their kids drug free, and give children a powerful reason to say no when offered drugs.

But zero-tolerance policies that impose expulsion can discourage students and their parents from speaking up if they suspect that a student is drinking or taking drugs. An unintended consequence of such a policy may be that teens who are experimenting with drugs sink into regular use, and students may be less likely to ask for help if one of their friends has a drinking or drug problem or needs medical attention for alcohol- or drug-related reasons.

Find out if your children's school has a zero-tolerance policy. If it does, find out what the consequences of alcohol or other drug use are and whether the school offers students an opportunity to avoid or ameliorate punishment if they seek treatment. And train your child never to leave a friend or classmate who is in trouble or passed out from drug or alcohol use, but to help him or her or call 911.

Daniel Reardon's son, Danny, was killed in an alcohol-related hazing incident at a school that has a zero-tolerance expulsion policy. Danny's friends could have saved him by calling 911, but they were afraid of getting kicked out of school, and so they left him to "sleep it off" instead. Danny never woke up.

BEWARE OF SEE-NO-DRUGS, HEAR-NO-DRUGS, SPEAK-NO-DRUGS PRINCIPALS

Some of America's middle and high school principals are living in an unrealistic, sometimes self-serving cocoon when it comes to the presence of drug use in and around their schools. Unlike their students, few principals ever see drugs sold on school grounds. Most claim that their students do not smoke at their schools either. Yet if some students are to be believed, the presence of drugs in schools is as common as pen and paper.

Principals are much less likely than students to admit that drug use is happening on their campuses: nine out of ten principals say their campuses are drug free, but, as you now know, more than half of students say their campuses are not drug free.

Principals are also less likely to think that drugs are a big problem for students. Principals rank drugs behind family problems and social pressures as the top issues facing teenagers, even though teenagers themselves are more concerned about drugs than anything else.

By graduation, Janet's oldest son was on the path toward harder drugs, a path that would eventually lead him to an extended stay in rehab, mere days away from trying heroin because it was cheaper than the cocaine and prescription drugs he had been using.

Janet readily admits her son's situation was the result of his own "stupid choice," but she also points the finger at school administrators.

"Drugs are incredibly easy to find in Pennridge," she said. "[The school] didn't really acknowledge that they had a problem."

Theresa Hegel, Danny Adler, and Marion Callahan, "Drugs Find Their Way into Local Schools," PhillyBurbs.com, May 26, 2013.

HELP YOUR KIDS NAVIGATE THE CHALLENGES OF A DRUG-INFECTED SCHOOL

Put yourself in your child's shoes for a moment and ask yourself, What would it be like to be twelve or fourteen or sixteen years old and witness a drug deal on the football field? Or see your friend stash pills in his or her locker? Or be offered pot or Molly by an upperclassman? How would you feel? How would you react? Would you say or do anything?

Or try it another way: How would you feel if your coworker on a dangerous construction site were smoking pot or swigging vodka? Or if someone who works in the office cubicle next to yours or in the stockroom offered you pot or pills to get high? Or suggested that you do a line of cocaine in the bathroom? Would you feel uncomfortable? Suppose that someone was your boss? Would you say or do anything?

If these scenarios make you feel at all uneasy, imagine how difficult it must be for your children to confront such issues at school.

If you have established a comfortable rapport with your kids, you may find it easy to talk to them about drugs in their school. If this is an issue of concern for your kids (as it is for many of the kids we survey at CASA), and if they feel that you are on their side, they'll likely want to talk to you. Listen closely to your children. Once you raise the issue with your kids, you will have ample opportunity to revisit it. You don't need to accomplish everything in a single talk.

Our research statistics cannot tell you what your child is experiencing or witnessing at school, but they do say something about your children's learning environment. If your daughter or son is in high school, whether it's public, private, or religious, the odds are overwhelming that alcohol and other drugs are there. If your child is in middle school, the odds are one in three that he can buy a joint or a pill there. So there's a good chance that your kids are concerned about what's going on in their schools and would like to be able to talk to someone about it.

Be the person they can talk to. Tell them you've read about the problem of drugs in school; ask them if this (or how much of this) is going on at their school. Find out if they are worried about this or have questions about it. Let them know you are available to talk to them and that you can help them come up with ways to respond if they see classmates using or if someone offers them drugs. Share with your teenagers the information you learn in this book about the

impact of substance use on the developing brain and school performance, and the slippery slope of addiction.

If your child tells you there are no drugs in school, that may be the
reality, or it may just be that your child is unaware of the situation. In
either case, it's good news. It's also likelier to be the case when your
child is young.

If your child tells you there are drugs at school, or you suspect that
may be the case, encourage other parents to join you in talking to the
school principal, headmaster, and teachers. When seeing other parents and school officials, let them know why you are concerned about
drugs at school. Share the information in this chapter with them. You
are likely to find them just as concerned, and most schools will take
steps to deal with the problem.

For parents who strive to raise healthy, substance-free kids, coun-
tering the influence on their children of drug-infected school days can
be an uphill battle. But do not leave your child to fend for herself in
this environment: acknowledge it if there's a problem in the school
and communicate with your child about it.

IT DOESN'T HAVE TO BE THAT WAY:
DEMAND DRUG-FREE SCHOOLS

You do not have to accept the presence of drugs as an inevitable part
of your child's school experience. And you should not. You have the
Parent Power to do something about it.

You do not have to take on this struggle alone. If you are concerned or even just curious about drugs in your child's school, you'll
find that many other parents are concerned. Teachers and school administrators also want their schools and students to be drug free.

Most parents believe that drugs or alcohol are used, kept, or sold
on the grounds of their teen's school. Almost 90 percent of these parents do not hold administrators responsible for this sorry state of af-

fairs. Indeed, six out of ten parents believe that making their child's school drug free is not a realistic goal. These parents are wrong!

Parents have successfully pressed for better schools, higher academic standards, and quality education. Some have lobbied to get legislation passed so that their children could attend charter schools or receive vouchers to attend parochial schools. If you get a group of parents to understand how the presence of drugs in schools can savage their children's academic achievement and threaten their children's safety and future, they will join you in insisting that the schools do everything in their power to insure that the schools are drug free. The creation of drug-free school environments for our teens is a matter of parental and administrative will.

Q. Do you get any support from your child's school, religion, or extended family in keeping your kid drug free? What support would you like to get? Does your child's school or religious organization offer parent education programs on teens and substance use?

A. Yes, all of the above . . . Once a year, the school offered a parents' night regarding this information. I would've loved to have a presentation on all types of drugs, what they are made of, how they affect kids, how much they cost, etc.—all the details. That could help parents determine if their child could be using or, even better, *not* using.

Parent posting in CASA's "How to Raise a Drug-Free Kid" online discussion forums.

Parents have the right to demand drug-free schools for their children. Every state requires children to enroll in school (or be homeschooled) until at least age sixteen, seventeen, or eighteen. The state that requires you to send your children to school has an obligation to provide a safe and nourishing school atmosphere for them. You should not let your school board, or state or local education authorities, force you to send your children for at least half of their waking hours, nine months out of the year, to a place that is infected with drugs.

In talking to other parents, point out that if asbestos were found in your children's school, they would raise hell and refuse to send their children to class until every speck of the dangerous dust had been removed. Moms and dads who spend thousands of dollars each year to send their children to private schools demand that these schools get their children into Harvard, Yale, Stanford, Holy Cross, Georgetown, and Princeton—and the schools deliver. If they demanded that these schools clear out the drugs, the schools would do that too. If parents made it clear that they care as much about their children's exposure to drugs, alcohol, and cigarettes as they do about their children's exposure to asbestos and achievements on College Board test scores, principals and headmasters would clear the fog of tobacco, alcohol, and drugs from their schools.

This will not be an easy task, getting your child's school drug free and keeping it in that condition. Schools have tried a variety of methods: testing all students randomly, testing student athletes, assembling parents and asking for their help by not allowing alcohol at parties. But this is a battle worth waging—and it can be won.

Use your Parent Power to mobilize other parents and energize the school, teachers, administrators, and students, to make your child's school drug free. You're likely to find that most teachers and administrators will be receptive. Ask your school directly about any programs or policies they have in place to help keep students substance free. Some schools have a variety of zero-tolerance policies, as I discussed earlier in the chapter. Other schools require parents to attend forums on the dangers of teen drug and alcohol use and to sign contracts that they will not permit any alcohol use at teen parties at their home. Many schools have other rules or contracts that can be put in place at your own middle or high school with just a little community support.

Here are a few examples.

Episcopal High School, just outside Houston, has established a school program called Choices to help keep their teens and school safe and substance free. Choices engages community members, families, students, and the school to come together to reduce risky behaviors of students, including drug and alcohol use. At the core of this program is the idea that the path a teen takes to getting drunk or high is usually no different from the path toward other risky behaviors, like dating violence, dangerous driving, and eating disorders. For that reason, Choices believes all of these risky behaviors can be prevented using the same techniques, activities, and education. Choices has licensed counselors and addiction specialists in the school at all times.

In deciding which risky behaviors to target, Choices asks students to identify their greatest concerns and makes those the focus of the program. (Drinking and drug use always come up as a top concern.) Educational materials and discussion topics on the student concerns are sent home with the teens so that their parents can get actively engaged in the prevention process. In just three years of Choices, the Episcopal High School community experienced a decline in risky behaviors by teens. Choices prepared the chart below to illustrate its successes. (You can find more information on Choices at its website: www.ehshouston.org/page.cfm?p=1839.)

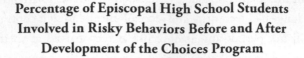

Percentage of Episcopal High School Students
Involved in Risky Behaviors Before and After
Development of the Choices Program

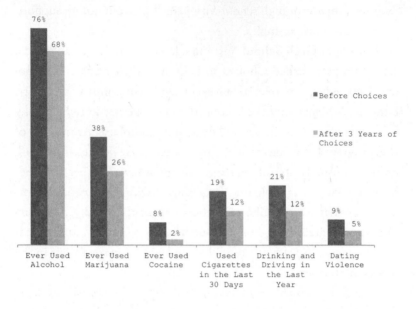

Before Choices

After 3 Years of Choices

76%
68%
38%
26%
19%
12%
21%
12%
9%
5%
8%
2%

Ever Used Alcohol | Ever Used Marijuana | Ever Used Cocaine | Used Cigarettes in the Last 30 Days | Drinking and Driving in the Last Year | Dating Violence

Raw data obtained via email from the Council on Alcohol and Drugs Houston, 2013.

Mt. Lebanon High School, just outside of Pittsburgh, requires students to uphold its drug and alcohol policy, which prohibits drinking, using, selling, or having any drug or drug-related paraphernalia on and off school grounds. After a first offense of an off-campus violation, students must either complete a drug and alcohol evaluation by a licensed counselor and follow the recommendations of the counselor or face a thirty-day restriction on school activities.

The Park School in Baltimore has Park Connects, a comprehensive program to teach its students to avoid risky and unhealthy behaviors. The Park Connects program brings together parents, teachers, and students for educational programs, seminars on alcohol and other drugs, and ongoing community dialogues to promote healthy behaviors.

The Middletown Township Public Schools in Middletown, New Jersey, randomly drug tests students in athletics and other extracurricular activities, such as theater and school government, and students who want a pass to park on school grounds. The school allows any parents of any other student to opt to have their child drug tested randomly.

Conor Wilson, 16 and a junior at Demarest, said that most students opposed [random drug] testing, but that he was not one of them. He said the threat of being kicked off a team or out of a club could help students fight off peer pressure to use drugs.

"Now I can say, 'No, I don't want my number to be pulled,'" Conor said. "It's a stronger stance for kids who want to say no to drugs and alcohol."

Daniel E. Slotnik, "Drug Testing in Schools Divides North Jersey District," New York Times, *October 6, 2013.*

These are just four examples of school programs. If your own school does not already have any, you can be the guiding force to start one. For information about effective substance use prevention and education programs that could be implemented in your community or at your child's school, see SAMHSA's Evidence-Based Programs and Practices database at www.nrepp.samhsa.gov.

PARENT TIPS

- Talk to your child about whether students are smoking, drinking, or doing or selling drugs at school.

- Bring the information in this book to your school's PTA meeting. Talk to the other parents about joining you in raising the issue with the school leadership.
- Join or put together parents to establish effective substance abuse programs if your child's school has none.
- Insist that the school take steps to become substance free. Providing a robust substance abuse prevention curriculum is important. Establishing and enforcing substance-free rules and policies are also essential.
- Urge your child's school to help coordinate support services for students and their families, and insist on parental involvement.

18

HOW DO I HELP MY TEEN COPE WITH THE COLLEGE YEARS?

I added this chapter to this revised edition of *How to Raise a Drug-Free Kid* for three reasons.

First, because I have been asked this question repeatedly by parents since the first edition was published. I'll never forget speaking at an Atlanta Chamber of Commerce luncheon when a father said, "With all the drinking on campuses, I'm scared to death about the safety of my daughter who is a freshman at Georgia Tech. What can I do?"

Second, because since that edition went to press in 2008, scientists have learned a lot about the developing brain, confirming that it is not fully developed until the midtwenties. That means a college student's impulse control and ability to foresee consequences are more like a high school teen's than an adult's—and college students away from home are detached from any immediate, intimate parental control and observation.

Third, because I want to offer ways in which you can help select a better college environment for your child and establish that you continue to be interested and concerned during your child's college years. You are simply not ready to cut your child loose.

SO HOW CAN I PREPARE MY
KIDS FOR COLLEGE?

Actually, you've been preparing your child for this moment for years: teaching him to get a good night's sleep before a big exam, to eat balanced meals, to study hard, to make friends with kids who don't drink or use drugs, to spend money wisely—setting a foundation for your child to make independent decisions.

Q. How would you prepare your children to manage the new social pressures to drink alcohol and use drugs that come with the transition to college and their new independence?

A. You start at the beginning, as soon as they understand bad and good . . . This could be six months, two years old—but by the time they are six, you have already done a lot of work, every day, every second, every year . . . If you have truly shown your unlimited love by doing your work, by the time they reach college, the new independence turns into productivity, planning ahead, great grades, good healthful habits, and knowing when partying and fun have their place . . . Love, discipline, and respect—there is no secret here. These three qualities need to be instilled by your unending actions throughout their formative years.

Parent posting in CASA's "How to Raise a Drug-Free Kid" online discussion forums.

For many teens, college is a stepping-stone toward adulthood, but college campuses are far from mature environments—"college bubbles," as many students call them. When you say good-bye, you will leave your new collegian surrounded by thousands of other teenagers, all free from any parental supervision, almost all for the first time in their lives. Due in part to this newfound freedom, your child will face a new world of opportunities, challenges, and temptations—among them, alcohol and other drugs.

Sending your children to college without coaching them about how to deal with drugs and alcohol would be like giving them the keys to the car without teaching them how to drive. When faced with unlimited access to drugs and alcohol—and plenty of free time to party—unprepared college students can ruin their lives or accidentally end them.

"I went on spring break a boy and came back an alcoholic."

This is why your influence is more important now than ever: 70 percent of college students say that their parents' concerns or expectations influence whether or how much they drink, smoke, or use drugs. So even though you won't be on campus with your children, you will have a big impact on their conduct.

In this chapter, I'll explain the steps you should take to prepare your children for college. First, I'll describe the college substance use scene and its dangers, so that you and your children will know what to look out for. Second, I'll give you tips about how and when to talk to your children about substance abuse on college campuses. Then I'll give you some suggestions for ways to help your children pick a college and choose their college housing. Last, I'll tell you how you can stay engaged and continue to empower your children to make good choices once freshman year begins.

EDUCATE YOURSELF AND YOUR TEEN ABOUT SUBSTANCE ABUSE ON COLLEGE CAMPUSES

If you needed to sit down when you read about the situation in our high schools, you'd better get back into that seat as you learn about the world your child will enter in college.

The use of alcohol and other substances among college students presents a pervasive and perennial public health challenge. At the most serious level, it has been estimated that excessive drinking contributes to approximately 1,800 deaths and [hundreds of thousands of] injuries among college students each year . . . Vandalism, community disturbances, physical assaults, and sexual assaults are also strongly related to college student substance use.

Conference sponsored by the Conversations in the Disciplines Program of the State University of New York, The Challenge of Reducing College Student Substance Use, held November 8–9, 2012.

Perhaps you're inclined to think that kids will be kids, and that college is the time when they should be permitted to take a walk on the wild side. Maybe you're thinking back to your own college years, and the drinking and partying that took place: "Sure, we got a little crazy, but so what? We had fun, we graduated, and now we're all healthy, productive adults. The same will be true for my kids."

What you may not be thinking—but should know—is that the college experience today is vastly different from the days when you were a student. Male college students may have been more prone to excessive drinking than females; today women have caught up and are drinking just as recklessly. Many college campuses are encircled by bars that sell beer and alcohol at low prices to attract students. Fake IDs are a dime a dozen.

Many colleges have reduced or abandoned altogether any parental role toward students. Technology gives students greater access to instant information about parties and drugs and how to get them and use them. Students have more time than ever to party; they can set their schedules so that they have no Friday (or even Thursday) classes and fewer morning classes. The weekend can begin on Wednesday or Thursday evening and extend far into Monday. The amount of free time your child can have in college will be a dramatic lifestyle change that can set the stage for abuse of alcohol and other drugs. And remember: since the brain is developing until the midtwenties, those controls on impulses, and the ability to appreciate consequences of actions, are not yet fully in place.

A POTENT MIX OF POT, PILLS, AND POWDERS

The mix of drugs that is available on college campuses today is new and ever changing, and the dangers of these drugs are misunderstood and underappreciated by students. Nine in ten college students say that alcohol is easy to obtain for those who are underage, and two-thirds say that addictive prescription drugs (without a doctor's order) and marijuana are just as readily available.

The abuse of prescription drugs among college students has exploded, just as it has among high school students. On some campuses, prescription drug abuse is more common than marijuana use. College students know well the abuse (partying and performance-enhancing) potential of prescription drugs such as Vicodin, OxyContin, Xanax, Valium, Ritalin, and Adderall. College students abuse Ritalin and Adderall to help them cram for an exam or pull an all-nighter writing a paper. They abuse Vicodin and OxyContin to get high, and Xanax and Valium to relax, chill out, and sometimes to sleep. They often mix these prescription drugs with beer, vodka, rum, or other alcohol. They also dip into drugs such as Molly and cocaine so that they can keep partying all night—or all weekend—long.

Alex [a student at Miami University] remembers the impressive assortment of drugs he once used.

"I used pretty much everything," he said. "Adderall, Ambien, Xanax, Klonopin, Percocet, morphine, Suboxone, ketamine . . . Now I only use Xanax once in a while."

He used each drug, he said, for a different purpose.
"Adderall helps me study," he said. "The benzos chilled
me out and helped my anxiety, and the opiates made me
feel great and forget about my problems."

*Victoria Slater, "Prescription Drug Epidemic on
the Rise," Miami Student newspaper, Miami
University of Ohio, December 3, 2013.*

The reasons that college students use these drugs—party, relax, study, or disengage and avoid something stressful—are no different from the reasons high school students report using the same drugs. But the big difference for college students is their permissive and independent environment. As opposed to most sixteen-year-olds, a college freshman doesn't need to be home, waking up Mom and Dad before midnight and having his breath smelled, or be awake and feeling well enough to attend church service early Sunday morning with the family. To college kids, the nights are longer, the parties are harder, and the access to drugs and alcohol is easier.

Not long ago, a New York University student went to
a "white trash" party with a bottle of Xanax rattling in
her purse. The student health center had prescribed the
antianxiety drug, along with a cocktail of antidepressants,
after she told a campus doctor of her panic attacks. That
night two friends made a play for the bottle and started
distributing them to everyone at the party. The morning
after the place was littered with crushed pills; the party had
moved to the roof (they managed to break the lock and
latch) and been busted by the cops. "It was out of control

and irresponsible," says the student. "But these kinds of things are really popular."

Sara Peck, "Generation Rx: Recreational Drugs of Choice on College Campuses," Forbes, August 11, 2010.

Women Drinking More Than Ever

I can drink my liquor
Faster than a flicker.
I can drink it quicker,
And get even sicker!

Annie Oakley, singing "Anything You Can Do," bragging to lead male character about her drinking prowess in the hit Broadway musical Annie Get Your Gun.

Women on college campuses today are drinking lots more than their mothers or grandmothers ever did. When asked why, women say they drink to reduce stress and keep up with the boys. They also say that the pressure to have sex leads them to use alcohol as a disinhibitor to help deal with that pressure. A generation ago, college women were more inclined to forgo alcohol for fear of letting down their guard and ending up having sex. Today's college women (and men) are likelier to use alcohol to shed their inhibitions and increase the likelihood of "hooking up"—a student euphemism for sexual activity without any commitment.

Maria attributes the hookup culture first and foremost to a lot of drinking. This enables students to do things they won't remember the next day. "I know some girls have hopes that it will turn into more if they hook up with a guy," Maria says, expressing a common opinion about why women are willing to hook up that I heard repeated many times by both the men and women I interviewed. But "some girls just do it because they are drunk and they think it is fun, and boys . . . want to say they hooked up with a girl that night."

> Donna Freitas, Sex and the Soul: Juggling
> Sexuality, Spirituality, Romance, and Religion
> on America's College Campuses.

One of the points you should make with your daughter is that getting drunk (or high on drugs) puts her at higher risk for sexual assault. Alcohol is far and away the campus's number one date-rape drug. Roughly one in twenty college women are raped each year; most of them are drunk at the time of the assault.

Universities Are Not Surrogate Parents

At some universities, especially large institutions, students have little opportunity to form personal relationships with their professors, counselors, or other adults on campus. In such environments, your children are left to their own devices, without the benefit of adult supervision to encourage responsibility. No one is hovering over them like parents to make sure they don't abuse drugs and alcohol. However, some institutions of higher learning, such as the University of Notre Dame, continue to foster a culture of stewardship with respect to their students' behavior and development.

Alcohol will always be available[;] encourage your son or daughter to make decisions to protect future plans of going abroad, getting into graduate schools, the Peace Corps or other future endeavors. Most students do not think ahead and instead live in the moment, or believe it won't happen to them. Developing a drinking pattern is a process. The more time that passes without "getting caught" leads to the increased belief that it won't happen. It is a roll of the dice, and every opportunity creates the possibility something bad can happen.

University of Notre Dame, Office of Alcohol and Drug Education, http://oade.nd.edu/for-parents.

The supervisory relationship between many institutions of higher learning and their students (who are overwhelmingly under twenty-one) is shaped, in large part, by the school's degree of legal liability for the consequences of student behavior. Increasingly, courts are holding universities liable for foreseeable harms to students—including alcohol-abuse-related injuries, sexual assaults, and deaths—if the university failed to use reasonable care to prevent the harm. However, the university's duty of care does not extend to off-campus incidents, including many fraternity- or sorority-related drinking events. As a result, some universities seek to avoid liability by banning parties on campus and forcing students to move them off campus, or by imposing regulations and policies aimed at curbing alcohol and drug use by students. Indeed, at some schools, fraternities and sororities have two houses: one on campus and the other off campus for unsupervised partying.

"I joined an online fraternity."

Few schools keep careful track of alcohol- and substance-related incidents among students, and they rarely notify parents of such incidents. Most colleges and universities will state their notification practice within their drug and alcohol policy or student handbook, which is frequently available for all students and parents to find on the school's website.

Many parents do not want to know if their children in college experience legal difficulties resulting from underage alcohol or drug use. When the University of Missouri attempted to institute a parental-notification policy as part of a broader effort to reduce student substance abuse, parents fought back. Many said that they send their children to college to experience, as they did, "life as it really is," and that drinking is part of the college experience and the real world. Other parents worried that being notified of their children's substance-related legal troubles might harm their relationship with their children. In the face of this denial and resistance from parents, we instituted a less strict parental-notification policy than we otherwise would have.

Manuel T. Pacheco, PhD, former president, University of Missouri System and University of Arizona.

Federal education law requires colleges and universities to keep track of the school's enforcement of consequences for violations of its drug and alcohol policies. But the standards of what conduct is reportable vary, and there is considerable underreporting and little, if any, auditing of these reports by the US Department of Education. Colleges and universities are also required to publish certain information related to drug and alcohol crimes committed on and around campus, but only if such crimes lead to an arrest or a documented disciplinary action by the university. At most schools, the true picture of (widespread) student substance abuse remains hidden.

I understand that there are traditions that people would like to be upheld, but to what degree is the University willing to accept this culture that has been created? I am just unable to see how anyone can justify going to class drunk, taking shots before classes, or finding any excuse for ridiculous behavior because it is a weekend where the University chooses to look the other way. [This weekend event] only brings to light even more the serious drinking problem on this campus because it becomes openly acceptable to be continuously drunk for the entire weekend . . . The support [by the college administration of this event] just fuels student's justification for drinking and gives off the impression even more that the unsafe, underage drinking is allowed.

Anonymous letter written by a student to the president of Bucknell University, 2013.

The situation at Pennsylvania State University became so serious that the school paid local restaurants and bars $167,000 either not to serve alcohol or to close during the university's annual "State Patty's Day—a student-organized, communitywide party celebrating Saint Patrick's Day. Many other schools in recent years have decided to cancel campuswide events (often called "traditions") that have been celebrated for decades but have morphed into dangerous alcohol-infested weekend-long parties for students.

I have seen too many students get themselves into trouble with alcohol, physically and academically. These students risk serious harm to themselves and others . . . [H]igh-risk drinking can lead to death in the blink of an eye, and has at colleges and universities across the country. High-risk drinking is alarming and sad, not only for all of us at Bucknell who care about our students but also of course

for the parents and friends of the individuals who put
themselves at risk.

Bucknell University president John Bravman in
a letter to students and alumni canceling the
school's annual House Party Weekend, 2013.

Instant Communication = Instant Access

Cell phones, smartphones, iPads, laptops—college students are connected in more ways than ever before. Being connected means always
knowing where the party is and where the drinking games and open
beer kegs, Jell-O shots, marijuana, pills, and other drugs are. With
WiFi, students can order drugs online from their laptop or cell phone
in class and have them sent to their mailbox or their dorm room.
There is no longer the need to go off campus or even down the hall in
search of drugs. In California, one drug-dealing student was busted
after sending his "faithful clients" a mass text message promoting a
cocaine sale.

Students Have More Time to Party

The urge to let loose and party on the weekend is natural because Sat-
urdays and Sundays are days when you don't have to get up and go to
work. But for many college students, *every* day is the weekend. Some
students choose classes that meet only in the afternoon so they can
go out drinking every night. Some universities have stopped holding
classes on Friday altogether, because so many students are partying
Thursday night and skipping classes on Friday, and because so many
faculty want long weekends or another day for consulting or research.
Not having to get up and go to class on most days encourages students
to spend more evenings drinking and doing drugs.

A DETAILED PICTURE OF
COLLEGE SUBSTANCE ABUSE

With rampant substance abuse on our college campuses, we're talking about a significant segment of our nation's best and brightest having a diagnosable substance abuse problem.

One in ten people in the general population, age twelve and older, meet the medical criteria for a diagnosis of alcohol or drug dependence or abuse. In contrast, nearly one in four full-time college students meet the same clinical criteria. Each month, almost four million full-time college students—nearly 50 percent—binge drink, abuse prescription drugs, and/or abuse illegal drugs.

College drinking is, simply stated, out of control:

- Ask the mothers of the nearly 2,000 college students who die each year from alcohol-related causes.
- Ask the fathers of the almost 200,000 college students who become the victims of sexual assault or rape each year due to alcohol abuse.
- Ask the 700,000 college students who are assaulted each year as a result of alcohol abuse.

Am I trying to scare you? No.

But I do want to splash some cold water on your face so that you wake up to the fact that college drinking and drug use is a serious matter. The point is not for you to be frightened but to be informed. Remember, parent knowledge is Parent Power. And parent ignorance is not parent bliss.

Everett Glenn, 19, a popular student whose friends said he was destined for great things, died of acute alcohol poisoning.

It happened May 5 after he took part in an outlawed fraternity's recruiting drive that started before dawn on All-College Day, traditionally a day of hard-charging partying on College Hill as students toast the ending of the spring semester.

Glenn was found dead early that afternoon in his dorm room as wild parties raged on college-owned properties around campus. His blood-alcohol level was 0.34, more than four times the legal limit for driving, according to the Northampton County Coroner's Office.

Jim Deegan, "Lafayette College Keeps Its Secrets—and Its Lips—Tight," Express-Times (Lehigh Valley, PA), January 27, 2013.

You might be thinking, however, Aren't college students practically adults? A lot of adults drink or take pills to relieve tension, and they don't have a problem. So what makes college students so different? It is true that most adults who drink are not problem drinkers and most adults who take pills never become addicts. But college students are different from the average adult. The average adult over twenty-five has a fully developed brain—and usually a full-time job and family responsibilities. College students have a still-developing brain and the time and opportunity to party, constantly if they want.

Featured as the drug of choice in recent rap songs and at concerts, Molly has been gaining popularity and notoriety over the past few months.

With recent fatalities linked to the abuse of the substance . . . it's time to bring more awareness to college campuses . . .

Students need to understand what Molly is and what the dangers are, so that this increasing trend can be controlled.

Editorial Board, "Editorial: Students Deserve Education on MDMA, Molly," Virginia Tech Collegiate Times, October 2, 2013.

A Warning About Drinking Games

Ever hear of beer pong, Beirut, flip cup, keg race, quarters, screw the dealer, power hour, or Edward Fortyhands? If those names don't make sense to you, they definitely will to your college-age son or daughter. They're the names of popular drinking games on college campuses.

In beer pong (also called Beirut), players throw a Ping Pong ball across a table, trying to get it into a cup. If the player gets it in, the opposing team has to drink all of the beer in that cup. Flip cup is an alcohol relay race in which each team member must chug the entire contents of the cup before him, and then set down the cup on the edge of the table and try to flip it so that the cup lands on its opposite end. Once the cup is flipped successfully, the next teammate must drink and flip, and so on, until the entire team has done it. In Edward Fortyhands, each player duct-tapes a forty-ounce bottle of alcohol (usually malt liquor) to each of his or her hands and is not allowed to remove them until both bottles have been consumed. Power hour is an hourlong game in which sixty songs are chosen and played back-to-back for one minute each. Every time the song changes, players take a big gulp of their drink.

A common college twenty-first-birthday game is to encourage the birthday girl or boy to consume twenty-one drinks in the first hour or so after midnight.

Everyone's so much friendlier after a couple of drinks.
It takes the pressure off. And if you want to get drunk
quickly, shots are key. There's a sense that you need to be
wasted to go to a party, and if you're not, you won't have
fun. Certain events, like Halloween and homecoming,
it's kind of guaranteed that kids are going to end up in
hospitals.

> *Helene, a twenty-year-old junior in college in*
> *Colorado, quoted by Emily Listfield, "The Underage*
> *Drinking Epidemic," Parade, June 12, 2011.*

The goal of these games is straightforward: get drunk and get drunk fast. This is achieved by forcing the participants to chug alcohol (drink a large amount in a short period of time). Chugging alcohol bypasses the body's normal defense mechanisms (feeling full, sick, or tired, and vomiting). That's why the amount of alcohol consumed during these games can reach dangerous levels so easily, causing alcohol poisoning and sometimes death.

The devastating effect of these drinking practices on campuses has forced several schools and communities to start banning drinking games. Unfortunately, many schools permit them or look the other way, and many bars around campuses encourage them by offering "beer pong tournaments" or "flip cup challenges" to local college students.

Talk to your kids about the dangers of drinking games before they leave for college.

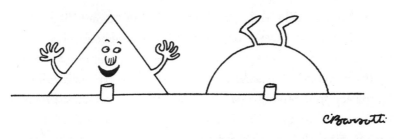

"I win. I win."

The circle passes out after losing a drinking game to the triangle.

START PREPARING YOUR CHILDREN IN HIGH SCHOOL

Your Parent Power to influence your kids positively will persist through the college years—especially if that influence is cultivated before college starts. Parents of students about to enter college have the best chance to prevent substance abuse by their children if in middle school and in high school they developed a positive, open, nurturing relationship; demonstrated explicit disapproval of substance use; and had a history of monitoring their children's behaviors and not being overly permissive.

The truth is that most college students who drink and use drugs in college were doing so in high school—or even before.

- Two-thirds of college students who drink alcohol or use illicit drugs began using them in high school. Almost one in ten began using in middle school.
- College students who began using drugs in middle school use them twice as frequently as students who began using them in high school (six days a week versus three days a week).

- Students who are drug and alcohol free throughout high school are much likelier to remain that way throughout college.

If you adopt the strategies in the earlier chapters, you will do a lot to keep your children safe when they go to college. Resisting peer pressure and avoiding risky situations are acquired skills, and the best time to teach them is when your teen is living at home with you. If you can keep your son or daughter drug and alcohol free before going to college, that child will have the best chance of staying sober over the next four years.

In my four years at UW–Madison, I can't recall a single experience where a friend or acquaintance openly acknowledged the potential dangers of alcohol and binge drinking—until they experienced the consequences, of course. It simply is not discussed.

Emily, a former University of Wisconsin–Madison student
Emily quoted by Colleen Jurkiewicz, "Is Peer Pressure Worse for Adults?," OnMilwaukee.com, February 13, 2013.

Even if you have not consistently discussed the dangers of substance use in the past with your children, brief parent-teen interventions about your expectations and the dangers of substance abuse prior to your child's entering college can help to form a baseline for appropriate and healthy behavior in college. Especially at this time both parents need to be involved and to present a united front when it comes to expectations about substance abuse.

HELPING YOUR TEEN PICK A COLLEGE AND COLLEGE HOUSING

Choosing a college is among the most important decisions that you and your child will have to make. You have the Parent Power to be quite influential in the choices that your children make in the process of selecting, preparing for, and attending college. Parents are consulted more often than peers, other adults, teachers, college resources, and media for every possible college-related choice: academic, institutional, personal, social, and financial.

Finding the Right Campus Environment

Colleges and their surrounding communities often create or enhance an environment that enables or even promotes substance abuse among students. Attending a college where the culture encourages substance abuse can threaten not only your child's education but also the health and future of your child.

About 25 percent of college students report academic consequences of their drinking including missing class, falling behind, doing poorly on exams or papers, and receiving lower grades overall.

National Institute on Alcohol Abuse and Alcoholism, "College Drinking," July 2013.

Many campuses and communities lack strong and well-enforced policies on substance use. Different schools have different inherent risks for substance abuse; "party schools" often live up to their reputations for heavy alcohol and drug use. When your child starts the process of picking a college, you can take a look at the lists of top party schools, beer-drinking schools, marijuana-smoking schools, and more on websites like that of the Princeton Review (www.princetonreview .com/college-rankings.aspx).

Party schools are usually characterized by widespread binge drinking and drug use; an uninhibited fraternity, sorority, or other club scene; and less focus on getting a good education. If your son or daughter is interested only in attending a big party school, ask why. If your child is thinking only about the potential for an exciting social life, remind him of some of the negative consequences of substance abuse on campus, such as vandalized rooms, rapes and sexual assaults, vomit in the dorms, lack of sleep, and having to rush a drunk roommate to the hospital. You can refuse to pay for your child to attend such a school.

Confirm whether the schools your child is considering have peer education or university-sponsored student support programs to deal with substance abuse, and educate students about the dangers of binge drinking, hazing, alcohol poisoning, and prescription drug abuse. Tell your child what you learn so that she may know what services are available for her and her friends once she gets there.

During the school-selection process, you should research the alcohol and drug policies of colleges that your child is considering. Find out what policies the school has for protecting students from substance abuse. You can look many of them up on the National Institute on Alcohol Abuse and Alcoholism website at www.collegedrinking prevention.gov/policies. Ask the guidance counselors or teachers at your teen's high school what they know about the colleges your child is interested in applying to—they frequently know more "behind-the-scenes" type information that you won't necessarily be able to discover from just looking at a university's website.

When you go on a campus tour, ask questions about the social scene: Does the school have alcohol-free events on campus? Are fraternity and sorority parties the only (or biggest) social things to do? Does getting accepted into a fraternity or sorority involve dangerous hazing or drinking activities? Are there substance-free dorms? Is smoking allowed in public places and dorm rooms? Do most of the class schedules allow for extralong weekends? Is the school a big "tailgating" school, permitting drinking and partying in preparation for a big sports game?

Find out if classes are held on Fridays and if students can arrange their class schedules to avoid Friday and morning classes. Find out if the administration keeps track of how many students have been hurt or injured from substance abuse in addition to keeping legally required records of violations of school policies or laws. What actions, if any, does the school take when students are caught with drugs or alcohol? You should also find out what steps the school is taking to restrict dangerous drinking games on campus and in the surrounding community.

Some universities have taken steps to curb binge drinking. Find out whether the schools your child is considering have taken steps or adopted programs or policies to reduce substance use and drinking on campus, such as:
- banning smoking on campus;
- providing mandatory education about alcohol and drug abuse and addiction to incoming freshmen;
- supporting peer education programs;
- offering substance-free housing options;
- providing counseling for students who are substance abusers or become addicted to alcohol or drugs;
- banning alcohol in dorms, in most common areas, and at on-campus student parties and college sporting events;
- offering alcohol-free events and activities;
- requiring trained servers where alcohol is offered and banning open kegs;
- requiring the presence of a faculty member at fraternity/sorority parties where alcohol is served;

- closing down fraternities or sororities where drinking is excessive or where hazing takes place;
- reporting substance use infractions of students to parents; and
- providing amnesty to students who may call 911 or on-campus police to get help for a friend who may have drunk too much or popped too many pills.

How Readily Available Is Alcohol?

Here's another rule of thumb: The greater the number of alcohol outlets available to students, the greater the likelihood of problem drinking.

Having a bar on campus increases the risk that underage students will drink and binge drink. In environments where binge drinking is common and alcohol is readily available and cheap, students are more likely to become binge drinkers than those in environments where alcohol is hard to get and/or drinking is discouraged or even prohibited. In some environments, students can obtain alcohol for free at parties or at deeply discounted prices from bars catering to college-age clientele.

College bars offer specials designed to draw heavy-drinking crowds. Some bars have ladies' hours, during which women can drink cheaply or for free in the early evening. The hope is that men will be attracted to the bar later, when it is full of tipsy women, a situation fraught with danger of sexual assaults and date rape. Other bars offer drink specials so cheap that anyone can afford to get wasted; still others promote drinks that are mixed with energy drinks such as Red Bull so that people can stay awake longer and drink more—a dangerous combination. And getting wasted is the goal: these bars prosper on binge drinking.

The women, in the pre-fall evening-out uniform of tiny shorts and four-inch heels, had fortified themselves for the outing with tequila shots at home. They sat in Level B, a basement bar on the southwestern edge of the Cornell campus in Ithaca, New York, snapping photos of their two $18 fishbowls (each contains a half-bottle of vodka, or about 16 shots, and a plastic animal) and texting them to friends (no explanation necessary) to coax them to hurry over before the fishbowl special ended at 12:30. The bar was as dead as a strobe-lighted library until shortly after 11, when suddenly, as if the campus belltower chimed at a frequency only students could hear, the place was sweat-inducingly full.

Courtney Rubin, "Last Call for College Bars," New York Times, *September 26, 2012.*

When visiting college campuses with your children, you should take note of the number of bars and liquor stores in close proximity, and you should remind your son or daughter of your expectations regarding underage drinking. Alcohol use is common on many campuses, but it does not mean that excess drinking and binge drinking—or, for that matter, any drinking—has to be the norm.

Is the Health Clinic Keeping Kids Healthy?

For many students, visiting the student health center may be their first trip to the doctor without parental supervision.

College students can obtain prescription drugs on campus by faking symptoms and getting a prescription from the school health clinic. They can find out how to fake symptoms on the internet. Many students say that they can get a prescription for Adderall just by saying they need help concentrating. But unlike high school students who may use the same excuse, students in college can usually get such a prescription from the on-campus clinic without you, their parents, ever having to know about it.

Students in CASA's focus groups report the ease of obtaining prescription drugs from school health centers and how a student with a legitimate prescription for a painkiller or a stimulant medication may use some of the dose but then share the rest with friends. Several students mention receiving large amounts of opioid pills for athletic injuries or dental problems, using only a few to ease their legitimate pain and then sharing the excess medication with classmates or selling it to them.

Talk to the administration or the staff at the health center to learn the clinic's policies for prescribing medications and monitoring their use, and its practices for dealing with substance-abusing students. Have a conversation with your teen about the abuse of prescription drugs on campus, and how tempting it may be to join in, but how dangerously important it is to his health, education, and future that he stay strong and say no.

CONSIDER HEALTHY HOUSING OPTIONS

Substance-Free and Single-Sex Dorms

In looking at colleges with your child, find out whether there are any substance-free dorms where smoking, drinking, and drugs are banned.

More and more, students choose to live in such substance-free housing. What substance-free housing does best is protect students from experiencing some of the adverse consequences of other students' substance abuse, particularly their binge drinking. Nobody wants to clean up after a drunk roommate or have drug users crashing in their bed. Substance-free housing can be a great way to avoid these problems and stay safe while still enjoying college and having an active social life. Although students living in substance-free dormitories do sometimes drink, they generally drink less, and less often. Substance-free dorms can also help cut back on the likelihood of your teen's taking part in "pregaming," or drinking large amounts of alcohol quickly in a dorm room before going out to a party or bar.

Among students living on campus, those who live in coed dorms report more alcohol-related nuisances and binge drinking than those in single-sex dorms do. When the time comes to pick housing for freshman year, it is a good idea to encourage your son or daughter to consider substance-free housing or single-sex dorms. Neither choice will preclude going to parties and enjoying college life, but either choice can reduce some of the nastier consequences of substance abuse in dorm life.

Don't Tolerate a Substance-Abusing Roommate

Having a roommate who abuses drugs or alcohol can have a negative impact on your son or daughter. Adjusting to new roommates is an integral part of the college experience, and the housing office can often be hesitant about changing roommates haphazardly. But if a roommate's drug or alcohol abuse is putting your child at risk, it is your responsibility as a parent to speak with the administration to resolve the situation promptly to protect your child.

Consider Your College Student's Living at Home

Students whose parents live close to their university may choose to live at home and commute to school. Research shows that students who live at home during college are less likely to drink or use other drugs than students living on campus. Although moving away from home is an important step in a student's personal development, having a high-risk student live at home, at least during freshman year, can be an effective way to prevent substance abuse.

PARENTAL ENGAGEMENT
CONTINUES INTO COLLEGE

The nest may be empty, but your job is far from over. Your Parent Power doesn't end when college begins.

Staying engaged and continuing to incorporate the lessons from this book will help keep your sons and daughters safe as they go through this significant chapter in their lives. Let the college officials know that you expect them to discourage drinking and drug use and that you want to be notified if your child is found to be abusing any substance.

Here are some additional things you should consider once college begins.

Spending Money

If you're paying your child's credit card bills or sending your child spending money, keep an eye on how much your child is spending. A sudden increase in spending habits could indicate substance abuse. Also, look over the credit card bills carefully: illegal prescription drugs and other drug paraphernalia may show up as cosmetics, food, soap, or other seemingly innocuous and random items. Keeping track of how the money you send is being spent can be helpful in spotting signs of potential substance abuse. Keep an eye open for excessive amounts spent at bars or restaurants, or of cash your child takes out of ATM machines.

If you send your child spending money, make sure the amount is moderate. As in high school, teens with too much disposable income are more likely to be substance users.

Find New Ways to Stay in Touch

Maintaining a relationship with your child during college is an important step in keeping him substance free. Although college should be a time for children to grow on their own, there are still many opportunities for parent participation that won't feel overbearing or intrusive. Try going to parents' weekend or a football (basketball, soccer, hockey) game on campus. Even dinner at a nice restaurant will be a welcome opportunity for your son or daughter after a few months of cafeteria food. And just as when she was in high school, these opportunities can also be a chance for you to get to know your teen's new friends and their interests.

I had occasion to visit the emergency room a few times at the University of Arizona. I was surprised that students who were being treated for bruises from fights that happened while they were drunk implored me not to tell their parents they were intoxicated. It gave me a strong sense that the possibility of parental displeasure about their children's behavior and drunkenness can have a moderating effect on students' behavior in many cases. Parents can positively influence their children's behavior at college if they tell their children what their expectations about substance use are and that they have asked to be informed by the school if the children's behavior in this regard is unacceptable.

Manuel T. Pacheco, PhD, former president, University of Arizona and University of Missouri System.

While your child is away at school, you can still keep in touch, but bear in mind that you may have to be more flexible. Students may not always be able to chat on the phone or in person, so try to be more available through email or text message. Sending a quick email or text takes only a few seconds, but it will let your child know that you are there—while still giving him the necessary space to grow. Nowadays, you'll probably Skype, FaceTime, Google Chat, or be Facebook friends with your college-student son or daughter. Take advantage of the digital age we're living in and stay a part of your teen's life in college.

Don't forget that the transition to college can be incredibly stressful and scary for many teens and requires a big transition period. Having Mom or Dad to call and check in with every few days, or video chat with regularly, can make for a nice, comforting reminder of home and ease the leap into adulthood for them. This in turn can help give them the confidence and self-assurance they need to stick to their values and not get caught up in an excessive drinking and drug culture on campus.

Many students say they are aware of the adverse consequences of substance use, including lower academic performance and sexual violence, but this knowledge does not seem to be enough to dissuade them from abusing alcohol, smoking, or using drugs. That "It won't happen to me" excuse that led them to take unnecessary risks when they were younger is still alive and well. But consistent messages from parents—of caring and of expectations—will have a greater impact than any public service or college administration internet message.

Staying in touch with your children during the college years is especially important because you will have little contact with their college except for its requests to pay bills or make donations. The school will likely not inform you of your children's schedules or grades (considered confidential), much less their conduct or personal situations. Only your children can do that.

PARENT TIPS

Before College

- Discuss your expectations and the dangers of substance abuse with your children.
- If you are divorced parents, make sure that you are both sending the same message about expectations during college for your child. You should each review the following tips and agree on them.

When Picking a College, Consider the Following

- Is the campus smoke free?
- Does the college have a clearly defined alcohol policy that is enforced consistently? What is the policy on notifying parents about students' alcohol- and drug-related behavior?
- Does the college ban smoking and drinking in public areas? Dorm rooms?
- Does the college sponsor alcohol-free social activities?
- Does the college allow alcohol to be involved in rushing for fraternities and sororities?
- Is attending fraternity and sorority parties the dominant social activity?
- Is the college surrounded by a high density of bars and liquor stores?
- Are there substance-free or single-sex housing options?
- Does the college keep track of alcohol and other drug incidents?

After Your Child Goes Off to College

- Let the school know that you want to be informed if your child is involved in an alcohol- or other drug-related incident.
- Keep an eye on your child's spending habits. If he seems to be spending an excessive amount of money at restaurants or bars or withdrawing a lot of cash from ATMs, ask about it.
- Keep an eye on your child's grades at the end of each term. If they seem lower than what you expected, have a conversation with her about what may be getting in the way of devoting enough time to studying.
- Communicate regularly with your child—and continue to discuss the temptations and dangers of drinking and drugs.

PART 3

CONFRONT IT

19

WHAT ARE THE SIGNS OF USE? WHAT SHOULD I DO IF I SEE THEM?

Plants can't tell you when something is wrong, but if you are a gardener, you can detect signs of ill health in your plants by observing them. You can inspect a plant's leaves for signs of trouble or disease, and the leaf will sit still in your hand as you check its texture, color, and health. If there are signs of a problem, you can buy a spray treatment at the store to fix it, and the plant will not resist your spraying.

But children are not plants. Though children can talk, they won't always tell you when something is wrong. If your child starts drinking or experimenting with drugs, it won't necessarily be obvious. Your son or daughter is more likely to hide it than to tell you. If your child develops a substance abuse problem, there are no quick fixes to cure it. Indeed, your child may resist your efforts to deal with the problem.

The early signs of substance use are subtle, if not obscure. That's why it is so important for you to recognize the risk factors that often precede use. If you respond to the risk factors early on, you will reduce the likelihood that your child will ever start using drugs. These risk factors include:

- A genetic predisposition;
- A learning disability;
- An eating disorder;
- An emotional, developmental, or behavioral problem;
- Being stressed out;
- Feeling perpetually bored;
- Having a family member who uses;
- Lacking self-esteem;
- Exhibiting sensation-seeking behavior;
- Having sex at an early age; and
- Dating someone several years older.

Timely and consistent parental engagement can mitigate these risk factors; lack of it will increase your child's likelihood of smoking, drinking, and using drugs.

SPOTTING THE SIGNS OF USE

Early signs of substance abuse are often indistinguishable from normal teenage behavioral changes, such as mood swings, erratic sleeping patterns, an increased demand for privacy, and changes in hobbies, interests, or friends. So how can you differentiate between normal teenage behavior and indications that your child might be using drugs and needs your help? It's a matter of degree. You should be concerned about changes that are sudden or drastic; these may indicate that something is wrong, drug related or otherwise. You should also be concerned if several changes occur simultaneously. Be open to the possibility that your child could be using drugs and avoid falling prey to the illusory comfort of denial.

You are more likely to detect the early signs of use if you are engaged in your child's life, know your child's world, and have established a foundation of communication that will allow you to discuss any issues that arise. A parent's best early detection device is an ongoing dialogue with teens concerning their thoughts, feelings, friends, and activities. If you wait until you spot some of the more glaring warning signs of drug abuse—such as finding marijuana, OxyContin, a bottle of vodka, or a syringe in your son or daughter's backpack—you will have missed the opportunity to catch the problem early on, when your parental influence has a better chance of promoting positive changes in your child's behavior.

At CASA, we have spent almost twenty-five years identifying the early warning signs of drug use because the sooner you recognize that your teen may be smoking, drinking, using marijuana, or abusing prescription pills or other drugs, the greater chance that you will be able to intervene before drug use escalates to dependence or addiction.

THE SIREN SIGNALS

Some changes in behavior send an alarm that your teen is likely using drugs or alcohol. I call these the Siren Signals. I want you to recognize when changes in your teen's behavior are sending these signals and be prepared to take action. Here are the most common Siren Signals to watch out for and suggestions about what to do.

Dropping Old Friends and Getting New Ones

What adult can keep up with the rapidly changing social life of a teenager? Best friends who spend hours each day texting, talking, and hanging out can become enemies overnight. Relationships and crushes that seemed bigger than life can fizzle in less than a week. Childhood friends may suddenly become uncool, and joining a sports team may cause a move to another social group. Trying to keep up with your teen's circle of friends can be confounding. But observing the changes and talking to your teen about the reason for the changes can help you distinguish a typical teen shift in friends or activities from a Siren Signal of trouble.

Merely changing friends does not suggest that your child may be drinking or using drugs, but who your child's new friends are might. In a teen's world, friends often reflect one's social identity. New friends can be a good thing; they may reflect a new interest in sports, theater, science, or some other healthy activity. Teens tend to spend their time with other teens who are engaged in similar activities, such as theater, debating, art, music, computer programming, sports—and yes, doing drugs.

Teens who drink or use drugs tend to flock together; they often give up old friends who don't drink or use drugs in favor of new friends who do. If your child's new friends are using substances, it is a Siren Signal that your child may be using too.

If your teen has a new group of friends, try to get to know them. At the very least, find out who the new friends are and talk to your teen about why he or she is hanging out with this new group and what they share in common. If you suspect that these new friends are smoking, drinking, or taking other drugs, discuss your concerns with your teen, reiterate your expectations about not using substances, and monitor your teen's behavior for other Siren Signals. If your teen admits that her new friends are drinking or using drugs, tell her that she should consider finding others who don't. If she continues to spend time with friends who are a bad influence, you may need to use discipline such as grounding to prevent her from associating with alcohol-drinking and drug-using peers.

Borrowing or Stealing Money

Cigarettes, alcohol, and drugs cost money. Some drugs—a few Vicodin or a fifth of vodka—may be within the weekly allowance of many teens. Other drugs, such as Ecstasy and cocaine, are more expensive.

When drinking or drug use becomes frequent, the cost rises faster than Jack's beanstalk.

Teens tend to have limited resources—an allowance or a salary from a part-time job. For most teens, these resources are enough to cover social activities such as moviegoing and having pizza with friends. But if a teen is using drugs, these resources may start to run out. Teens who have a substance problem may resort to borrowing money (from friends and family members), stealing it, or selling drugs in order to satisfy their own cravings.

Be on the lookout for changes in your child's spending patterns. Does his allowance suddenly run out before the end of the week, week after week? Is she constantly asking you for extra money? Keep track of any cash that you keep in your wallet or around the house, so that you notice if money is missing.

Dropping Activities

Sometimes when teens start drinking or using drugs, they lose interest in activities that used to occupy their time, like playing on sports teams, robotics, hiking, or biking. It may be that the old activities become boring in comparison to partying, or that your child is too tired or out of it to enjoy the activity. Your child's substance use may also be causing a culture clash if the friends who engaged in the old activities disapprove of your child's new behavior.

If your child loses motivation or interest in activities he used to enjoy, find out why. Has your child simply grown out of them? Has he found new activities? If you suspect that your child is forgoing productive activities to get drunk or high, you should intervene. Talk to your child about your concerns. Also talk to others in your child's life to find out what they suspect the problem might be. Reengage with your teen; create enjoyable opportunities to spend more time together. If you discover that there is an underlying problem, get your child the necessary help.

Other Common Siren Signals to Look Out For

- Increased secrecy
- Missing or skipping school
- Declining grades
- Constant discipline problems
- Sudden, frequent mood swings
- Aggressiveness
- Irritability
- Depression
- Chronic restlessness
- Sleeping too much or too little
- Marked change in appetite and weight (some drugs, like marijuana, can greatly increase a teen's appetite, while others, such as amphetamines, can decrease it)
- Difficulty concentrating
- Use of stimulants to study
- Loss of interest regarding physical appearance or personal hygiene

SYMPTOMS OF SUBSTANCE ABUSE

Some secrets are easy for kids to keep. You may not notice that your son borrowed the car without your permission. Your daughter may be able to hide the fact that she hooked up with a boy while she and her friends were at the movies. But like Edgar Allan Poe's story "The Telltale Heart," some secrets are too big to keep hidden, and an observant parent will notice that something is going on.

The behavioral changes described in the previous section indicate that your teenager may be experimenting with or using drugs. However, if your child is actually drunk or high, or is using drugs habitually, there are a set of distinct, clear symptoms.

Teenagers using drugs will try to hide the evidence from you. But if you know the telltale signs, their secret won't be secret very long. The abuse of each substance is associated with a cluster of unique symptoms, which are described in detail in the "Parent Power Glossary for Parents and Teens" at the end of this book.

Here are some of the general symptoms that may reveal current drug abuse:

- Excessive talking, rapid or slurred speech
- Bizarre or paranoid comments
- Excessive forgetfulness
- Difficulty expressing thoughts
- Nervous twitches or ticks
- Erratic or violent behavior
- Lack of coordination, poor balance, tipsy walking, or dizziness
- Nausea or vomiting
- Spaciness, inability to concentrate or follow a conversation
- Bloodshot eyes
- Dilated or very small pupils
- Excessive sweating, jitters, jaw-clenching, and jumpiness
- Excessive scratching or picking at the skin
- Nodding off (eyes closing, head falling forward)
- Nosebleeds, excessively rubbing or wiping nose
- Constantly popping breath mints, chewing gum, or drinking a flavored drink immediately before talking to you (to cover the smell of alcohol or smoke)
- Missing prescription drugs like OxyContin, Vicodin, or Xanax
- Possession of drug paraphernalia such as tin foil, rolling papers, pipes, straws, plastic bags
- Increased accumulation of inhalable products such as glue, hairspray, or nail polish

- Increased accumulation of over-the-counter cold medicine
- Use of incense, room deodorant, or perfumes to hide smoke or chemical odors on clothing or in a room
- Use of eyedrops to clear red eyes

WHAT TO DO IF YOU SEE
THE SIGNS OF USE

Early intervention is a potent prevention tool. By being alert to signals that your child may be drinking and using drugs, you can stop the behavior in its early stages. Ending the behavior early significantly reduces the risk that your child's use will lead to harm: an accident, poor school performance, legal problems, brain damage, experimenting with riskier and more harmful drugs, or addiction.

You are your child's first line of defense. You are uniquely positioned to detect the early signs of drug use. You have the Parent Power and motivation to do something about it.

Think about it. If your son's friends knew that he was smoking pot, would you want to rely on them to tell you? That makes you the best—and perhaps only—chance your child has that someone will intervene and help stop the behavior.

As a parent, you've known your child intimately since birth. You can judge when something is going wrong in your child's life. If you see some of the Siren Signals, or are otherwise worried or suspicious that your child may be smoking, drinking, or using other drugs, there are several steps you can take.

Like so many parents, we didn't heed the warning signs.
We found an empty beer bottle in the backyard, we
smelled pot on his clothes, we found an unidentifiable pill
in the laundry room; we chalked these things up to normal

teen behavior, but we were wrong. One day I found his backpack sitting on his bedroom floor, the contents spilling out. Inside was the tie we had given him for Christmas. Only, it was cut in half, and he had been using it as a tourniquet. Also in his bag were several bags of heroin and some syringes.

> *Jim Bildner, whose son died of a heroin overdose; a*
> *supporter of Addiction Recovery Management Service*
> *(ARMS) at Massachusetts General Hospital in Boston.*

You might start by engaging your inner Sherlock Holmes and investigating the matter further. Ask your child specific questions about his or her activities, friends, and spending habits, and observe your child's response and behavior. The information you collect may confirm or dispel your suspicions.

My then fifteen-year-old son spent a summer periodically using marijuana at a friend's house. I was suspicious, so I called the friend's parent, who denied it could be happening in their house. But when the parent asked a younger sibling, she found out it was true.

I talked to both of the boys at our home. I told them how disappointed I was in their behavior, [that I] believed they were stronger than that, told them it would stop immediately but they were now going to be under my microscope until they were out of high school, and that I hoped they could rebuild my trust in them by stopping.

Then I talked to my son alone to find out if he was feeling anxious, depressed, or other reasons for why he was using it. He just said they were trying it out (and, of course, gave all the arguments about how safe and nonaddictive it is, how it should be legal like cigarettes, etc.). I responded by telling him I expect him not to smoke cigarettes either and that no matter what the arguments, pot is still illegal [in my state]. At the end of a long tearful talk, he admitted he wanted to stop because he was sick of losing friends.

Thankfully, in the next few months, all those old friends started being around and calling more again, and his friend who had initiated the using came to me in their senior year of high school and thanked me for being stronger than his parents by not just punishing them but talking about the emotional letdown they had been and giving them the belief that they could be stronger and better kids.

Parent posting in CASA's "How to Raise a Drug-Free Kid" online discussion forums.

Follow your intuition if you think there is a problem; your kids may be inclined to lie about their drinking or drug use. Ask probing questions if the things your child tells you don't add up, but be open to the possibility that drugs aren't the root of the problem. In the next section, I will discuss what to do if you confirm that your child is smoking, drinking, or using drugs.

Some suspicious parents choose to search their child's room or possessions, or require their child to take a drug test. As a suspicious parent, you have a right—and it is your job—to search your child's room, cell phone, iPad, and computer. A search may turn up evidence of drugs, but if it doesn't, you still can't be sure that your child isn't using. If you conduct a search without your child's permission, your child will likely be angry and will conclude that you don't trust him or her. Tell your child that it is your responsibility to take actions that enable you to protect him and help him lead a healthy, drug-free life; that this is not a matter of distrust but of verifying that he is safe and drug free. It is important that both parents be on the same page in this situation.

"Your mother and her drug-sniffing dog were cleaning your room and happened upon this."

Q: Do you regularly search your kid's bedroom or schoolbag? Would you if you suspected that he or she might be drinking or using drugs?

A: I have open discussions with my children about sex, drugs, and alcohol. They know that I will and have checked their rooms (since I am graciously letting them live there for free) and that it is better to come to me (even if they know I am not going to like what they bring to me) rather than having me find out later. It is much worse of a consequence if I find out in any other way than them telling me.

A: I raised an amazing daughter by being honest. From the time she was in preschool, I told her that her room is her domain for quiet time and space from others—we all need that. However, I also told her that I would search her room randomly because I love her so much. If kids are raised this way, then it won't be a shock to them in their teen years.

A: I don't routinely go through my children's room/ things. I, however, don't avoid it either. I do the laundry and sometimes pick up things in their rooms. Recently I smelled something a little funny in my son's closet while collecting empty hangers. Thanks to *Moonshiners* [a reality television show on the Discovery Channel], he had decided to try to make some of his own. Trust is a really difficult thing to rebuild, and I will be in his room much more often for the next few months. I made sure he understood that by breaking the rules he forfeited his right to privacy.

A: I do search my kids' bags. It started by making sure they weren't hiding bad grades and notes from the teacher. We randomly check our thirteen-year-old son's cell phone. We found inappropriate pictures from a girl. This led us to check his phone and bag daily. A lot of times, we worry the boys are saying nasty things to girls, but I have since found it can be more the girls. After checking his bag daily, I found a letter from a girl laughing about inappropriate things. This led to us talking to him about sex, pregnancy, STDs, HIV, sexting, and drugs. He had a lot of questions. It was a good talk. Now he shows us the letters because he knows his bag will be searched, and it is better to show us than let us find it. We can't stop the girls from writing, but we have taught him that he can talk to us without getting in trouble.

*Parent postings in CASA's "How to Raise a
Drug-Free Kid" online discussion forums.*

WHAT TO DO IF YOUR CHILD IS SMOKING, DRINKING, OR USING OTHER DRUGS

Perhaps you noticed that your daughter has a new set of friends and quit the tennis or softball team. When you asked her about it, she admitted that she has been smoking pot on the weekends. Maybe you found a bottle of vodka hidden in the back of the closet in your daughter's room, or some pills in the pocket of your son's jeans when you were doing the laundry. How should you react?

Though you are not likely to think so at the time, this cloud has a silver lining, because now that you've identified the problem, you can do something about it. As a parent, you can change your child's behavior through ongoing dialogue, setting clear rules, monitoring your child's conduct closely, and enforcing consequences when he or she breaks the rules. That's Parent Power in action. Many teens experiment with tobacco and alcohol, some may experiment with drugs, but most don't go on to develop a substance abuse problem. How you respond to the discovery of your child's substance use may spell the difference between your child's stopping it or sinking into trouble.

Discuss Your Concerns with Your Child

If the signs themselves are a problem (your child is skipping school, for example) or if your investigation suggests that your child is drinking or doing drugs, calmly discuss your concerns directly with your child.

Your conversation will be most effective if you are able to express your concern and disapproval of your child's substance use while also affirming your unconditional love and support: "I notice that your grades are slipping and that you've been sleeping most of the day on the weekends. I'm concerned that something is wrong, and I'm worried that you may be doing drugs. I love you, and I will help you no matter what the problem is, but I need you to tell me honestly what's going on." You should avoid labeling your child as "bad" or "irresponsible" or a "druggie." Your teen can deal with your condemning his or her mistakes, but if you condemn your child, that child is less likely to respond to your parenting and may lose even more self-esteem— something that could have been a trigger for his starting to use drugs or drink in the first place.

The next actions you need to take are to enforce consequences for your child's behavior and to monitor him closely for signs of continued use so that you can seek professional help, if necessary, on a timely basis.

Enforce Consequences

Hopefully, before you caught your child smoking, drinking, or getting high, you had already talked about substance use. Ideally, in those conversations you discussed your expectations for your child's behavior and the consequences for violating those expectations. If so, and your child has broken the rules, then you should say: "I'm disappointed that you decided to drink [use drugs], and I'm concerned about your safety. I'd like to talk about what happened and why you did it, and how you plan to avoid doing it again. In the meantime, you know what the consequences for breaking the rules are: you can't use the car [or you're grounded] for a week [month]."

It's important to enforce consequences if you catch your child drinking or using drugs. There's no upside to letting it slide. It's also likely that your child may have broken other rules in order to drink or use drugs, such as lying about where he was going or whom he was going with, or sneaking out of the house after curfew. As I explained in chapter 1, children need parents to set boundaries so they can establish their own boundaries; children whose parents fail to enforce consequences, or enforce them unevenly, are more likely to abuse substances. Being lackadaisical about your child's behavior will not make you a cool parent and will not help your child learn responsibility or self-control. Instead, your child will get the message "Anything goes," or "My parents don't care enough to parent me."

Q: If you discovered that your child was drinking alcohol or smoking marijuana or cigarettes, what did you do?

A: First time: conversation, increased time together as a family, a session with a therapist.

Second time (involved catching our daughter coming home at 3:00 a.m., after having snuck out of the house at 11:00 p.m.): conversation, grounding, weekly Friday-night family nights, insistence that she join a sports team (that turned out to have been a great idea), insistence that she join student government at school (another good idea—she met some new friends and felt part of things more).

Third time, two years later (she turned eighteen, and after two years of no use of drugs/alcohol): She refused to promise she'd not use pot, refused to promise not to keep drug stuff in the house, refused to honor family rules. She

left the house and went from friend's house to friend's house
for two months, trying to wait us out so we'd let her live at
home and smoke/drink as she pleased.

Now, another two years later: she's in rehab for all sorts
of junk. She has thanked us for "buying her time" in high
school, when she stayed sober.

We'd probably do what we did before, but also bring
her for an addiction evaluation after the second time. We'd
also probably have gone to Al-Anon ourselves then.

*Parent posting in CASA's "How to Raise a
Drug-Free Kid" online discussion forums.*

If you haven't talked about consequences previously, you can in-
troduce the concept now, but don't worry about finding the perfect
solution in the heat of the moment. If you've just found out that your
child has been drinking or smoking pot, both you and your child may
be upset, angry, or simply not thinking clearly. The better approach is
to put off talking about specific consequences until you've had some
time to calm down and think about it. In your initial encounter, discuss your concerns about your child's behavior and the risks to his or
her health and safety, and mention that there will be consequences:
"Your father [or mother] and I are concerned about the fact that
you've been drinking [smoking marijuana/popping prescription pills].
We need to discuss what we think the consequences for your behavior
should be. We want you to think about it too, and tomorrow we'll sit
down to discuss your behavior and the consequences."

Appropriate consequences might include taking away privileges
that matter to your child: for example, grounding, or, if your child
has a driver's license, taking away driving privileges. Keep in mind
that discussing the problem should not be considered a punishment;
discussion is a healthy family activity. If you choose to ground your
child, don't let her hide in her room watching TV. Try to take ad-

vantage of this opportunity to build your relationship with your child. Remember, your child needs parenting, which means she needs you.

Assess the Situation

If you've discovered that your child is smoking, drinking, or using drugs, you need to assess how serious the situation is. Was it a one-time event? If your son was at a party and had a few beers, did he risk getting in trouble and decide to call you for a safe ride home instead of getting into a car with a drunk driver? Does your child have an underlying problem that needs to be addressed? Is there a history of addiction in your family? You should discuss the situation with your child, but be aware that children who are frequent smokers, drinkers, or marijuana users are more likely to lie about it.

You should also determine, with professional help if necessary, whether your child is struggling with other issues, such as depression, anxiety, or stress, that need to be addressed. If you are unsure whether your child just tried a drug once or is using regularly, have your child evaluated by a professional.

Caught in the Act

Your daughter comes home from a party, reeking of alcohol, and runs into the bathroom to throw up. You come home early from work one night and find your son smoking pot on the porch.

What should you do?

Wait until your child is sober to talk about it. Having a rational conversation with a teenager can be difficult enough, but it is nearly impossible if she or he is drunk or high. This doesn't mean that you should ignore what's going on. If she is sick, take care of her; if he is stoned, tell him, "I don't want to talk to you about this while you're high. We'll discuss it tomorrow morning."

Monitor Your Child Closely

Once you find out that your child has started using, you need to monitor him or her more closely. Be on the lookout for the Siren Signals of use, and for lying that may indicate your child continues using. If your child is going to a party at a friend's house, call the friend's parents to check that they will be home and there will be no alcohol or drugs available. Set a curfew and enforce it. Make it a habit to wait up for your kids when they return home after going out, or require them to wake you up once they get home. Talk to them before they go to bed. If your child knows that she has to look you in the eye, talk to you, and kiss you good night, she is not likely to drink or smoke pot. Keeping close tabs will keep your kid safe.

Should you do home drug testing? It comes down to a very personal and individual decision, and there is no clear or easy answer to this question. The home drug tests are not perfect, and there are risks associated with the testing process, but if you don't think you can keep your kids safe any other way, then maybe home drug testing is worth doing. If your child does have a history of drug use, then the arguments toward testing get a lot more compelling, and if your child has a history of lying to you about his or her substance use, then you may not need to worry much about eroding your trust relationship.

If you do decide that you need to test your children, make sure you have a reasoned talk with them explaining why you're doing it, and that you are testing them only because you love and worry for them. Parenting teens is a tough job, and there are rarely easy answers.

Parent posting in CASA's "How to Raise a Drug-Free Kid" online discussion forums.

Some parents make their children take regular drug tests. You should speak to a doctor, psychiatrist, or counselor if you think that drug testing might be necessary or appropriate for your child.

Seek Professional Advice

If you discover or suspect that your child is drinking or using drugs regularly, consult someone who can help you to assess the problem, such as your child's doctor, a therapist, a school counselor, or your priest, minister, or rabbi. Your child may be more likely to open up and accept help from someone who is not in a position of authority and to whom he or she can speak confidentially. Pediatricians, clergy, and school counselors aren't necessarily trained to deal with substance abuse problems, but those who are may be able to judge the severity of the problem. Those who aren't may be able to recommend a professional who can provide screening and, if necessary, treatment. If you don't know whom to talk to, your local Al-Anon or Alateen chapter may be able to point you in the right direction. Simply call its national hotline (888-4AL-ANON or 888-425-2666) and explain that you're concerned about your child's drug or alcohol use.

PARENT TIPS

- Keep an eye out for the Siren Signals, such as dropping old friends, borrowing money in larger amounts or more frequently, a sudden loss of interest in activities, declining grades, and drastic changes in personality.
- Although some signs of use may be the result of typical teenage moods and the adolescent desire to develop independence and one's own identity, listen to your gut about whether this is the case for your teen.
- If you are concerned that your child is using drugs or drinking alcohol, if he comes home smelling like cigarette smoke or vodka, consider searching his bedroom, backpack, or other personal space. Your child will likely be angry about this "invasion of privacy," but remind him that you will do whatever it takes to keep him healthy, safe, and substance free. Make sure both parents are in agreement.
- Set limits and enforce consequences for your teen, whether it be grounding him for a weekend if he misses curfew, or revoking her driver's license if you find a joint in her jacket pocket.
- If you determine that your child is using drugs or alcohol, discuss your concerns with him when he is sober. Explain why you are worried and provide explicit examples. Be prepared for him to get angry or to possibly act hurt. Remember that you are just doing your job as a good parent.
- If your child is using drugs or alcohol, and your intuition tells you that he is in trouble and that it was not just a onetime experimentation or thrill-seeking behavior, seek professional advice from your child's doctor or a professional experienced in drug and alcohol abuse and addiction.

20

WHAT IF MY CHILD
NEEDS TREATMENT?

So you've been trying your best to keep your child away from drugs. But now you're concerned. You've talked to your spouse, you've talked to your child, you've talked to your child's teachers, your priest or rabbi, your physician or pediatrician, your closest friend. You've called the hotlines, you've done your online research, you may even have contacted Alcoholics Anonymous (AA) or Narcotics Anonymous (NA), and you've come to the traumatic, I-can't-believe-this-could-happen-to-me-or-my-child conclusion: my child needs treatment.

But what kind of treatment? Residential or nonresidential? Mental health counseling along with alcohol or drug addiction treatment? How do you find the "right" person or place? Is there *any* "right" person or place? How do you even get your child to accept the fact that she needs treatment?

Well, none of this will be easy. If your child had a heart condition or cancer, traumatic as that would be, you could probably find out pretty quickly where to get help—and convince your child to go without much hassle. Your family physician would surely have a recommendation of a specialist. But, sadly, that's not likely to be the case in this situation. Instead, you now have to confront the following agonizing question: From whom and where is my child going to have the best chance of stopping her drug use and recovering from her addiction?

Discovering that your child is abusing any substance or is addicted to one is heartbreaking. But don't let it paralyze you, freeze you into a state of despair. And don't let your feelings of guilt or shame—they're quite normal—keep you from reaching out to find help for your child. There is help out there. It's likely to take some hard work on your part to find it, but your child is certainly worth the effort. The importance of finding the best place for *your* child should squelch any embarrassment that you might feel.

At this point, you, as well as your child, will need help in dealing with the situation. As a parent, you should seek support and counseling for yourself. Professional counselors and therapeutic groups such as Al-Anon, or parenting support groups in your community, church, or temple can help you to deal with your own anxiety, and provide assistance in facing this emotionally wrenching situation and obtaining treatment for your child. Taking care of yourself will put you in a better position to help and take care of your child. (Remember the airline crew's instruction to passengers: put on your own oxygen mask *first* before trying to help your young child.)

TALKING TO YOUR CHILD
ABOUT SEEKING TREATMENT

The conversations that you may need to have with your child about addiction or treatment will not be easy. It's possible that your child may not respond to your first, second, or even third attempt to get him to stop using. In this chapter, I'll give you some suggestions on how you can best prepare to talk with your child about his alcohol or drug abuse, and then how to best handle the search for a treatment program for your teen.

Starting the Conversation

When you decide you need to have that conversation with your child, it's important that you and your spouse prepare for it in advance. If you are a single parent, or separated or divorced, and others are actively involved in your child's life, make a plan ahead of time with the other parent, or stepparent, grandparent, or aunt or uncle, to discuss how you will approach your child about her or his drinking or drug abuse. Doing this serves two purposes.

First, it will help insure that all of the "parenting" adults in your child's life are prepared to send consistent messages about acceptable behaviors, family rules, need for treatment, consequences, and values.

Second, preparing in advance for the conversation will help you stay calm and more levelheaded during the real thing. Talks with your teen about abusing (or addiction to) drugs and alcohol and the need for treatment can quickly become highly charged, upsetting, and emotionally volatile for all involved. Your child may respond with anger, denial, name-calling, lies, walking away, even violence, but you've got to have the self-control to keep your cool through all of it. It's essential that the conversation stay focused on your concerns for your child's health and safety, not on who can scream louder or slam doors harder.

Although some specific things parents should say to their child in this situation are different for every family, a few key elements of the conversation are the same for just about everyone.

One is to make sure, to the best of your ability, that your child is sober when you decide it's time to discuss his or her drug use or drinking. Your child needs a clear head and the ability to listen and to process what you are saying. Even with a clear head, it will be difficult for your child to listen and hear what you are saying, but his being high or drunk is bound to make any communication impossible. If you have planned the time for the conversation but discover, or even suspect, that your child may be under the influence of alcohol or drugs at that time, hold off; postpone this discussion until he or she has sobered up.

When you do talk to your child, be prepared with specific examples of the changes you've noticed in behavior, or evidence of her being high or drunk, or drugs or alcohol you might have found in her room or backpack, that are cause for your concerns. Why? Because the odds are that your son or daughter will deny any drug or alcohol use, or claim, "I can handle it," or "It only happened once," or "The pot you found is someone else's; I was just holding it for her." Having direct examples to share can be important in such situations. For example: you've discovered that you are missing some of your prescribed pain or anxiety medication; you've recognized the smell of marijuana on his clothes after the last few times he's gone out with friends; you found marijuana in a handbag; you've noticed significant changes in his sleep patterns. For more of these red flags and behavior changes commonly seen in children who use drugs and alcohol, go back to chapter 19, "What Are the Signs of Use? What Should I Do If I See Them?"

Most importantly, when you talk to your child, express your love for him and your concern for his well-being and happiness. This is likely to be a difficult conversation about the dangers of drug and alcohol abuse and addiction and the need for treatment. It's one in which you need to make it clear to your child that she must get professional help—as would be the case with any disease—and one in which your child is likely to strenuously resist any such action. The goal is to make your child understand that your insistence on the need for treatment stems from your love and support. But I know you can achieve that understanding as long as you prepare for this conversation. You are, after all, trying to get your child to stay off of drugs and alcohol and avoid consequences that could ruin his life. If he knows that you will love him regardless of the mistakes he's made and the lies he's told, it's likelier that he will feel safe enough to admit his use and accept your help.

FINDING THE MOST
SUITABLE TREATMENT

Addiction is a serious and complex disease, and you should explore treatment options just as you would if your child had any other major illness. There are people in your community who may be able to help you find a treatment program for your child. Ask your pediatrician or family doctor, friends, and relatives. Look on your medical insurance company's website, or call your local Al-Anon, Alcoholics Anonymous, or Narcotics Anonymous chapter and ask for a referral.

Unfortunately, it can be very difficult to find professional drug or alcohol treatment programs for children. Even if you're lucky enough to have insurance that covers substance abuse treatment, there may not be effective and affordable programs designed for adolescents in your area. Don't give up—keep calling.

To help parents like you navigate the different type of treatment options out there, CASA has put together our *Patient Guide* for finding quality care. The guide is available online for free at www .casacolumbia.org/addiction-treatment/patient-guide and will walk you through the step-by-step process of how to find the right treatment option for your teen and what to expect throughout the process.

A similar resource you may find helpful when considering treatment options is the Child Mind Institute's *Parents Guide to Getting Good Care*—another step-by-step guidebook you can access for free online to help you best manage the maze of treatment options. Visit its website to download the guide at www.childmind.org/en/parents -guide-getting-good-care/.

Another useful tool for finding an appropriate treatment program for your child is SAMHSA's Substance Abuse Treatment Facility Locator, an online US government system that allows you to identify treatment options by city and state. The website address is www.find treatment.samhsa.gov/locator. You can call its toll-free number: 800-662-HELP (4357). You might also be able to find an appropriate treatment program through your state or city health department; many states and some cities have set up toll-free hotlines for people seeking help for a substance abuse problem.

You can also visit the Partnership for Drug-Free Kids' website for parents at www.drugfree.org/get-treatment or call its toll-free Helpline at 855-DRUGFREE (378-4373) to identify local treatment programs. The staff manning this hotline can give ideas about how to talk to your child about getting treated and, if you'd like, put you in touch with another parent who has been through a similar experience.

As a parent, your intuitions and gut feelings about what's best for your child's health and safety are strong and exist for a reason. Although you may face hurdles when you start your search for good treatment options for your son or daughter, staying determined and getting help early on will greatly increase your kid's likelihood of recovery in the future.

Addiction treatment must help the individual stop using drugs, maintain a drug-free lifestyle, and achieve productive functioning in the family, at work, and in society. Because addiction is a disease, most people cannot simply stop using drugs for a few days and be cured. Patients typically require long-term or repeated episodes of care to achieve the ultimate goal of sustained abstinence and recovery of their lives.

National Institute on Drug Abuse, Principles of Drug Addiction Treatment: A Research-Based Guide, *3rd ed., 2012.*

Questions to Ask When Selecting a Treatment Program

Once you've identified some good options for a treatment program, it may seem overwhelming to choose the one that will best suit your child's needs. As in so many of life's situations, the key to finding the best answer is to know what questions to ask. So as people suggest potential treatment programs for your child and you examine those programs, here are some questions you should ask. The answers you get will help highlight the differences between programs, and give you and your child an idea as to what the treatment process will be like with each provider.

Is the treatment program specifically for children and teens my child's age?

Many programs follow a one-size-fits-all treatment process. But teens have their own unique needs and problems, and they are best served by treatments that are designed with those needs in mind. Such programs will understand their emotional, psychological, spiritual, and social situations, as well as the stages of development for their developing brains. So it's important to find a program for teens like your child.

Chances are, when your child was born and you needed to find him a doctor, you searched for a pediatrician, someone that specialized in children's health and medicine. The search for your child's drug or alcohol treatment program should be no different, and the professionals should be no less specialized.

Is the treatment program licensed, certified, accredited?

All states have some kind of certification process for drug and alcohol treatment programs. Make sure the programs you are considering are certified by appropriate state agencies.

How are counselors on staff trained?

Treating your teen is a job for professionals, just as with any other treatment for a serious disease. So ask potential programs how their counselors are trained. Some simply require counselors to have been addicts themselves and may not have strict requirements about education or professional experience. For you to know that your child is getting the best quality treatment, you want counselors who have been professionally trained in addiction and have worked with teens before.

Is there a doctor in the house?

Good treatment programs have physicians readily available when needed. So ask the program you're considering if it has a doctor on call should your child require medical attention during treatment.

The best treatment programs will have a psychiatrist who specializes in addiction. Dr. Herbert Kleber, one of the nation's premier addiction specialists, says, "As a parent, I would not send my child to a program unless it had an addiction psychiatrist on its staff or at least available part-time."

What assessments, counseling, and support services will my child receive?

Most treatment programs will include a combination of these three elements. The assessment will help determine the extent and seriousness of your child's drug use, and should be conducted by a doctor or other health care professional trained in addiction and recovery. It will likely involve a physical examination and discussions about your child's current use and your family history of substance abuse and addiction. Once the assessment is completed, the provider will create a treatment plan based on your teen's needs and will explain the treatment options, counseling, and support services likely to be most beneficial for him.

There are many different types of counseling and therapy offered by most inpatient and outpatient treatment facilities, and it's likely that your teen may be involved in more than one kind at a time. Counseling can be done in an individual setting involving just your teen and a therapist, in a group setting that includes other recovering adolescents, or in a family setting involving you and other immediate and extended family members. Each type of counseling provides your teen with a different set of tools to help him stay clean and sober.

The treatment program should also explain what support services it offers. Since the impact of drug and alcohol use usually creeps into different areas of a teen's life, your son may need tutoring or homework help in order to get his grades back up to where they were before he began drinking alcohol, or your daughter may need help in developing positive social skills so she can gain the confidence and strength needed to resist the peer pressure to get high. Services like these can give your child additional support and positive influences that will help him or her navigate the road to recovery.

Does the treatment facility offer girls-only or boys-only services?

Especially for girls, single-sex treatment is likely to be more effective in helping treat addiction and maintain sobriety. When boys are present in group therapy sessions, girls are less likely to discuss their experiences of being high or drunk. This may be due to the shame or embarrassment felt by many girls about sexual abuse they have experienced or things they have done while under the influence of drugs or alcohol. When among other females exclusively, girls appear more willing to open up during group therapy sessions; in part this may be because they hear other girls talking about similar experiences. So if your child is a girl, it's worth looking for a treatment facility with a girls-only program or at least with girls-only group therapy sessions.

Will my teen receive mental health services?

Most teens require some mental health services as part of any successful treatment. For many teens battling an addiction to drugs or alcohol, hidden mental health issues such as anxiety, depression, and bipolar disorder are often involved. You or your teen may not even recognize the issues yet, but having them addressed professionally during treatment may be essential to your child's recovery.

Are parents and siblings required to participate at any stage of treatment?

For most teens, drug and alcohol addiction is a family affair. Almost all good treatment programs require participation at some stage by the teen's parents and by siblings as well. This is important not only for successful treatment of your child but also to enhance your ability to provide a supportive environment during nonresidential treatment or when she returns home after residential treatment.

What is the success rate of the treatment program?

Listen to the answer to this question with special care. Make sure that you know how the program calculates the rate of success. Does it include only those who stay the course for treatment as long as needed? Is it the rate for teens being treated for the first time? Does it include whether teens go to Alcoholics Anonymous or Narcotics Anonymous or other support programs regularly after returning home from treatment? How and when does the program follow up on its teen patients? And how often? These factors and more can all greatly impact the success rate a treatment program claims.

How can I pay for my teen's treatment?

You should find out whether your health insurer pays for addiction treatment and if it has any restrictions on what services are covered. Common restrictions include a limit on the number of days in treatment, kinds of programs, and whether mental health treatment is required. You should also find out if your treatment provider will work this out with your health insurer directly and if the provider will accept the financial limits of your insurance coverage. You can learn more about what services your provider will and will not cover by going to its website or calling directly.

Even if you have no insurance and insufficient resources, don't give up. Get your child into a free AA or NA program that is focused on teens as soon as possible, and do whatever you need to do to make sure he or she goes to meetings regularly. Look around for treatment programs that may work better for your financial situation. They may take longer to locate, but there are still some options available for your teen. For example, look for programs that offer payment assistance or use a sliding fee scale to determine the cost of treatment based on your income. Go to Al-Anon to learn productive ways to support your child. The SAMHSA Substance Abuse Treatment Facility Locator mentioned earlier in this chapter allows you to search for treatment programs that accept different methods of payment like these.

WHAT TO EXPECT AFTER SELECTING A TREATMENT PROGRAM

Once you find the best treatment program, your child may refuse to go. It's certainly better if you can convince your child to enter treatment voluntarily, but you should not hesitate to use every carrot and stick available. This may even mean forcing your teen into a program against his will (prior to eighteen years of age, parents usually have the right to do so). Even though committing your teen to treatment should be used as a last resort, it is still far better than trying to handle this problem on your own, and there is ample evidence that involuntary treatment can still be effective.

Treatment does not need to be voluntary to be effective. Sanctions or enticements from family, employment settings, and/or the criminal justice system can significantly increase treatment entry, retention rates, and the ultimate success of drug treatment interventions.

National Institute on Drug Abuse, Principles of Drug Addiction Treatment: A Research-Based Guide, *3rd ed., 2012.*

When your child returns home from treatment in a residential facility, or after he completes nonresidential treatment, you will be an important influence on his ability to maintain sobriety. Your teen is likely to need to attend AA or NA meetings—and you may be well advised to go to Al-Anon meetings or join another support group.

Teens also face the difficult challenge of returning to school. Often, maintaining sobriety requires an individual to change his or her friends and social situations. This may seem overwhelming and nearly impossible to a teenager returning to the same school he attended when he first began using drugs or alcohol. Here it is important for you to help your teen, encourage him or her to make new friends and try new activities or clubs, and talk to the teachers and counselors at the school to make sure they are sensitive to your child's new circumstances. It is critical to take action to insure that your teen is not returned to the same environment—the haunts and "friendships"—that precipitated the substance abuse. This may even require placing your teen in another school.

In an effort to ease the transition home, your teen's treatment program might suggest that he or she temporarily move into a sober living facility. These facilities and other step-down programs seek to offer some services in a sober environment—free of drug and alcohol temptations—as your teen transitions back to a normal life. If you consider a sober living facility for your child, be cautious in your selection. These facilities are not subject to licensing or accreditation guidelines as treatment programs are, so parental vigilance is imperative. Make sure the facility is professionally run with trained staff and effective precautions to ensure that no alcohol or drugs are on the premises. For specific characteristics you should look for in such a facility, consult the nonprofit organization Safe Sober Living at www.safesoberliving.org.

HANG IN THERE AS A GOOD PARENT

Recognize that treatment for your child involves not only him or her but also you and your spouse—and potentially the whole family, including siblings. The drug abuse didn't start overnight, and you can't expect it to be fixed that quickly. It's going to take awhile and perhaps a leave of absence from school. But the sooner the treatment starts, the better; dealing with your teen's drug abuse and addiction is not something that can wait until the school year ends or the semester is over. And there may be some uncomfortable consequences for you as a result of the family counseling. But saving your child is more than worth this effort.

Even with the best treatment, your child may slip back into drug or alcohol abuse and addiction. Remember, addiction, like high blood pressure or diabetes, is a chronic disease. Just as someone with high blood pressure may stop taking his pills, your child may stop going to AA or NA meetings because he feels he no longer needs to. Similarly, just as someone with diabetes may give in to the temptation to over-indulge on sweets, your child may use drugs or drink alcohol again.

Don't despair. Don't blame yourself. Don't give up. Don't condemn or abandon your child. Get her to try and try again. It may seem like an uphill battle, but your continued engagement and involvement with your son or daughter may be what saves your child.

"Am I going to be okay?" I asked the nurse who was monitoring my heart rate. "I don't know," she said. "If you are, I hope you stop destroying your life."

It was not the first time substance abuse had landed me in the emergency room. But, though I didn't know it then, it would be the last.

. . . Writing this blog a year ago would have been impossible, because of the shame and the deep guilt I felt about being an addict. I have never been abused or neglected. I didn't grow up in an alcoholic home. I have been blessed with an unconditionally loving family, and I have been given every opportunity to thrive. Why then? Why cause the people who love me so much pain? Why be seemingly intent on throwing it all away?

The honest answer is: I don't know. What I do know—and I have grappled with this [since becoming sober]—is that addiction is a disease. It is progressive, it can be fatal, and it can touch anyone.

Christina Huffington, assistant editor of HuffPost Women, sober since March 5, 2012, at twenty-two years old, "Addiction Recovery: Getting Clean at 22," Huffington Post, April 13, 2013.

In the last meal I had with my close friend and partner Edward Bennett Williams, when the legendary criminal lawyer was close to death, I asked him, "What's the most important thing you've ever learned?"

"Always leave a light in the window. For the kids. So they know they always have a home to come to whatever happens to them, whatever they've done."

Given the ravaging effects addiction can have on family members, supporting your child through treatment and relapses can be painfully difficult. Reach out to others for support and never give up. Always leave a light on in the window for your child.

PARENT TIPS

- If you're concerned that your child may need treatment for substance abuse or addiction, prepare yourself for what may be a very difficult yet very necessary conversation.
- Plan a time to confront your child and express your concerns to him. Make sure your spouse and any other parent figure or close family member, like a stepparent, grandparent, or aunt or uncle, is present too.
- Use the resources around you to help you navigate through the various treatment options that are available for your teen. Check out the SAMHSA Substance Abuse Treatment Facility Locator, and talk to your child's pediatrician or psychiatrist. The contact information for this resource and others is listed in the back of this book.
- Do your homework. Know what questions to ask of a treatment program ahead of time, such as availability of social skills services, costs, and whether psychiatrists are on staff.
- Make sure you are taking care of yourself, because you're not able to be the best parent you can be if you aren't looking out for yourself too. Check out local Al-Anon support groups or talk to a counselor or psychiatrist on your own or with your spouse.

21

YOU CAN DO IT

We [parents] are the only ones who have our children's best interests at heart all the time.

Susan Cassell, mother of four.

Because you have your children's interests at heart all the time, you are the most important person in their lives.

In this book, I've tried to give you practical tools and ideas—informed by decades of research by CASA and others—to help you raise healthy, drug-free children. The concepts reflect the latest science—including the new knowledge about the developing brain—and the successes and mistakes of mothers and fathers. They are also enriched by the thousands of parents, clergy, school nurses, counselors, child and adolescent psychiatrists, and others that I have met with over the past five years as I discussed the first edition of the book in sessions across the country. There's a lot here to help you help your teen negotiate the dangerous decade from ten to twenty-one without smoking, drinking, or using drugs.

Simply by reading this book, you have shown how determined you are to do just that.

But when all is said and done, it's you—your instincts, your love for your children, your willingness to make sacrifices big and small for your daughter and son—that matters most.

From the time they are infants, you know what makes your children tick. Your instincts as a parent helped you to decipher their "tired" cry from their "hungry" cry from their "dirty diaper" cry from their "sick" cry. You knew what to say to them on their first day of school to help calm their nerves, how to soothe them when they hurt themselves, how to make them feel better after the first time they fought with their best friend.

You know your child. Trust in that knowledge to help you parent your son or daughter about everything, including drugs and alcohol.

Let's not be afraid of intuitive parenting. Make use of the good information available, but remember there is no single right way to parent. Dr. [Benjamin] Spock [pediatrician and renowned author of *Baby and Child Care*] was on to something when he said: "Don't be overawed by what the experts say. Don't be afraid to trust your common sense."

Motherhood is the ultimate learning curve, the ultimate stretch, but it pays the ultimate reward. Don't overthink it, or overanalyze it, but by all means, "overenjoy" it.

Michaela Fox, writer and mother of three, "Overdoing It, or Over-Thinking It?," Huffington Post, November 19, 2013.

Because your child's brain is still developing, he or she is going to take risks. And just as one of those risks may be speeding on a bike without a helmet and without holding on to the handle bars, or running a red light after getting a driver's license, it's possible that one of those risks may be trying drugs or alcohol. If this happens, listen to your gut. You should find out the circumstances, remind your child of the dangers, enforce the consequences you've set out earlier. Your gut will help clue you in on whether this may be an instance of typical teenage risk taking—and that's all you have to deal with—or whether it may be something more dangerous and worth discussing with a professional—perhaps your child's pediatrician—to see if he or she needs help.

Knowing your child well also positions you to be the first to notice behavioral changes, even small ones, which might signal risk factors or even smoking, drinking, or drug use. Be confident in your ability to assess these nuances of your child's personality and conduct, and act on your assessment.

If you have read this book, you'll have a good sense of your teen's world and the things in it that make raising substance-free kids challenging, such as social media, cell phones, advertising, entertainment, availability of alcohol and cigarettes, drug-infected schools, marijuana, and pills at parties. But you now also have a host of practical suggestions for helping your teen deal with that world.

Over many years as a lawyer, public servant, researcher, and writer, working with all sorts of people, and a father and grandfather, I've come to the conclusion that what makes the biggest difference among adults is not whether they are women or men, rich or poor, black or white, believers or nonbelievers. The biggest difference is whether or not they have children. Something just clicks the moment you become a parent, and it is a life-defining switch.

Deep within every parent is the unconditional and selfless love you have for your child. Trust in this love to help guide you down the parenting path. Use the ideas in this book—as well as professionals if you need them; the advice of your own parents, relatives, and friends; religious community; your child's teachers and physicians; and other committed parents of your child's classmates—to help you become the best and most engaging parent you can be. I hope and believe that this book can be enormously helpful to you, as it has been to the thousands of parents who have read the first edition.

But know that the root of good parenting comes from within you. Parenting may be the most challenging job you'll ever have—it's certainly the most important—and as you succeed in raising healthy and drug-free children, it will prove to be the most satisfying. Raising drug-free kids will not only help give them a healthy childhood, it will also set them on the road to a healthy, productive, and happy life as adults because a child who gets to age twenty-one without smoking, abusing alcohol, or using drugs is virtually certain never to do so.

The one thing I'm sure of is that you can do it. You can succeed.

Acknowledgments

This new and revised edition is based on a quarter century of research at the National Center on Addiction and Substance Abuse at Columbia University (CASA) and the work of countless dedicated scientists, pediatricians, psychiatrists, psychologists, and other experts at universities and at the National Institute on Drug Abuse and the National Institute on Alcoholism and Alcohol Abuse at the National Institutes of Health. It also reflects my experiences as secretary of health, education, and welfare in the Carter administration, President Lyndon B. Johnson's chief domestic aide, and New York governor Hugh Carey's special counsel on drug and alcohol abuse.

This edition is uniquely enriched by what I have learned from the thousands of teens and parents (as well as teachers, counselors, physicians, and other professionals) I have met travelling the country in the years since the first edition was published in 2009.

I am particularly indebted to Brean Flynn, MA, whose intelligence, judgment, resourcefulness, and meticulous research have been essential to writing this book. She is just beginning a career in public health, and I am confident that she will make significant contributions to the field and to health policy in our nation.

This edition especially benefits from the suggestions of a number of experts and practitioners who reviewed the entire manuscript: Claudia Califano, MD, an adolescent and child psychiatrist and assistant clinical professor at the Yale Child Study Center; Susan Foster, MSW, substance abuse and addiction researcher; Herbert D. Kleber, MD, professor of psychiatry and director, Division on Substance Abuse at Columbia University and the New York State Psychiatric Institute, and one of the nation's top experts in substance abuse and addiction; Ralph I. Lopez, MD, professor of clinical pediatrics at Weill Cornell Medical Center, author, and extraordinary physician specializing in adolescent medicine; Elizabeth Planet, JD, executive vice president and chief strategy officer at the Child Mind Institute; Jeanne Reid, EdD, research scientist at the National Center for Children and Families at Teachers College, Columbia University; Joseph L. Woolston, MD, renowned child and adolescent psychiatrist and Albert J. Solnit professor of pediatrics at the Yale Child Study Center.

The generosity of the American Express Foundation and its chairman, president, and CEO, Ken Chenault, provided the grant that made this book possible. He also made available an American Express consulting team composed of Crystal Ammari, Jonathan Bachrach, Melissa Golub, Liana Kohn-Gardner, Sonny Shah, and Andrea Zaretsky to help launch this book.

Jeffrey Lane, board chair of CASA, and Sam Ball, president and chief executive officer of CASA and professor of psychiatry at Yale School of Medicine, have made several staffers available to help: librarian David Man, PhD, MLS, checked to make certain that the citations and data were accurate; Aaron Hogue, PhD, and Charles Neighbors, PhD, associate directors of Health Treatment Research and Analysis, reviewed the "Parent Power Glossary for Parents and

Teens"; manager of digital strategy Andrea Roley, communications specialist Ali McSherry, director of marketing Kathleen Manning, and director of communications Lauren Duran are working on plans to make parents aware of how this book can help them raise healthy, drug-free kids.

Steven Wagner, president of QEV Analytics, has conducted much of the teen and parent survey research and led numerous CASA focus groups for more than a decade.

Loren Fishman, Steve Kelley, and Rob Rogers for donating their cartoons, and the *New Yorker* magazine and CartoonStock for making their cartoons available.

The data from Choices, the program at Episcopal High School in Houston, was assembled for me thanks to board member Mindy Hildebrand and the director of the Behavioral Health Institute at the Council on Alcohol and Drugs Houston, Crystal Collier.

I am indebted to the individuals and organizations who hosted me during my appearances over the past five years, the countless parents who attended those events, and especially the many parents who participated in the *How to Raise a Drug-Free Kid* online discussion forums.

JoAnn McCauley kept me reasonably on schedule during this process, and Sue Brown kept the wheels at CASA turning, as she has since the doors opened in 1992.

The Touchstone/Fireside team at Simon & Schuster has been superb: my editor, Michelle Howry; Chief Executive Officer Carolyn Reidy; Publisher Susan Moldow; Editorial Director Sally Kim; Publicity Director Shida Carr; Associate Publisher David Falk; Touchstone Art Director Cherlynne Li, who designed the cover; and Senior Production Editor Tamara Arellano.

I owe special thanks to my wife, Hilary, who (once again) put up with the weekends, early mornings, and late evenings I worked in the spectacular study she has created for me in Westport, Connecticut. She is the love of my life and has been for more than thirty-one years, during which time she has showered me with love, sage advice, and her wonderful sense of humor.

I am indebted to all of the above; this book would not be possible without them. But responsibility for what's on these pages rests on my shoulders alone.

JAC Jr.

August 2014

Parent Power Glossary for Parents and Teens

COMMONLY USED TERMS

Addiction is a chronic, relapsing disease characterized by compulsive drug seeking, cravings, and continued use despite harm. The social consequences of addiction include low academic achievement, troubled interpersonal relationships, inability to thrive, underemployment or lack of employment, and social isolation.

Dependence occurs when a user develops a tolerance to a drug and suffers withdrawal when the drug is discontinued. The terms *addiction*, *dependence*, and *alcoholism* are interchangeable—they are all characterized by a lack of control over one's drug use.

Drug means nicotine, alcohol, illegal drugs, prescription drugs, and toxins, such as inhalants.

Substance refers to any drug, such as nicotine, alcohol, illegal drugs, prescription drugs, and toxins, such as inhalants.

Substance Abuse involves making a choice to use a drug in spite of the negative legal, health, and safety consequences, and/or the inappropriateness of the drinking/drugging experience.

Tolerance describes (1) the body's ability to absorb a drug without feeling its effects and (2) the body's need for higher doses of a drug after prolonged use in order to feel the same effects.

Withdrawal is the syndrome of often painful physical and psychological symptoms that occur when a person stops taking a drug.

CIGARETTES, TOBACCO, AND MENTHOL

What are cigarettes, tobacco, and menthol?

Tobacco is made from the dried leaves of a plant that contains many chemicals, including nicotine. Tobacco comes in several forms:

- Cigarettes and cigars—including flavored cigars, menthol cigarettes, and minicigars, or "cigarillos"—are made by rolling tobacco leaves in paper. Tobacco companies add other chemicals to cigarettes, some of which have been linked to cancer.
- Dip, chew, and pipe tobacco are forms of pure tobacco that are sold in tins. Rolling tobacco is sold in pouches and is used for hand-rolled cigarettes.
- Electronic cigarettes, or "e-cigarettes," have recently become a popular alternative to smoking traditional cigarettes and have been marketed heavily toward teens. Unlike traditional cigarettes, e-cigarettes can come in fruity or sweet flavors that make them more attractive to younger consumers. These cigarettes run off of a battery and contain a cartridge inside holding nicotine, flavoring, and other chemicals, and are designed to be smokeless.
- Menthol can be found in cigarettes, cigars, and e-cigarettes. Menthol gives a cooling or minty sensation in the throat and lungs when smoked and can therefore taste better or be easier to inhale, especially for new, young smokers. Additionally, menthol is the one "flavor" excluded in the US Food and Drug Administration's 2009 ban on cigarette flavorings.

What do cigarettes, tobacco, and menthol do?

Cigarettes contain stimulants that increase the heartbeat and blood pressure. The most important stimulant is called nicotine. Some users experience a mild euphoria or rush after smoking and a feeling of stress relief. Smoking may decrease the appetite.

Young smokers frequently report symptoms such as wheezing, shortness of breath, coughing, and an increase in phlegm production. In general, teen smokers have a greater susceptibility to colds and flus than nonsmokers do.

How are cigarettes, tobacco, and menthol used?

Cigarettes and cigars are the most popular form of tobacco. Cigarettes are inhaled into the lungs; cigars are not meant to be inhaled. The chemicals from the tobacco make their way into the user's bloodstream. Some people also put a pinch of tobacco directly into their mouth and hold it between their cheek and gum so that the chemicals can be absorbed through the lining of the mouth and cheek.

What other names do people use for cigarettes, tobacco, and menthol?

Beedi, Camel, cancer stick, chew, cig, ciggy, dip, e-cig, e-cigarette, fag, looseys, smoke, smokeless cigarette, snus, snuff, and stoge/stogie.

What are the signs of use?

Signs of cigarette, tobacco, and menthol use include the smell of smoke on your child's clothing, skin, or hair, yellowing of the teeth, wheezing or shortness of breath, and a persistent cough.

How bad is it? What are the long-term side effects?

Tobacco use is a leading cause of death in the United States. Cigarette smokers have an increased risk for heart disease, blood clots, cancer, strokes, bronchitis, emphysema, poor circulation, and ulcers. Cigar and pipe smokers and chewing tobacco users are at risk of developing cancers of the mouth and neck.

Teenagers who smoke are much more likely to be addicted to cigarettes as adults. A child who makes it to twenty-one before trying her first cigarette is less likely to become addicted later in life. Teenagers who have never smoked a cigarette are also unlikely to try other drugs, including marijuana and cocaine.

How addictive is it?

Cigarettes are highly addictive, due to the nicotine found in tobacco. Some experts consider nicotine to be more addictive than heroin or alcohol. People who start smoking before the age of twenty-one find it very hard to quit later in life. Recent research has shown that menthol cigarettes may also lead to increased addiction.

ALCOHOL

What is alcohol?

The oldest and most widely used drug in the world, alcohol is also the drug most frequently used by teens. More likely than not, your child has or will try it.

Alcohol is a distilled liquid that is made from fruits, grains, and vegetables. The most common forms of alcohol are beer, wine coolers, malt beverages, wine, and liquor (examples: bourbon, gin, scotch, vodka). Alcohol companies also make sweet, teen-friendly drinks and market them to your children. Sometimes called "alcopops," these drinks include Mike's Hard Lemonade, Smirnoff Ice, and Bacardi Breezer.

The concentration of alcohol in each of these beverages differs. Beer has the lowest percentage of alcohol, wine has slightly more, and liquor has the most alcohol. In the United States a 12-ounce bottle of beer, a 5-ounce glass of wine (about a half cup), and a 1.5-ounce shot of liquor all have the same amount of alcohol. Alcopops often have more alcohol than beer.

What does alcohol do?

Drinking can seriously affect your teenager's judgment, reaction times, and coordination. Alcohol works by depressing the central nervous system, affecting motor coordination, reflexes, visual and other sensory perceptions, and emotions. It can relax the drinker and reduce social inhibitions.

Teenagers who drink too much may become confused or depressed, suffer short-term memory loss, and vomit or pass out. Teenagers who binge drink (drink large amounts of alcohol in a short period of time) can develop alcohol poisoning, a potentially life-threatening condition.

How is alcohol used?

Alcohol is a liquid that people drink. Some teenagers prefer to mix liquor with soda, juice, or some other beverage that disguises the smell and taste of the alcohol. Adolescents who want to get drunk will often drink "shots," which are small glasses of straight liquor, because the body absorbs the alcohol much faster that way.

What other names do people use for alcohol?

Booze, brew, brewskies, cold one, juice, sauce, hooch, cocktail, moonshine, shots, and vino.

What are the signs of use?

Signs of teenage drinking include the smell of alcohol on your child's breath, slurred speech, lack of coordination, nausea, vomiting, and hangovers.

How bad is it? What are the long-term side effects?

Teenage drinking can physically damage the developing brains of teenagers in ways that impair learning, memory, abstract thinking, problem solving, and perceptual-motor skills (such as eye-hand coordination). Drinking at an early age can interfere with social and behavioral development, interrupt academic progress, increase the chance of risky sexual behavior, and increase the risk of serious injury and death. Heavy drinking also increases the risks of cirrhosis of the liver and other diseases, like heart disease and breast cancer, later in life.

Teen drinking and driving can be fatal; car crashes are the leading cause of death in the United States for sixteen- to twenty-four-year-olds, and alcohol is the major factor in most of these fatal crashes.

Teenage drinking can also lead to more serious substance abuse problems. Kids who start drinking regularly in their early teens (between the ages of eleven and fourteen) are more likely to develop alcoholism than those who start drinking at twenty. Almost all adults who are addicted to alcohol began drinking before the age of twenty-one. Teenagers who binge drink (consuming more than five drinks in one day) are more likely to use illicit drugs than teens who don't.

How addictive is it?

Alcohol can be psychologically addictive, which means the user feels like he needs to drink in order to feel good, deal with life, or cope with stress. In addition, frequent users of alcohol can develop a tolerance to the drug. Alcohol abuse can lead to physical dependency, or addiction. Withdrawal from alcohol can be painful and even life threatening. Symptoms of alcohol withdrawal range from shaking, sweating, nausea, anxiety, and depression, to hallucinations, fever, and convulsions.

MARIJUANA AND SYNTHETIC MARIJUANA

What are marijuana and synthetic marijuana?

Marijuana is the most popular illicit drug among teens. It comes from a plant called *Cannabis sativa* and looks like a dry, shredded greenish-brown herb. Each part of the plant—the flowers, stems, seeds, and leaves—can be used to get high. The main active chemical ingredient in marijuana is THC (delta-9-tetrahydrocannabinol).

What do marijuana and synthetic marijuana do?

Marijuana and synthetic marijuana affect the pleasure receptors in the brain the same way as other drugs like tobacco, alcohol, heroin, and cocaine. They cause a hazy euphoria, or high, often called being "stoned." Some people experience pleasant sensations. For example, colors and sounds may seem more intense. However, it's not all fun and games. Marijuana and synthetic marijuana can also cause anxiety, paranoia, distrust, panic, and depression. It also causes temporary cognitive defects, including short-term memory loss and lack of attention span.

How are marijuana and synthetic marijuana used?

Marijuana and synthetic marijuana are usually smoked. Either one can be rolled in paper and smoked like a cigarette (called a "joint"), rolled in a cigar that has been emptied of tobacco (called a "blunt"), smoked out of a regular pipe, or smoked out of a water pipe ("bong"). Marijuana and synthetic marijuana can also be mixed in or cooked in food (such as brownies) or candy (lollipops), or brewed as a tea. Marijuana and synthetic marijuana can also be combined and used together.

What other names do people call marijuana and synthetic marijuana?

Marijuana: bud, blunt, chronic, dope, ganja, grass, hash, herb, hydro, indo, joint, Mary Jane, pot, sinsemilla, skunk, reefer, and weed.
Synthetic Marijuana: fake weed, K2, moon rocks, skunk, spice, Yucatan fire.

What are the signs of use?

Signs of marijuana use include dry mouth; red or bloodshot eyes; pungent smell on clothing, skin, or hair; short-term memory gaps; excessive giggling; hunger ("munchies") or thirst ("cotton mouth"); and impaired reaction time.

In addition to the signs of marijuana use, the signs of synthetic marijuana use may also include hallucinations, extreme anxiety, vomiting, agitation, confusion, dilated pupils, and increased heart rate.

Other signs of use of both marijuana and synthetic marijuana include burning incense or using other deodorizers to cover the smell, frequent use of eyedrops, and owning paraphernalia, such as pipes and rolling papers.

How bad is it? What are the long-term side effects?

The effects of marijuana and synthetic marijuana are particularly damaging for the developing minds of adolescents. Both can impair critical cognitive functions related to attention, memory, and learning, lasting up to twenty-four hours after use. Using marijuana and synthetic marijuana at a time when these skills are particularly important for succeeding in school may cause children to fall behind in their intellectual, emotional, and psychological development. Withdrawal from marijuana use also causes symptoms that interfere with learning, including restlessness, irritability, and sleep disturbance.

Someone who smokes marijuana regularly can develop the same respiratory problems that tobacco smokers do, including a persistent cough, an increased risk of colds, flu, and lung infections, and an increased risk of cancer of the respiratory tract and lungs.

Although synthetic marijuana is still fairly new and requires continued scientific study as to its short-term and long-term effects, it has been associated with heart attacks due to a reduced blood supply to the heart.

Marijuana and synthetic marijuana use may signal other future drug use. Although most kids who use marijuana will not move on to harder drugs, twelve- to seventeen-year-olds who smoke marijuana are eighty-five times more likely to use cocaine than those who do not.

How addictive is it?

Frequent users of marijuana can develop a higher tolerance. Marijuana users may become dependent upon it to feel good, deal with life, or handle stress. Teens who use marijuana are more likely to become dependent on it than adults are, and the younger the teen starts using, the more likely that child is to become addicted. Teens who are depressed or have prior serious antisocial problems are more likely to become addicted to the drug.

INHALANTS

What are inhalants?

Believe it or not, kids can use everyday products that they find in your house to get high. Inhalants are carbon-based substances such as glue, aerosol gases, lighter fluid, cleaning fluids, and paint products that, when inhaled, produce effects similar to alcohol or anesthetics. Inhalants are popular among younger teens, ages twelve to sixteen. They are easy to get, relatively cheap, legal for kids to buy, and easy to carry and hide.

What do inhalants do?

Inhalants are similar to anesthetics, which slow the body's functions. They act on the central nervous system (CNS), reducing heart rate and breathing. In small doses, inhalants create a feeling of intoxication similar to alcohol. In large doses, inhalants can produce psychoactive, or mind-altering, effects. The effects do not last long—only a few minutes to an hour at most.

An overdose will cause disorientation, loss of control, and even unconsciousness, although the user generally recovers quickly. When using some products (particularly aerosol gases and cleaning fluids), a prolonged sniffing session can cause irregular and rapid heartbeat and even lead to heart failure and death. So-called sudden sniffing death can result from a single session of inhalant use. However, such deaths are rare.

How are inhalants used?

The product is inhaled or sniffed to get high. Some kids try to intensify the effect by sniffing the product from inside a bag placed over the head, which is extremely dangerous.

What other names do people use for inhalants?

Air blast, ames, amys, boppers, bullet, buzz bomb, glue, hardware, heart-on spray, huff/huffing, laughing gas, moon gas, oz, pearls, poppers, quicksilver, rush, snappers, snotballs, whippets, and whiteout.

What are the signs of use?

Signs of inhalant use include dizziness, drunk or dazed appearance, and missing household items.

How bad is it? What are the long-term side effects?

Chronic use of inhalants can cause serious damage to the heart, lungs, liver, and kidneys. In rare cases, abusing inhalants can be fatal.

How addictive is it?

Inhalants are not very addictive, but children who use inhalants regularly will develop a tolerance to them, and some users become psychologically dependent on them. Most children do not use inhalants for more than a short period of time, but some continue to use them for several years.

STEROIDS

What are steroids?

Anabolic steroids are manufactured drugs that mimic the naturally occurring male hormone testosterone. When anabolic steroids are abused for athletic or cosmetic purposes, they can have dangerous side effects.

Anabolic steroids are distinguished from corticosteroids, which have no abuse potential, and are used to treat conditions such as asthma, chronic lung disease, skin conditions, and allergic reactions.

What do steroids do?

Steroids increase muscle mass, strength, and endurance, and reduce body fat. People generally use steroids to improve performance or appearance.

Because steroids act like hormones, they affect women and men differently.

- Women who use steroids can develop excessive body and facial hair, male pattern baldness, a deepening of the voice, shrinking of the breasts, menstrual irregularities, and genital swelling.
- Men may experience baldness, breast enlargement, sterility, impotence, shrunken testicles, difficulty or pain in urinating, and increased risk for prostate cancer.

Other physical effects include liver tumors, jaundice, water retention, and high blood pressure.

In addition, steroids can cause severe emotional and cognitive side effects, including uncontrolled aggression and violent behavior, severe mood swings, manic episodes, depression, paranoia, jealousy, extreme irritability, and even delusions.

How are steroids used?

Tablets or liquid forms are generally swallowed, but steroids can also be injected. Combining different steroids to intensify their effect is called "stacking."

What other names do people use for steroids?

A's, anabolics, arnies, balls or bulls, gym candy, juice, pumpers, roids, stackers, and weight trainers.

What are the signs of use?

Signs of steroid use include rapid weight gain or muscle development, acne flare-ups, fluid retention, yellow tint in the eyes and on the skin (jaundice), mood swings such as depression or aggressive behavior, and premature balding.

How bad is it? What are the long-term side effects?

Steroids can have a magnified effect on teenagers, since their bodies are still growing. Any substance that physically alters the body while it is still growing can result in stunted growth, which is permanent.

Over time, steroid buildup can become toxic to the body, and can lead to hypertension, high cholesterol, kidney disease, and heart damage. Some synthetic steroids can cause diabetes.

How addictive is it?

Steroid use can lead to increased psychological and physical dependence. Withdrawal symptoms may include depression, irritability, and paranoia.

OVER-THE-COUNTER DRUGS CONTAINING DXM

What are over-the-counter drugs?

Over-the-counter cold and cough medicines are sold without a prescription. Some contain the cough-suppressing ingredient dextromethorphan (DXM), which some people take to get high. Many different products contain DXM, including Robitussin-DM, DayQuil, and some Vicks products (such as DayQuil Cold and Flu and NyQuil Cough); often these products have *tuss* or *DM* in their names.

What does DXM do?

If taken in large quantities, DXM can cause hallucinations, loss of motor control, and "out-of-body" (or dissociative) sensations.

Side effects of cold and cough medicine abuse include fever, confusion, impaired judgment, blurred vision, dizziness, paranoia, excessive sweating, slurred speech, nausea, vomiting, abdominal pain, irregular heartbeat, high blood pressure, headache, lethargy, numbness of fingers and toes, dry and itchy skin, loss of consciousness, seizures, brain damage, and even death.

How are cough and cold medicines used?

Cough and cold medicines, which come in tablets, capsules, gel caps, and lozenges, as well as syrups, are swallowed in large doses to achieve intoxication. DXM can also be extracted from cough and cold medicines, turned into a powder, and snorted.

What other names do people use for over-the-counter drugs?

Candy, c-c-c, dex, DM, drex, red devils, robo, robotripping, rojo, skittles, triple C, tussin, velvet, and vitamin D.

What are the signs of use?

Signs of cold or cough medicine abuse include missing medicine or empty medicine containers, intoxication, lethargy, spaciness, slurred speech, and flushed face.

How bad is it? What are the long-term side effects?

Excessive use of DXM can produce hallucinogenic and other psychiatric effects, and can lead to brain damage and death.

How addictive is it?

Regular abuse of cough and cold medicines can lead to psychological dependence.

PAINKILLERS (PRESCRIPTION OPIOIDS)

What are painkillers?

Prescription opioids are strong painkillers used by doctors to treat serious and chronic pain. Commonly abused prescription painkillers include OxyContin, Vicodin, fentanyl, Dilaudid, codeine, Demerol, and Percodan. Opioids are derived from or structurally related to morphine.

Between 1992 and 2003, the incidence of first-time uses of painkillers among teens increased an astounding 542 percent, more than four times the rate of increase among adults.

What do painkillers do?

Painkillers attach to the opioid receptors in the brain, blocking the transmission of pain signals. They may produce a quick, intense feeling of pleasure, which is followed by a calm drowsiness, and feelings of relaxation and contentment.

Painkillers also bring about an inability to concentrate, apathy, lack of energy, constipation, nausea, vomiting, and, most significantly, respiratory depression.

How are painkillers used?

Painkillers are typically sold as pills that are meant to be swallowed, but some can also be crushed up and inhaled ("snorted"). Some painkillers come in liquid form and can be injected.

What other names do people use for painkillers?

80s, blue, china white, hillbilly heroin, hydro, kicker, norco, OC, oxy, OX, oxies, oxycotton, percs, pills, and vikes.

What are the signs of use?

Signs of use include constricted pupils, slow reaction time, hazy thinking, missing medicine bottles, change in appetite and sleeping patterns, shallow breathing, constipation, and nausea.

How bad is it? What are the long-term side effects?

When used for nonmedical purposes, painkillers can alter brain activity and lead to dependence and addiction. Opioid withdrawal symptoms include insomnia, bone and muscle pain, diarrhea, and vomiting. Taking a large dose of opioids at one time, or mixing them with alcohol or other drugs, can cause severe respiratory depression and death.

How addictive is it?

Prescription opioids, like their illicit counterpart heroin, are addictive. These opioids are tightly controlled by the Food and Drug Administration (FDA) and the Drug Enforcement Administration (DEA). However, some painkillers are more addictive than others. The strongest painkillers, such as OxyContin and Zohydro ER, have the highest potential for abuse and addiction.

STIMULANTS (UPPERS)

What are stimulants?

Stimulants are prescription drugs that physicians use to treat asthma, respiratory problems, obesity, attention deficit/hyperactivity disorder (ADHD), and sleep disorders such as narcolepsy. The most commonly abused stimulants are Ritalin, Adderall, and Dexedrine.

What do stimulants do?

Stimulants stimulate the central nervous system (CNS). They help people to stay awake and focus by causing feelings of exhilaration, energy, and increased mental alertness. Teenagers often take stimulants (with or without a doctor's prescription) to stay awake, boost energy, or get high, or as a study aid to increase alertness and concentration. When used improperly (that is, in significantly greater dosages or frequency than medically prescribed), they may cause euphoric effects and feelings of being high.

Side effects include increased heart rate, blood pressure rate, and metabolism; irregular heartbeat, heart failure, chest pain with palpitations; reduced appetite, weight loss, vomiting, abdominal cramps; dilated pupils, loss of coordination, dizziness, tremors, headache, excessive sweating; feelings of restlessness, anxiety, jitters, panic, delusions, hostility and aggression, and suicidal or homicidal tendencies. Paranoia, often accompanied by auditory and visual hallucinations, may also occur. Stimulants can cause heart attacks in patients with underlying cardiac disease, such as chronic high blood pressure.

How are stimulants used?

Commonly prescribed stimulants are pills that are meant to be swallowed. Some pills can also be crushed up and then snorted or mixed with alcohol. Teenagers who are prescribed stimulants for ADHD can save up their pills and share them with friends or sell them.

What other names do people use for stimulants?

Bennies, black beauties, crosses, dexies, hearts, LA turnaround, rippers, ritz, speed, truck drivers, uppers, and vitamin R (Ritalin).

What are the signs of use?

Look for signs of alertness, increased energy or attention span, excessive talking, anxiety, or decreased appetite.

How bad is it? What are the long-term side effects?

Stimulants can alter brain activity and may lead to dependence, especially when not taken as prescribed by a doctor. Withdrawal symptoms may include depression, disturbance of sleep patterns, fatigue, and apathy.

How addictive is it?

Stimulant use can lead to tolerance and addiction when not taken as prescribed by a doctor.

DEPRESSANTS (DOWNERS)

What are depressants?

Depressants are prescribed by doctors to treat anxiety and sleep disorders, and have three different chemical forms: benzodiazepines, barbiturates, and nonbenzodiazepine sleep medications like Ambien, Lunesta, and Sonata. Benzodiazepines are prescribed more frequently, the most common of which are Valium, Restoril, and Xanax. The most commonly prescribed barbiturate is Nembutal.

What do depressants do?

Depressants depress the central nervous system, causing slower breathing and a general sense of relaxation, reduced pain and anxiety, a feeling of well-being, and lowered inhibitions.

Side effects include impaired coordination, memory, and judgment, respiratory depression, sensory depression, fatigue, confusion, and irritability. Psychological side effects include poor concentration or feelings of confusion and lowered inhibitions. Barbiturates may also cause sedation, drowsiness, depression, unusual excitement, fever, irritability, poor judgment, slurred speech, and dizziness.

The effects of depressants can be dangerously intensified by mixing them with alcohol.

How are depressants used?

Depressants are pills that are swallowed.

What other names do people use for depressants?

Barbs, downers, jellies, sekkies, sleepers, temazies, tranx or tranks, and Vs.

What are the signs of use?

Signs of depressant use include dilated pupils, slurred speech, relaxed muscles, intoxication, dizziness, sedation, drowsiness, and fever.

How bad is it? What are the long-term side effects?

When used for nonmedical purposes, depressants can alter brain activity and lead to dependence; they can be fatal when taken in large quantities or when mixed with other drugs.

Long-term use of some depressants has been associated with increased aggression, significant depression, memory problems, cerebral atrophy (brain shrinkage), decreased motivation, irritability, impaired sexual functioning or menstrual irregularities, weight gain, sleep disorders, emotional disinhibition, and rage.

How addictive is it?

Users can quickly develop a tolerance to depressants. Continued use of benzodiazepines and barbituates can lead to addiction. Users who become dependent can experience withdrawal symptoms, and in some cases can experience life-threatening seizures.

HEROIN

What is heroin?

Heroin is an opioid and a highly concentrated derivative of morphine, which is extracted from the poppy plant. Due to its similarity to prescription-strength painkillers, heroin is frequently used by people that first become addicted to pills such as Vicodin and OxyContin, and then move on to this cheaper and sometimes more accessible alternative.

Heroin is typically sold in small bags and looks like a white or brownish powder. Sometimes it comes in the form of a black, sticky substance called "black tar."

What does heroin do?

Heroin enters the brain quickly and binds with the opioid receptors, slowing down cognitive functions, reaction time, and memory. Short-term effects include a surge of euphoria followed by feelings of calm or contentedness, drowsiness, and cloudy mental functioning.

The concentration of heroin varies widely from dose to dose, so users are always at risk of an overdose (especially if the drug is injected). Heroin overdose is fatal if not treated immediately.

How is heroin used?

Heroin can be injected, smoked, or inhaled ("snorted"). Before the 1990s, people needed to inject the drug to get high because the product was so impure. Starting in the 1990s, high-purity forms of heroin became widely available. Snorting or smoking the high-purity form creates an intense high and eliminates the need to use needles.

What other names do people use for heroin?

Big H, black tar, brown sugar, cheese, china white, dope, H, horse, junk, mud, skag, and smack.

What are the signs of use?

Signs of heroin use include constricted pupils, drowsiness, nodding off, impaired mental functioning, suppressed respiration, nausea and/or vomiting, reduced appetite, slurred speech, and scars at injection sites ("track marks"). Heroin paraphernalia includes straws, rolled-up dollar bills, razor blades, pipes, burned aluminum foil, tourniquets, hypodermic needles, and burned spoons.

How bad is it? What are the long-term side effects?

The risks of heroin use include fatal overdose and addiction. If injected with an intravenous needle, risks also include diseases such as HIV and hepatitis. Chronic use can lead to infections of the heart lining and valves, abscesses, cellulitis, and liver disease. Heroin's depressant effects on breathing increases the risk of contracting lung diseases such as pneumonia.

Heroin withdrawal is painful: symptoms include severe restlessness, muscle and bone pain, insomnia, chills, sweats, diarrhea, vomiting, and other intense flu-like symptoms.

How addictive is it?

Heroin is highly addictive.

MDMA (ECSTASY, OR MOLLY)

What is MDMA?

MDMA is a designer, man-made drug that is chemically similar to the stimulant methamphetamine and to the hallucinogen mescaline. Many Ecstasy pills contain additional drugs or drug combinations that can be harmful, including methamphetamine, caffeine, dextromethorphan (DXM), the diet drug ephedrine, and cocaine.

What does MDMA do?

MDMA acts as both a stimulant and a psychedelic, producing an energizing effect and intensifying emotions, as well creating distortions in time and perception, and enhancing enjoyment from tactile experiences (touch). The effects generally last four to six hours.

Short-term effects include feelings of mental stimulation, emotional warmth, enhanced sensory perception, and increased physical energy.

Side effects can include nausea, chills, sweating, teeth clenching, dry mouth, muscle cramping, and blurred vision.

Many Ecstasy users experience depression, paranoia, anxiety, and confusion. There is some concern that these effects on the brain and emotions can become permanent with chronic use.

Because MDMA can interfere with the body's ability to metabolize and excrete the drug, taking a lot of Ecstasy within short intervals can create potentially harmful levels in the body, leading to overdose. Ecstasy also raises the temperature of the body. This increase can sometimes cause organ damage and, in rare but unpredictable circumstances, death.

How is MDMA used?

MDMA comes in powder, tablet, or capsule form. It is usually swallowed in the form of a powder-filled capsule or a pill. The powder can be snorted. It is considered a party drug and is often used at concerts, raves, and other music-oriented parties. Adolescents and young adults also use Ecstasy in house parties and other social settings because it creates feelings of closeness and empathy, and reduces inhibitions.

What other names do people use for MDMA?

Adam, beans, clarity, disco biscuit, E, Ecstasy, eve, go, hug drug, Molly, rolls/rolling, X, and XTC.

What are the signs of use?

Signs of use include teeth clenching, dilated pupils, chills or sweating, and excessive displays of affection.

How bad is it? What are the long-term side effects?

Research using animals has shown that Ecstasy can cause long-term damage in the parts of the brain that are involved in mood, thinking, verbal memory, and judgment.

Many people suffer mild to severe withdrawal symptoms after using the drug, including fatigue, loss of appetite, depressed feelings, and trouble concentrating.

How addictive is it?

Ecstasy has not been proven to be physically addictive; however, teenagers who use it can become psychologically dependent upon it to feel good, deal with life, or handle stress.

LSD (ACID)

What is LSD?

Lysergic acid diethylamide (LSD) is a man-made hallucinogen that was popularized in the 1960s as a mind-expanding drug. It is an odorless and colorless substance with a slightly bitter taste. It is usually found in the form of tablets, capsules, "tabs," or liquid. Tabs are pieces of blotter paper that have absorbed liquid LSD and have been divided into small squares, with each square representing one dose.

What does LSD do?

We don't know exactly how LSD works, but it affects the areas of the brain associated with sensory stimulation and emotion.

The psychedelic effects of LSD vary depending on the amount taken, the mood the person is in, and the user's surroundings. Reported psychedelic experiences include intensified colors, distortion of vision and hearing, heightened self-awareness, mystical or ecstatic experiences, and a sense of being outside one's body. Hallucinations and delusions, such as believing that something exists when it does not, are rare, although they may occur at higher doses. Some users experience unpleasant reactions (a "bad trip"), including feelings of depression, dizziness, disorientation, fear, paranoia, and panic.

Physical side effects include dilated pupils, elevated body temperature, increased heart rate and blood pressure, sweating, appetite loss, sleeplessness, dry mouth, and tremors.

Deaths due to suicide or overdose are rare but can occur.

How is LSD used?

LSD is ingested orally.

What other names do people use for LSD?

Acid, blotters, doses, dots, hits, microdots, sugar cubes, tabs, and trips.

What are the signs of use?

Signs of use include dilated pupils, strange behavior or conversation, and paranoia.

How bad is it? What are the long-term side effects?

There is strong evidence that some healthy adolescents who use LSD will develop schizophrenia or severe depression as a result. It is not clear how LSD triggers these illnesses or whom it will happen to.

LSD users can experience flashbacks, during which part of the LSD experience can reoccur, even if the user stopped taking the drug days, months, or years before. These flashbacks may be disorienting and even dangerous if they occur, say, while the person is driving.

How addictive is it?

There is no evidence that LSD is physically addictive, although users can develop a tolerance to the drug.

METHAMPHETAMINE (METH)

What is methamphetamine?

Methamphetamine is an illicit drug, found most commonly in the Midwest and western states. It is a highly addictive stimulant that is often cheaper and easier to find than heroin or cocaine.

Almost all methamphetamine is homemade and resembles a white to yellowish fine or coarse powder, crystal, or chunks. It is sold in small plastic bags or wraps, aluminum foil, capsules, or tablets of various sizes and colors.

What does methamphetamine do?

Methamphetamine is a long-acting stimulant. People who take it experience pleasant feelings of euphoria, heightened alertness, and greater energy. Like other stimulants, the drug increases the heart rate and breathing, sometime inducing heart palpitations. Methamphetamine is a powerful appetite suppressant.

As the drug wears off, people often experience feelings of extreme fatigue or depression.

The physical side effects of long-term use also include hair loss, loss of teeth, and impaired mental capacity.

How is methamphetamine used?

Methamphetamine is a powder that can be injected, inhaled ("snorted"), smoked, or swallowed.

What other names do people use for methamphetamine?

Chalk, chicken feed, chris, christy, crank, crystal, crystal meth, glass, go-fast, ice, meth, shabu, speed, trash, tweak, yaba, yellow yam, and zip.

What are the signs of use?

Signs of methamphetamine use include dilated pupils, rapid speech followed by slurred speech, disturbed sleep patterns (staying up late, sleeping for long periods), nervous physical activity, jitteriness, decreased appetite, and excessive weight loss. Meth-related paraphernalia includes straws, rolled-up dollar bills, razor blades, pipes, and burned aluminum foil.

How bad it is? What are the long-term side effects?

Methamphetamine causes long-term damage to the part of the brain associated with emotions and pleasure. Chronic use reduces the user's ability to feel pleasure from anything. Other consequences of long-term use include paranoia, anxiety, mood and sleep disorders, and violent behavior. Heavy use can lead to coma, stroke, or death.

How addictive is it?

Methamphetamine is highly addictive.

COCAINE

What is cocaine?

Cocaine is a highly addictive stimulant that is derived from the coca plant. Cocaine is purified into a white powder and sold in most large and midsize cities. Crack cocaine is made by cooking cocaine powder with baking soda and water to form a concentrated solid substance ("rocks").

What does cocaine do?

Like other stimulants that affect the central nervous system, cocaine can produce feelings of euphoria or well-being, mental exhilaration, reduced appetite, and great physical strength and mental capacity. It can also cause jitteriness, anxiety, paranoia, and panic. Cocaine raises the heart rate and in large amounts can cause heart failure. While it is rare, some first-time users of even small amounts of cocaine can experience heart failure and/or sudden death.

How is cocaine used?

Cocaine powder is usually inhaled ("snorted"), but it can also be smoked or injected. Crack is smoked from a pipe.

What other names do people use for cocaine?

Blow, charlie, coke, flake, nose candy, perico, rock, snow, and tornado.

What are the signs of use?

Signs of cocaine use include dilated pupils, excessive talking, nose-bleeds, anxiety, and paranoia. Cocaine-related paraphernalia includes straws, rolled-up dollar bills, razor blades, and mirrors with white residue.

How bad is it? What are the long-term side effects?

The long-term health effects of cocaine include addiction, heart attacks, respiratory failure, strokes, and seizures. Chronic cocaine abuse can lead to premature death, permanent paranoia or psychosis, and damage to structures of the nose.

With long-term abuse, the brain loses its capacity to experience pleasure without the drug.

How addictive is it?

Cocaine is highly addictive.

OTHER DRUGS OF ABUSE

There are more drugs available to your children than you could imagine, and every year, new drugs are added to the list. Here are brief descriptions of some of the other drugs to which your child may be exposed.

Bath Salts. Bath salts are a synthetic drug in the form of a powder and can be purchased online and in some drug paraphernalia stores. They are commonly sold under names such as "Purple Wave," "Blue Silk," "Bloom," "Vanilla Sky," "Scarface," and "Hurricane Charlie."

Bath salts have only recently become popular, so very little is known about their short- and long-term effects. The drug can be inhaled ("snorted"), swallowed, or injected. Signs of use consist of chest pains, increased heart rate and blood pressure, hallucinations, and paranoia.

GHB (gamma hydroxybutyrate). GHB is an odorless and tasteless liquid made from industrial chemicals. It is classified as a sedative and produces long-lasting euphoric effects. GHB may be used as a date-rape drug because of its relaxing effect and its ability to impair judgment and memory; victims who were given GHB often forgot the details surrounding a sexual assault. GHB overdose can be fatal.

Hashish. Similar to marijuana, hashish is derived from the cannabis plant. It is a THC-rich, resinous material that is dried and compressed into hard balls as well as other shapes. Pieces of hashish are broken off, placed in a pipe, and smoked.

Ketamine. Ketamine (K, Special K, vitamin K) is an animal tranquilizer that is used by veterinarians. Ketamine became popular as a recreational drug because of its powerful hallucinogenic and dissociative effects; it impairs perceptions, creates feelings of euphoria, and distorts the user's sense of time and place. Ketamine comes in a powder or liquid form. Side effects include delirium, amnesia, damage to the motor system, and potentially fatal respiratory problems.

Mushrooms. Magic mushrooms or 'shrooms are wild mushrooms that contain the hallucinogenic chemicals psilocybin and psilocin. When eaten (fresh, cooked, or dried), mushrooms create hallucinogenic experiences similar to LSD but milder. Side effects may include vomiting, nausea, and stomach pains. As with other hallucinogenic drugs, users can have an unpleasant trip or experience a full-blown psychotic episode.

Methadone. Methadone is a synthetic analgesic developed to replace morphine and is a scientifically supported treatment for opioid dependence. It is available in oral solutions, in tablets, and as an injectable liquid. When used inappropriately, chronic methadone use can lead to addiction and is associated with prolonged withdrawal syndrome.

Opium. Opium is derived from the poppy plant and is a relative of morphine. It is sold as a dark, sticky, tar-like substance and is generally smoked from a pipe but can also be injected. Like all opioids, opium is addictive.

PCP. Phencyclidine (PCP, angel dust, ozone) is a powerful anesthetic. Users feel euphoric and spacey but may also experience acute anxiety, paranoia, violent hostility, and, in some cases, a psychosis indistinguishable from schizophrenia. PCP comes in a white crystalline powder that is often smoked but can be snorted or injected. It has a strong chemical smell, similar to ammonia. Overdose can lead to suicidal and hostile behavior, coma, convulsions, and possibly death from respiratory arrest.

Peyote / Mescaline. Peyote is a small cactus that contains the hallucinogenic ingredient mescaline. Peyote has been used by some Native American cultures as a part of religious rituals. Mescaline can be extracted from peyote or produced synthetically. The long-lasting hallucinogenic effects are intensely visual; side effects include anxiety, racing heart, dizziness, diarrhea, vomiting, headache, "bad trips," and possible psychosis.

Rohypnol. Rohypnol (roofie) is a powerful tranquilizer. Rohypnol pills can be swallowed or crushed and dissolved in drinks; the effects are similar to the intoxication of alcohol, plus sedation. The drug gained notoriety as the date-rape drug because of its combined sedative effect and its ability to literally erase the user's memory. The drug may be fatal if taken in excess or combined with alcohol.

Salvia. *Salvia divinorum* is a powerful herbal hallucinogenic, also known as diviner's sage. Salvia can be chewed, smoked, or mixed with a liquid, like water, and swallowed. The effects last for only a few minutes and range from uncontrollable laughter to intense hallucinations or delusions. Some users experience unpleasant or uncomfortable feelings. Salvia can be purchased over the internet, although it has been outlawed in several states.

Parent Power Reference List for Parents and Teens

The National Center on Addiction and Substance Abuse at Columbia University (CASA) website provides research-based reports on substance abuse prevention and treatment, information about Family Day, additional resources for parents and teens, and more at www .casacolumbia.org.

The following resources may be of particular interest to you and your family:

DRUG FACTS/DRUG POLICY

Legacy: www.legacyforhealth.org.

National Institute on Alcohol Abuse and Alcoholism (NIAAA): www.niaaa.nih.gov.

National Institute on Drug Abuse (NIDA): www.drugabuse.gov.

Office of National Drug Control Policy (ONDCP): www.white housedrugpolicy.gov.

Partnership for Drug-Free Kids: www.drugfree.org.

US Drug Enforcement Administration: www.usdoj.gov/dea.

PARENT AND COMMUNITY ORGANIZATIONS

Alcohol Policy Information System: Information on issues related to various alcohol policies in different states, and at the national level. Look up university drug and alcohol policies (http://alcoholpolicy .niaaa.nih.gov/).

American School Counselor Association: Tips and resources to prepare children for middle school and high school (www.school counselor.org).

Children Now, Talking with Kids About Tough Issues: Tips for parents on how to talk to children ages eight to twelve about sex, HIV/AIDS, violence, drugs, and alcohol (www.talkingwithkids.org).

Community Anti-Drug Coalitions of America (CADCA): Supports community coalitions in their efforts to create drug-free communities (800-54-CADCA / www.cadca.org).

FindYouthInfo: A government website that provides information, tools, and resources for parents and teens on topics affecting youth, such as mental health, bullying, substance abuse, and LGBT youth (http://findyouthinfo.gov).

Leadership to Keep Children Alcohol Free: Helps parents prevent the use of alcohol by children ages nine to fifteen, and helps parents find local and statewide chapters that they can join (www.alcoholfree children.org).

Mothers Against Drunk Driving (MADD): Information about the dangers of teen drinking, including drinking and driving, and drinking on college campuses (www.madd.org).

National Parent Teacher Association: Connect and chat with other parents, find after-school programs for your children, and learn how you can volunteer (www.pta.org).

Parents Helping Parents (PHP): Example of a community organization that provides support and services to parents of children abusing alcohol or other drugs (www.parentshelpingparents.info).

Partnership's Parent Toolkit: Federal government website that provides parents with advice and tools to raise drug-free kids (855-DRUGFREE / http://theparenttoolkit.org).

Princeton Review: Provides information for parents and teens about colleges, including which ones are party schools (www.princeton review.com/college).

Students Against Destructive Decisions (SADD): Provides children and teens with education and organization tools for making healthy and safe decisions, including saying no to drinking and driving (www .sadd.org).

Substance Abuse and Mental Health Services Administration (SAMHSA) Center for Substance Abuse: Provides prevention tools for communities and families (www.samhsa.gov/prevention).

MENTAL HEALTH ORGANIZATIONS

American Academy of Child and Adolescent Psychiatry (AACAP): www.aacap.org.

Mental Health America (formerly National Mental Health Association): www.nmha.org.

National Alliance on Mental Illness (NAMI): www.nami.org.

National Federation of Families for Children's Mental Health: www.ffcmh.org.

TREATMENT, RECOVERY, AND SUPPORT GROUPS

Al-Anon/Alateen: Support for people who have a friend or relative with a drinking or drug problem (1-888-4AL-ANON / 888-425-2666 or www.al-anon.org).

Alcoholics Anonymous (AA): Support for people who want to stop drinking (212-870-3400 [see phone book for local listing] or www.alcoholics-anonymous.org).

American Cancer Society: Free, phone-based programs to help people quit smoking (www.cancer.org).

Faces & Voices of Recovery: An advocacy organization for persons in recovery (www.facesandvoicesofrecovery.org).

Legacy EX Plan: Free online smoking cessation program (www.becomeanex.org).

Narcotics Anonymous (NA): Support for people who want to stop using drugs (818-773-9999, ext. 771, or www.na.org).

Parents Helping Parents: Support and education for parents of children abusing alcohol or other drugs (405-562-1919, or www.parentshelpingparents.info).

Safe Sober Living: An advocacy organization for the promotion of regulated sober living facilities to help ease the transition from residential treatment back home (www.safesoberliving.org).

SAMHSA Substance Abuse Treatment Facility Locator: Find a local treatment facility (1-800-662-HELP or 1-800-ALCOHOL [The Alcohol Treatment Referral Hotline] or http://findtreatment.samhsa.gov/locator.htm).

Bibliography

Arain, Mariam, Maliha Haque, Lina Johal, Puja Mathur, Wynand Nel, Afsha Rais, Ranbir Sandhu, and Sushil Sharma. "Maturation of the Adolescent Brain." *Neuropsychiatric Disease and Treatment* 9 (2013): 449–61.

Califano Jr., Joseph A. *High Society: How Substance Abuse Ravages America and What to Do About It.* New York: Public Affairs, 2007.

Califano, Jr., Joseph A. *How to Raise a Drug-Free Kid: The Straight Dope for Parents.* New York: Simon & Schuster, 2009.

CASA. *Addiction Medicine: Closing the Gap Between Science and Practice,* 2012.

CASA. *Adolescent Substance Use: America's #1 Public Health Problem,* 2011.

CASA. *Dangerous Liaisons: Substance Abuse and Sex,* 1999.

CASA. *Family Matters: Substance Abuse and the American Family,* 2005.

CASA. *Food for Thought: Substance Abuse and Eating Disorders,* 2003.

CASA. *Malignant Neglect: Substance Abuse and America's Schools,* 2001.

CASA. *National Survey of American Attitudes on Substance Abuse: Teens and Parents,* 1995–2012.

CASA. *Non-Medical Marijuana III: Rite of Passage or Russian Roulette?*, 2008.

CASA. *Patient Guide: How to Find Quality Addiction Treatment*, 2013.

CASA. *So Help Me God: Substance Abuse, Religion and Spirituality*, 2001.

CASA. *Substance Abuse and Learning Disabilities: Peas in a Pod or Apples and Oranges?*, 2000.

CASA. *The Commercial Value of Underage and Pathological Drinking to the Alcohol Industry*, 2006.

CASA. *The Formative Years: Pathways to Substance Abuse*, 2003.

CASA. *The Importance of Family Dinners*, 2003, 2005–2007, 2010–2011.

CASA. *Tobacco: The Smoking Gun*, 2007.

CASA. *Under the Counter: The Diversion and Abuse of Controlled Prescription Drugs in the U.S.*, 2005.

CASA. *Wasting the Best and Brightest: Substance Abuse at America's Colleges and Universities*, 2007.

CASA. *Women Under the Influence.* Baltimore: Johns Hopkins University Press, 2006.

CASA. *You've Got Drugs V*, 2008.

Centers for Disease Control and Prevention (CDC). *1991–2011 High School Youth Risk Behavior Survey Data.* http://apps.nccd.cdc.gov/youthonline (accessed February 13, 2014).

Colliver, J. D., Larry A. Kroutil, Lanting Dai, and Joseph C. Gfroerer. "Misuse of Prescription Drugs: Data from the 2002, 2003, and 2004 National Surveys on Drug Use and Health" (DHHS Publication No. SMA 06-4192, Analytic Series A-28). Rockville, MD: Substance Abuse and Mental Health Services Administration, Office of Applied Studies (2006). www.oas.samhsa.gov/prescription/TOC.htm (accessed February 6, 2009).

Crews, Fulton, Jun He, and Clyde Hodge. "Adolescent Cortical Development: A Critical Period of Vulnerability for Addiction." *Pharmacology Biochemistry and Behavior* 86, no. 2 (February 2007): 189–99.

Csomor, Marina. "There's Something (Potentially Dangerous) About Molly." CNN.com. www.cnn.com/2012/08/16/health/molly-mdma-drug/index.html (accessed February 12, 2014).

Desantis, Alan, and Audrey Curtis Hane. " 'Adderall Is Definitely Not a Drug': Justifications for the Illegal Use of ADHD Stimulants." *Substance Use & Misuse* 45, no. 1–2 (January 2010): 31–46.

Kaiser Family Foundation. "Daily Media Use Among Children and Teens Up Dramatically from Five Years Ago" (2010). http://kff.org/disparities-policy/press-release/daily-media-use-among-children-and-teens-up-dramatically-from-five-years-ago.

Kaiser Family Foundation. "National Survey of Adolescents and Young Adults: Sexual Health Knowledge, Attitudes and Experiences" (2003). www.kff.org/youthhivstds/3218-index.cfm (accessed February 12, 2014).

Levine, Amir, YanYou Huang, Bettina Drisaldi, Edmund A. Griffin Jr., Daniela D. Pollak, Shiqin Xu, Deqi Yin, Christine Schaffran, Denise B. Kandel, and Eric R. Kandel. "Molecular Mechanism for a Gateway Drug: Epigenetic Changes Initiated by Nicotine Prime Gene Expression by Cocaine." *Science Translational Medicine* 3, no. 107 (November 2011): 107.

Lubman, Dan I., Murat Yücel, and Wayne D. Hall. "Substance Use and the Adolescent Brain: A Toxic Combination?" *Journal of Psychopharmacology* 21, no. 8 (November 2007): 792–94.

Martin, Catherine A., Thomas H. Kelly, Mary Kay Rayens, Bethanie R. Brogli, Allen Brenzel, W. Jackson Smith, and Hatim A. Omar. "Sensation Seeking, Puberty and Nicotine, Alcohol and Marijuana Use in Adolescence." *Journal of the American Academy of Child and Adolescent Psychiatry* 41, no. 12 (December 2002): 1495–1502.

McQueeny, Tim, Brian C. Schweinsburg, Alecia D. Schweinsburg, Joanna Jacobus, Sunita Bava, Lawrence R. Frank, and Susan F. Tapert. "Altered White Matter Integrity in Adolescent Binge Drinkers." *Alcoholism: Clinical and Experimental Research* 33, no. 7 (July 2009): 1278–85.

Meier, Madeline H., Avshalom Caspi, Antony Ambler, HonaLee Harrington, Renate Houts, Richard S. E. Keefe, Kay McDonald, Aimee Ward, Richie Poulton, and Terrie E. Moffitt. "Persistent Cannabis Users Show Neuropsychological Decline from Childhood to Midlife." *Proceedings of the National Academy of Sciences of the United States of America* 109, no. 40 (October 2, 2012): E2657–64.

Mothers Against Drunk Driving (MADD). "MADD Analysis Finds Majority of Underage Drinking Deaths Not Traffic Related" (2013).

National Institute on Drug Abuse. "Commonly Abused Drugs Chart" (2011). www.drugabuse.gov/drugs-abuse/commonly-abused-drugs/commonly-abused-drugs-chart.

National Institute on Drug Abuse. "Drugs, Brains, and Behavior—The Science of Addiction" (2010). www.nida.nih.gov/scienceof addiction/brain.html.

National Institute on Drug Abuse. "Drug Facts." *NIDA for Teens—The Science Behind Drug Abuse.* http://teens.drugabuse.gov/drug-facts (accessed October 24, 2013).

National Institute on Drug Abuse. "Drug Facts: High School and Youth Trends" (2014). www.drugabuse.gov/sites/default/files/drugfactsmtf2013.pdf.

National Institute on Alcohol Abuse and Alcoholism. *Alcohol Alert 73: Underage Drinking—Highlights from the Surgeon General's Call to Action to Prevent and Reduce Underage Drinking.* Rockville, MD: US Department of Health and Human Services (October 2007).

National Institute on Alcohol Abuse and Alcoholism. *Underage Drinking.* National Institutes of Health. http://pubs.niaaa.nih.gov/publications/UnderageDrinking/Underage_Fact.pdf (accessed February 13, 2014).

National Research Council and Institute of Medicine. *Reducing Underage Drinking: A Collective Responsibility.* R. J. Bonnie and M.E. O'Connell, eds. Washington, DC: National Academies Press, 2004.

Office of National Drug Control Policy. "Fact Sheets." www.whitehouse.gov/ondcp/ondcp-fact-sheets (accessed February 14, 2014).

Partnership at DrugFree.org. "Partnership Attitude Tracking Survey (PATS)—Parents 2007 Report" (2008). www.drugfree.org/Files/new_pats_survey_2008 (accessed February 6, 2009).

Partnership at Drugfree.org and MetLife Foundation. "2012 Partnership Attitude Tracking Survey (PATS)—Teens and Parents Report" (2013). www.drugfree.org/wp-content/uploads/2013/04/PATS-2012-FULL-REPORT2.pdf (accessed February 13, 2014).

Pew Research Center. "Teens and Technology 2013." *Pew Internet and American Life Project* (2013). www.pewinternet.org/Reports/2013 /Teens-and-Tech.aspx.

Pew Research Center. "Teens, Kindness and Cruelty on Social Network Sites" (2011). http://pewinternet.org/~/media//Files /Reports/2011/PIP_Teens_Kindness_Cruelty_SNS_Report _Nov_2011_FINAL_110711.pdf.

Pew Research Center. "Teens, Smartphones, and Texting" (2012). www.pewinternet.org/files/old-media//Files/Reports/2012/PIP _Teens_Smartphones_and_Texting.pdf.

Pew Research Center. "Teens, Social Media, and Privacy" (2013). http://cms.pewresearch.org/pewinternet/files/2013/05/PIP_Teens SocialMediaandPrivacy_PDF.pdf.

Schwebel, Robert. *Saying No Is Not Enough.* New York: Newmarket Press, 1998.

Steiner-Adair, Catherine, with Teresa H. Barker. *The Big Disconnect: Protecting Childhood and Family Relationships in the Digital Age.* New York: HarperCollins, 2013.

Substance Abuse and Mental Health Services Administration. *Drug Abuse Warning Network, 2011: National Estimates of Drug-Related Emergency Department Visits.* HHS Publication No. (SMA) 13-4760, DAWN Series D-39. Rockville, MD: Substance Abuse and Mental Health Services Administration (2013).

Substance Abuse and Mental Health Services Administration. *Results from the 2012 National Survey on Drug Use and Health: National Findings* (NSDUH Series H-46, HHS Publication No. (SMA) 13-4795). Rockville, MD (2013).

Substance Abuse and Mental Health Services Administration. "Social Host Liability Laws." *Town Hall Meetings* (2012). www.stop alcoholabuse.gov/TownHallMeetings/pdf/GTO_SocHostLaws _Rev_F_13112.pdf.

TeensHealth. "Drugs: What You Should Know." www.kidshealth .org/teen/drug_alcohol/drugs/know_about_drugs.html (accessed February 6, 2009).

The Center on Alcohol Marketing and Youth. "Youth Exposure to Alcohol Advertising on Television, 2001 to 2009" (2010). www .camy.org/research/Youth_Exposure_to_Alcohol_Ads_on_TV

_Growing_Faster_Than_Adults/_includes/TVReport01-09 _Revised_7-12.pdf (accessed February 6, 2014).

US Department of Health and Human Services. Smokefree Teen Website. http://teen.smokefree.gov/default.aspx (accessed February 14, 2014).

US Department of Health and Human Services. "The Health Consequences of Smoking—50 Years of Progress: A Report of the Surgeon General" (2014). www.surgeongeneral.gov/library /reports/50-years-of-progress/full-report.pdf.

US Drug Enforcement Administration. "Drug Fact Sheets." www .usdoj.gov/dea/concern/concern.htm (accessed February 12, 2014).

US Drug Enforcement Administration. Just Think Twice Website. "Drug Facts." www.justthinktwice.com/factfiction/Marijuanais Harmless.cfm (accessed February 14, 2014).

University of Michigan. *Monitoring the Future* Annual Survey. Ann Arbor, MI (2013–2014).

Volkow, Nora. "Marijuana's Lasting Effects on the Brain." *National Institute on Drug Abuse, Messages from the Director* (2013). www .drugabuse.gov/about-nida/directors-page/messages-director /2012/09/marijuanas-lasting-effects-brain.

Volkow, Nora. Transcript of presentation at CASA conference, "Double Jeopardy: Substance Abuse and Co-occurring Mental Health Disorders in Young People" (October 18, 2007).

Volkow, Nora D., Joanna S. Fowler, Gene-Jack Wang, and James M. Swanson. "Dopamine in Drug Abuse and Addiction: Results from Imaging Studies and Treatment Implications." *Molecular Psychiatry* 9, no. 6 (June 2004): 557–69.

Volkow, Nora, and Ting-Kai Li. "Drugs and Alcohol: Treating and Preventing Abuse, Addiction and Their Medical Consequences." *Pharmacology & Therapeutics* 108, no. 1 (October 2005): 3–17.

Zeigler, Donald W., Claire C. Wang, Richard A. Yoast, Barry D. Dickinson, Mary Anne McCaffree, Carolyn B. Robinowitz, and Melvyn L. Sterling. "The Neurocognitive Effects of Alcohol on Adolescents and College Students." *Preventive Medicine* 40 (2005): 23–32.

Index

About the Author

Joseph A. Califano Jr. is founder of the National Center on Addiction and Substance Abuse at Columbia University (CASA), an independent nonprofit research center and think/action tank affiliated with Columbia University in New York City. Founded in 1992, CASA conducts public policy research and evaluates prevention and treatment programs involving all substances (alcohol; illegal, prescription, and performance-enhancing drugs; nicotine). Under its president and chief executive officer Sam Ball, PhD, professor of psychiatry at Yale University Medical School, CASA's mission is expanding to encompass addiction and addictive behaviors involving gambling, obesity and eating disorders, and compulsive sexual behaviors.

Mr. Califano has been adjunct professor of health policy and management at Columbia University's Medical School and School of Public Health. He is a member of the Institute of Medicine of the National Academy of Sciences. In 2010 he received the institute's highest honor, the Gustav O. Lienhard Award, for his contributions to improving public health, his leadership in catalyzing federal action to curb smoking, and his broader efforts to reduce the toll of addiction and substance abuse.

Mr. Califano was born on May 15, 1931, in Brooklyn, New York, where he grew up. He received his bachelor of arts degree from the College of the Holy Cross in 1952 and his LLB from Harvard Law School in 1955. After service in the US Navy and three years with Governor Thomas Dewey's Wall Street law firm, he joined the Kennedy administration and served in the Pentagon as general counsel of the army and as Secretary of Defense Robert McNamara's special assistant and top troubleshooter.

President Lyndon B. Johnson named Mr. Califano his special assistant for domestic affairs in 1965, and he served in that post until the president left office in January 1969. During his years on the White House staff, Mr. Califano served as the president's chief domestic aide, working on the Medicare and Medicaid programs and helping shape dozens of Great Society bills related to health care, education, children, criminal justice, the environment, consumers, and social welfare. The *New York Times* called him "Deputy President for Domestic Affairs." At the end of his term, President Johnson wrote to Mr. Califano, "You were the captain I wanted and you steered the course well."

From 1969 to 1977, Mr. Califano practiced law in Washington, DC, and served as attorney for the *Washington Post* and its reporters Bob Woodward, Carl Bernstein, and Richard Cohen during the Watergate years.

From 1977 to 1979, Mr. Califano was US secretary of health, education, and welfare and became the first voice to alert the nation to the explosion of health care costs and teenage pregnancy. He mounted the first national antismoking campaign, began the computer policing of Medicare and Medicaid to eliminate fraud and abuse, issued the first *Surgeon General's Report on Health Promotion and Disease Prevention, Healthy People,* to set health goals for the nation, and instituted Medicare reimbursement for hospice care and financed construction of the nation's first freestanding hospice in Branford, Connecticut. As secretary, he issued federal regulations to provide equal access for handicapped Americans, and Title IX regulations to provide equal opportunity for women in college athletics.

From 1979 to 1992, Mr. Califano practiced law in Washington, DC.

Mr. Califano is the author of twelve previous books (two with Howard Simons, former managing editor of the *Washington Post*) and has written articles for the *New York Times*, the *Washington Post*, the *Wall Street Journal*, *Reader's Digest*, the *New Republic*, *America*, the *New England Journal of Medicine*, and other publications. He is married to Hilary Paley Byers and lives in Westport, Connecticut. He has three children, Mark, Joseph III, and Claudia; two stepchildren, Brooke Byers and John F. Byers IV; and nine grandchildren.

His books include the original edition of *How to Raise a Drug-Free Kid*, published in 2009; *High Society: How Substance Abuse Ravages America and What to Do About It*; *Governing America*, about his years as secretary of HEW; his memoir *Inside: A Public and Private Life*; *The Triumph and Tragedy of Lyndon Johnson: The White House Years*; *America's Health Care Revolution: Who Lives, Who Dies, Who Pays*; *Radical Surgery: What's Next for America's Health Care*; and *The Student Revolution—A Global Confrontation*. His books are available as e-books or from Amazon.com or Barnes & Noble (www.bn.com).